1 SAMUEL

1 SAMUEL

by
John M Riddle

40 Beansburn, Kilmarnock, Scotland

ISBN-13: 978 1 907731 71 6

Copyright © 2012 by John Ritchie Ltd.
40 Beansburn, Kilmarnock, Scotland

www.ritchiechristianmedia.co.uk

All rights reserved. No part of this publication may be reproduced, stored in a retrievable system, or transmitted in any form or by any other means – electronic, mechanical, photocopy, recording or otherwise – without prior permission of the copyright owner.

Typeset by John Ritchie Ltd., Kilmarnock
Printed by 4edge Ltd., Essex

Contents

Preface	7
Introduction	9
Chapter 1	13
Chapter 2A	21
Chapter 2B	29
Chapter 3	38
Chapter 4	46
Chapter 5&6	53
Chapter 7	61
Chapter 8	70
Chapter 9	79
Chapter 10	88
Chapter 11	97
Chapter 12	104
Chapter 13	113
Chapter 14A	121
Chapter 14B	129
Chapter 15	137
Chapter 16	146
Chapter 17A	156
Chapter 17B	166

Chapter 18	176
Chapter 19	185
Chapter 20	194
Chapter 21	203
Chapter 22	212
Chapter 23	221
Chapter 24	230
Chapter 25A	238
Chapter 25B	248
Chapter 26	257
Chapter 27	267
Chapter 28	274
Chapter 29	284
Chapter 30	291
Chapter 31	301

Preface

This book represents the substance of Bible Class discussions on Friday evenings between September 2001 and November 2002 at Mill Lane Chapel, Cheshunt. Like the recently published book entitled *The Acts of the Apostles*, covering studies between January 2008 and July 2009, it does not purport to be a commentary in the usual sense of the word.

As stated in the Preface to *The Acts of the Apostles*, the Bible Class commenced in the mid-1980's, and was originally known as the Young People's Bible Study Group. In the Lord's will, the class is about to embark on the study of its forty-first book, namely, the prophecy of Hosea. This will complete studies in the so-called 'Minor Prophets', perhaps better described corporately as 'The Book of the Twelve'.

It has been the general practice, though not rigorously adopted, to alternate between Old and New Testaments. It has also been the practice since the commencement of the class to study the given passage for the evening on a verse by verse basis, which means that there is no escape from probing questions on 'difficult' passages. It should be said that this does not mean that every question is always answered satisfactorily at the time! However, since the notes are finalised after each session, they sometimes reflect 'second thoughts'. It is not always easy to answer 'non-standard' questions 'on the hoof'! It should also be said that answers are often given by more than one person! Dealing with questions is not the prerogative of 'the brother in the chair'. There is a certain joy and satisfaction in working through a passage together.

The studies in 1 Samuel predate those in Acts by some seven years, during which there have been changes in the constitution of the class. But some things remain happily constant, including the great help and encouragement given by brothers and sisters in the local assembly at Cheshunt, and elsewhere. It remains our firm conviction, without which we would be hopelessly lost, that "All scripture is given by inspiration of God, and is profitable for doctrine, for reproof, for correction, for instruction in righteousness: that the man of God may be perfect, throughly furnished unto all good works".

John Riddle
Cheshunt, Hertfordshire
September 2012

Introduction

Read the whole book

We must commence our studies in 1 Samuel by remembering that "whatsoever things were written aforetime were written for our learning, that we through patience and comfort of the scriptures might have hope" (Rom 15.4). We can therefore expect to hear God speaking to us throughout the book. The first chapter proves the point. It is brim-full of important lessons. But before we embark on chapter 1 we ought to say several things about the book in general.

1. The Name of the Book
In the Hebrew manuscripts, 1 & 2 Samuel form one book, and the same format applies to 1 & 2 Kings and 1 & 2 Chronicles. In the Septuagint translation of the Hebrew Scriptures into Greek, made at Alexandria in the third century BC (the work actually commenced in 280 BC), 1 & 2 Samuel and 1 & 2 Kings are called the First, Second, Third, and Fourth Books of the Kingdoms. (It is called the *Septuagint* because, it is alleged, seventy scholars were involved in the translation). The word "Kingdoms" refers, of course, to the two kingdoms of Judah and Israel. The Latin Vulgate translation repeated the Septuagint division of Samuel and Kings into two books each, but called them the First, Second, Third, and Fourth Books of the Kings (not "Kingdoms"). This is the origin of the sub-titles to these four books in our Authorised Version. For example, under the title "The First Book of Samuel", you will find *"Otherwise called the First Book of the Kings"*.

2. The Position of the Book
First Samuel covers the period of Israel's history commencing with the birth of Samuel to the death of Saul - approximately one hundred and fifteen years (1171-1056 BC). It was a most important period for at least two reasons. First, the era of the Judges ended, and the era of the prophets

commenced, and, second, the era of direct divine rule ended, and the era of the earthly monarchy commenced.

A) *The era of the prophets commenced*
Samuel was the last of the judges and the first of the prophets. See Acts 13.20. "And after that [the division of the land under Joshua] he gave unto them judges about the space of four hundred and fifty years, until Samuel the prophet".

a) Samuel the judge. See, for example 1 Samuel 7.6, "And Samuel judged the children of Israel in Mizpeh", and 7.15-17. "And Samuel judged Israel all the days of his life...and judged Israel...and there he judged Israel." Prior to Samuel, the judgeship was vested in Eli - see 1 Samuel 4.18. "And he had judged Israel forty years". In his latter years, Samuel "made his sons judges over Israel" (1 Sam 8.1-2), but they were rejected, for good reasons, by Israel.

b) Samuel the prophet. See Acts 3.24. "Yea, and all the prophets from Samuel and those that follow after, as many as have spoken, have likewise foretold of these days". Note, in this connection, 1 Samuel 3.20; 9.11,19; 1 Chronicles 9.22; 29.29; Hebrews 11.32. (In some of these passages, the word "seer" is used. For an explanation, see 1 Samuel 9.9). As C. E. Hocking observes, this did not imply "that there had not been prophets before him. From this time onward, however, they were given a specific and permanent place. The priesthood having failed irremediably, the prophet comes into his own".

B) *The era of the kings commenced*
Theocracy gave place to the monarchy. That requires some explanation, and 1 Samuel 8 now becomes compulsory reading. "Behold, thou (Samuel) art old, and thy sons walk not in thy ways. now make us a king to judge us like all the nations...Nevertheless (in spite of Samuel's protest) the people refused to obey the voice of Samuel; and they said, Nay; but we will have a king over us; That we also may be like all the nations; and that our king may judge us, and go out before us, and fight our battles" (vv.5,19-20). Up to this point in their history, Israel had been ruled directly by their unseen heavenly King. When they cried to Him, He heard and answered (see Judges 3.9,15). He had never failed them, and the stone between Mizpeh and Shen commemorated His faithfulness. It bore the name "Ebenezer", meaning "Hitherto hath the Lord helped us" (1 Sam 7.12). But now change was

afoot. Israel preferred visible human rule, rather than unseen divine rule. In God's own words, "They have rejected me, that I should not reign over them" (8.7). Years before, in different circumstances, Israel had asked Gideon to reign over them as king and to establish a dynasty. Listen to his splendid words. "I will not rule over you, neither shall my son rule over you: the Lord shall rule over you" (Jud 8.23). What a pity he spoiled it almost immediately! Read the rest of the chapter.

Church history, sadly, proves that little has changed. Professing Christians still prefer visible organisation and human wisdom to simple faith and dependence on God. Whilst God, in His mercy, allowed them a king, it was not long before the disadvantages of this arrangement became strikingly apparent. Israel chose the second-best. Faith in God, and obedience to His Word, cannot be bettered. We should not be satisfied with anything less.

3. The Plan of the Book
For sheer interest, 1 Samuel is unsurpassed. Not only does it recount eventful history, it is eventful history interwoven with the biographies of three colourful personalities, Samuel, Saul, and David. The book can be divided with reference to these three biographies.
In Chapters 1-7 *Samuel* is prominent.
In Chapters 8-15 *Saul* is prominent.
In Chapters 16-31 *David* is prominent.

Quite clearly, the three sections overlap. "Samuel lives well on into the reign of Saul, and also sees David rise to prominence; while Saul continues his reign until David is thirty years old" (J. Sidlow Baxter, *Explore the Book*). However, the three sections focus our attention on Samuel, David, and Saul respectively.

First Samuel begins where Judges ends. "In those days there was no king in Israel: every man did that which was right in his own eyes" (Judges 21.25). This does not mean that when the kings eventually came, everything turned out well. That was far from the case. It means that "the people themselves, individually and corporately, had the responsibility of checking ungodliness, and promoting holiness" (Michael Wilcock). The early chapters demonstrate that the priests were doing "that which was right in his own eyes" (2.12-17), and the people were doing "that which was right in his own eyes" in worshipping Baalim and Ashtaroth (7.4). The elders did "that which was right in his own eyes" by calling for the ark of the covenant in the conflict with the Philistines (4.3-4). Israel had sunk very low indeed when Samuel was born. He has been described as "God's emergency man". "When Samuel steps into the breach at the eleventh hour, we witness afresh the sovereignty and sufficiency of God. If all else has failed, God has not" (C. E. Hocking).

CHAPTER 1

The Birth of Samuel (1.1-28)

As we have already noted 1 Samuel 1-7 focuses our attention particularly upon Samuel himself. Chapters 1-3, which we will call *The growth of Samuel*, describe his birth, development, and call. Chapters 4-6, which we will call *The guilt of Israel*, describe the capture, triumph, and return of the ark. Chapter 7, which we will call *The guidance of Samuel*, describes his intercession for Israel.

1. Hannah's Sorrow (vv.1-8)
A) The home of Elkanah (vv.1-2)
"Now there was a certain man of Ramathaim-zophim, of mount Ephraim, and his name was Elkanah." Whilst Ramathaim-zophim, otherwise known simply as Ramah (v.19) was located in mount Ephraim, it actually lay in the territory of Benjamin. Samuel was born, lived, laboured, died, and was buried there (7.17; 15.34; 16.13; 19.18; 25.1; 28.3). Like most of the judges who preceded him, Samuel had an unpretentious background. He did not come from a leading family, or from a prominent city, which reminds us that it is not where we come from, but where we are going, that it is of supreme importance. We should never use our background, or surroundings, as an excuse for spiritual failure.

The place-names and people-names are interesting. You could construct a sermon from them! *Ramathaim-zophim* means "the two heights of the Zophites" (from his ancestor, Zuph). "Ephraim" means "fruitful". *Elkanah*, who was a Levite descended from Kohath (1 Chr 6.22-28), means "whom God possessed". *Jeroham* means "who is loved". *Elihu* means "whose God is he". *Tohu* means "low". *Zuph* means "flag", or "sedge", but he is also known as Zophai (1 Chr 6.26), meaning "honeycomb." Over to you! But do think particularly about Elkanah. Keil & Delitzsch point out that this was a most appropriate name for a Levite (they say it means "the man whom God has bought or acquired"), since the Levites were "set apart for service at the sanctuary, in the place of the first-born of Israel" (Num 3.13, 44-51). We too have been purchased by God: "Ye are not your own...for ye are bought with a price" (1 Cor 6.19-20).

"And he had two wives; the name of the one was Hannah, and the name of other was Peninnah. and Peninnah had children, but Hannah had no children." A.McShane *(Lessons for Leaders)* has a most helpful piece here. "This Levitical family, although devoted to God and the Tabernacle, was far from happy. Departure from the primeval law of Eden brought with it a crop of sorrows, for while at that time polygamy was widely practised and was tolerated by God, yet its evils are constantly brought out in the pages of Scripture. One cannot forsake basic principles without suffering the consequences." Hannah, like her namesake Anna in Luke 2.36, means "grace", or "gracious", whilst Peninnah means "coral." Coral is very beautiful, but Peninnah was far from beautiful when it came to her attitude towards Hannah!

B) The house of God (v.3)
"And this man went up out of his city yearly to worship and to sacrifice unto the Lord of hosts in Shiloh." The tabernacle was at Shiloh (Josh 18.1). It is called "the house of the Lord" (v.7), and the "temple of the Lord" (v.9). Both titles seem inappropriate at first glance. But only at first glance! Notice, for the first time in the Bible, the title "the Lord of hosts". It has its roots in Genesis 2.1: "Thus the heavens and the earth were finished, and all the *host* of them". Keil & Delitzsch explain as follows. "It is simply applied to Jehovah as the God of the universe, who governs all the powers of heaven, both visible and invisible, as He rules in heaven and on earth." Commentators have pointed out that the title is used particularly when Israel was weak. He is the all-powerful God, with infinite resources, and is quite able to help and deliver His people.

Circumstances were far from ideal. Politically, Israel was constantly harried by the Philistines; ecclesiastically, God's interests had become corrupted by evil men; domestically, Elkanah's two wives were far from friends. But these dark days did not prevent Elkanah from making the journey northwards every year to Shiloh, where he worshipped and offered sacrifices to "the Lord of hosts". Whether the annual visit to Shiloh was in addition to the three visits required in Exodus 23.14 etc, we do not know. But we do know that "the entire family circle went to the true centre, and each member shared in the eating of the peace-offerings before the Lord" (A.McShane). The lesson for us is clear. Even in difficult and discouraging times, we must still give the Lord His proper place in our lives, and that includes our assembly worship and service.

There is an ominous ring about the statement, "And the two sons of Eli, Hophni and Phinehas, the priests of the Lord, were there". They too had significant names. *Hophni* means "pugilist", and he certainly behaved like one! *Phinehas* means "mouth of brass" (Gesenius), although some say that it means "serpent's mouth". He certainly spoke like one! (2.16). They are called, here, "priests of the Lord", but they are also called "sons of Belial; they knew not the Lord" (2.12). There was no correspondence between their official position, and their actual practice. They ministered to themselves, rather than to the Lord. Their spiritual degeneracy was matched by their moral degeneracy (2.22).

C) The heartbreak of Hannah (vv.4-8)
The annual visits to Shiloh, which should have been happy occasions for the whole family, only intensified Hannah's grief. The following points are worthy of note.

i) Privileges were ineffective (vv.4-5). "And when the time was that Elkanah offered, he gave to Peninnah his wife, and to all her sons and her daughters, portions: But unto Hannah he gave a worthy (double) portion; for he loved Hannah." According to Keil & Delitzsch, this reads, literally, "one portion for two persons". They go on to explain that "he gave it as an expression of his love to her, to indicate by a sign, 'thou art as dear to me as if thou hadst born me a child'". But this was little or no consolation to her: "*But the Lord had shut up her womb*". (This was evidently a repetition of events in the life of Jacob - read Genesis 29.29-35. God does not look favourably on favouritism.) That was bad enough, but worse follows.

ii) Peninnah was insulting (vv.6-7). "And her adversary also provoked her sore, for to make her fret, because the Lord had shut up her womb. And as he did so year by year (i.e. as Elkanah gave her a double portion during the annual visit to Shiloh), when she (Hannah) went up to the house of the Lord, so she (Hannah's adversary, Peninnah) provoked her; therefore she wept, and did not eat." "Just as Elkanah showed his love to Hannah at every sacrificial festival, so did Peninnah repeat her provocation" (Keil & Delitzsch). Such conduct should have no place amongst God's people: "And whether one member suffer, all the members suffer with it; or one member be honoured, all the members rejoice with it" (1 Cor 12.26). All sorts of evil can flow from jealousy on the one hand, and superiority on the other.

iii) Elkanah was insensitive (v.8). He did not seem to understand Hannah's problem. Notice his battery of staccato questions. "Why weepest thou? and why eatest thou not? and why is thy heart grieved? am I not better to thee than ten sons?" He did not wait for the answer to any of his questions! He took no time to understand. There are important lessons here for husbands and wives, for parents and children, not to mention assembly relationships. How much do we care? Do we take time to visit, sit down, listen, and endeavour to understand the distress, difficulties, and problems of fellow-believers?

2. Hannah's Solemn Promise (vv.9-19)

Hannah arose "after they had eaten in Shiloh, and after they had drunk...and she was in bitterness of soul, and prayed unto the Lord, and wept sore" (vv.9-10). The woman who wept in the family circle, certainly before her husband (v.8), now wept before the Lord. She brought her sorrow to Him. Let us remember, "we have not an high priest which cannot be touched with the feeling of our infirmities" (Heb 4.15). As we shall see, an earthly priest was present when Hannah prayed, but he was *not* touched by her "infirmities." He didn't even perceive her distress!

A) The prayer of Hannah

Her prayer, in which she solemnly promised to give her son to God "all the days of his life" (v.11), is a striking example to us all. We must notice:

i) Her distress. Hannah "wept sore" (v.10 see also vv.15-16). She reminds us of Rachel, who cried, "Give me children, or else I die" (Gen 30.1). Both women were deeply distressed over their barrenness. In Bible times, it was a reproach to be childless. But we are often unmoved by *our* spiritual barrenness. Every assembly should cry, "Give me children, or else I die." Paul was able to say, "In Christ Jesus I have *begotten* you through the gospel" (1 Cor 4.15 see also Philem 10). Sadly, we almost regard it as normal when no one is saved.

ii) Her confidence. Hannah addressed the Lord as "O Lord of hosts" (v.11). We have already briefly discussed this title. Hannah was fully aware that God was able to help her. In fact, she realised that *only* God could help her.

We must approach Him with the same confidence. "Now unto him that is *able* to do exceeding abundantly above all that we ask or think..." (Eph 3.20). Where else can we look for help?

iii) Her motives. There was not an ounce of selfishness in Hannah's petition. She did not pray for a son to silence Peninnah. She did not pray for a son that she could display to her friends and neighbours. She did not pray for a son to keep her in old age. She prayed for a son whom she could give back to the Lord "all the days of his life." With that in mind, she was willing to part with him at a very early age. She was prepared to give back to God the very gift she wanted more than anything else in the world. More than that, she wanted God to have him perpetually. "I will give him unto the Lord all the days of his life, and there shall no razor come upon his head." He was to be a Nazarite. But in this case, "all the days of his separation he is holy unto the Lord" (Num 6.8 see Rom 15.16), meant his entire life. Hannah gave her best to God. How much are we prepared to give Him?

iv) Her humility. She describes herself three times as "thine handmaid" (v.11). She had no inflated thoughts about herself. Hannah placed herself completely at God's disposal.

v) Her perseverance. "And it came to pass as she *continued* praying before the Lord." (v.12). There was nothing perfunctory about Hannah's prayer. Her earnestness drove her to pray at length.

vi) Her reality. "Now Hannah, she spake in her heart; only her lips moved, but her voice was not heard." (v.13 see Mt 15.7-8) How real are our prayers? We must remember, "the Lord looketh on the heart" (16.7). It has been said that Hannah was a good NT sister. "Her voice was not heard!" (1 Tim 2.11-12). But let us look at this positively. Hannah's voice was silent, but she was certainly praying, which reminds us that in the assembly prayer meeting we all pray, both brothers and sisters! We don't just listen to other people praying! The brother who prays expresses the desire of everyone present. That is one reason why we should say "Amen!"

B) The priesthood of Eli
His name is mentioned five times in the passage (vv.9,12,13,14,17), and each reference is thought-provoking. However, we will concentrate on the following.

i) "Eli...sat" (v.9). We are not accustomed to a seated priest in the tabernacle! See Hebrews10.11-12 which contrasts the Levitical priests standing, because their work was never finished, and the Lord Jesus, our great high priest, who is seated "on the right hand of God" because His redeeming work is eternally complete. According to Gesenius, the word "seat" means "throne", and if this was the case, then Eli had an unwarranted position. He was elevated above the people he was called to represent. Compare this with Hebrews 5.1-4. The Lord Jesus is the only priest with the right to sit upon a throne.

Eli evidently sat where he could see what was happening. However, whilst he could see some things (Hannah's mouth, for example), he could not, or would not, see everything (2.12-17). In any case, when he did find out, all he did was reprove his sons. He did nothing to retrieve the situation, and failed to implement the word of God.

ii) "Eli thought" (v.13). "Eli thought she had been drunken." He could not distinguish between a drunken woman and a distressed woman. As A McShane puts it, "His sharp rebuke to this exercised soul was in sad contrast to his mild treatment of his wicked sons. Apparently he knew more about the motions of the drunken than the behaviour of the devoted." Eli evidently counted her "a daughter of Belial" (v.16), but failed to count his infamous sons as "sons of Belial" (2.12). Eli came to the wrong conclusion about Hannah, but the Lord Jesus is perfectly aware of our circumstances!

iii) "Eli answered" (v.17). "Then Eli answered and said, Go in peace. and the God of Israel grant thee thy petition that thou hast asked of him." At last Eli appears in a better light. He functions as a man in touch with God, and assures Hannah that her prayers would be answered. Hannah's changed countenance and restored appetite prove that, like Abraham, she believed that "what he (God) had promised, he was able also to perform" (Rom 4.21). Her "bitterness of soul" and "sorrowful spirit" disappeared, and she was "no more sad." Hannah had cast her "burden upon the Lord" (Ps 55.27), and had no intention of retrieving it! She is not named in Hebrews 11, but she triumphed by faith. "She lived in the good of the answer before it was granted" (A.McShane).

The family worship the following morning must have been infused with great joy. Faith brought Hannah "beauty for ashes, the oil of joy for mourning, the garment of praise for the spirit of heaviness" (Is 61.3). Her joy was soon justified for "The Lord remembered her" (v.19)

3. Hannah's Son (vv.20-23)
"She bare a son, and called his name Samuel, saying, Because I have asked him of the Lord." Samuel actually means "heard of God", and his name commemorates the fact that God had heard Hannah's prayer. It reminds us that "if we ask anything according to his will, he heareth us" (1 Jn 5.14).

We should notice, first, that during the next annual visit to Shiloh, Elkanah offered "unto the Lord the yearly sacrifice, and his *vow*" (v.21). This suggests that Elkanah shared Hannah's vow to God (see v.11). Husband and wife were of one mind in their devotion to God. Second, Hannah had no intention of revoking her vow (v.22). She did not say, "It was an error." (Read carefully Ecclesiastes 5.1-7). Keil and Delizsch quote 2 Maccabees 7.28 (an Apocryphal book) which indicates that "Hebrew mothers were in the habit of suckling their children for three years." Hannah intended that Samuel should "appear before the Lord, and there abide for ever." Her devotion to God was stronger than the strongest human instincts. Third, Elkanah expected God to "establish his word." This evidently refers to the promise made by Eli, "Go in peace: and the God of Israel grant thee thy petition that thou hast asked of him" (v.17). That is, that Samuel would be devoted to God "all the days of his life."

4. Hannah's Selflessness (vv.24-28)
Hannah was as good as her word, but at what a cost! "And when she had weaned him, she took him up with her...and brought him unto the house of the Lord in Shiloh: and the child was young...And they...brought the child to Eli." The reference to the bullocks, flour, and wine takes us to Numbers 15 which refers, amongst other things to "a sacrifice in performing a vow." (v.8). This specifies one bullock; the other two were, presumably, connected with the annual sacrifice made by Elkanah and his family.

No further comment is really necessary. We can only listen with wonder to Hannah herself (vv.26-28). It was a permanent loan! But God is no man's debtor, and in due course we shall find that He pays the highest interest rates in the world, five hundred per cent!

The chapter ends with worship. The subject is mentioned in verses 3,19 and 28. A little sermon here! It isn't too easy to ascertain who worshipped in v.28. Some translations say, "And *they* worshipped the Lord there." Even the French Bible (La Sainte Bible) has it: "Et *ils* se prosternerent la devant l'Eternel." However, it is more likely that the singular was originally employed, and that it refers to Elkanah. "Elkanah first of all worshipped before the Lord in the sanctuary, and then Hannah worshipped in the song of praise which follows in 2.1-10", Keil and Delitzsch. They gave Samuel to God, not with resentment, but with worship.

What a marvellous way to end the chapter!

CHAPTER 2A

Hannah's Praise (2.1-11)

If our information is correct, Hannah took Samuel to "the house of the Lord in Shiloh" when he was three years old. She then returned home without him. In her own words, "I have lent him to the Lord; as long as he liveth he shall be lent to the Lord" (1.28). Sacrifice for God is always costly. Hannah was not devoid of "natural affection" (2 Tim 3.3), but she was willing to give her only son (at that time) to God. So was Abraham. How much are **we** prepared to give God? Remember, He gave His "only begotten Son."

In the circumstances, it is remarkable that the next thing we hear is Hannah praising God! "And Hannah prayed, and said, My heart rejoiceth in the Lord, mine horn is exalted in the Lord." 1 Samuel 2 commences with a woman praising God, but it continues with men profaning His name.

We can divide the chapter as follows. **(1)** The prayer of Hannah (vv.1-11); **(2)** The perversity of Eli's sons (vv.12-17); **(3)** The progress of Samuel (vv.18-21); **(4)** The protest of Eli (vv.22-25); **(5)** The prophecy of judgment (vv.26-36).

1. The Prayer of Hannah (vv.1-11)

Hannah's psalm of praise should be compared with the thanksgiving of Mary in Luke 1.46-56. To quote N.Crawford *(What the Bible Teaches - Luke)*, "If two columns are made of the two songs, there is a unique parallelism." Hannah praised God at the birth of a son. Mary praised God at the birth of **the** Son. That should engender some very fruitful meditation!

Whilst Hannah "prayed", it was "not quite in the sense in which we generally understand prayer. Her prayer here asks for nothing; it is rather a song of thanksgiving for the past, a song which passes into expressions of sure confidence for the future." (Ellicott's Commentary). She expresses her gratitude to God (v.1), and then extols the glory of God (vv.2-10).

1 Samuel

A) The gratitude of Hannah (v.1)

The woman who **"prayed** unto the Lord, and wept sore" (1.10), now **prayed,** and said, "My heart rejoiceth in the Lord, mine horn is exalted in the Lord: my mouth is enlarged over mine enemies; because I rejoice in thy salvation." (Hebrew *"yeshuah"*, whence Joshua, and Jesus!) We must notice Hannah's "heart...horn...mouth."

i) "My **heart** rejoiceth in the Lord." In her distress, she "spake in her **heart**" (1.13), and "poured out her soul before the Lord" (1.15). Now that same heart is full of joy. "My **heart** rejoiceth in the Lord." Hannah experienced the "oil of joy for mourning" (Is 61.3). God had heard her prayer, and seen her tears. See Isaiah 38.5. One day, God will "wipe away all tears." In the Bible, the word "heart" signifies the entirety of inner life. Hannah was full of joy! But it was joy "in the Lord." He had answered her prayer. Compare Psalm 126.6.

ii) "My **horn** is exalted in the Lord." In her distress, Hannah humbly described herself as "thine handmaid" (1.11). Her humility led to her exaltation. Solomon reminds us that "before honour is humility" (Prov 16.33;18.12. See 1 Peter 5.5-6). The word "horn" denotes strength. The imagery is taken from oxen and other animals whose strength lies in their horns. See, for example, Deuteronomy 33.17. John saw the Lord Jesus as "a Lamb as it had been slain, having **seven horns** (perfect power) and seven eyes (perfect perception), which are the seven Spirits of God sent forth into all the earth." (Rev 5.6). We must not, for one moment, conclude that Hannah was proud of herself. She does not say, "Mine horn is exalted", but "Mine horn is exalted ***in the Lord.***" Paul says the same thing, but in a different way, in Philippians 4.13.

iii) "My **mouth** is enlarged over mine enemies." In her distress, "only her lips moved." Eli "marked her mouth" (1.12), and so do we! Her inaudible prayer now gives place to audible praise. Her mouth was not filled with "arrogancy" (v.3), but with thanksgiving. Compare Ephesians 4.29. Whilst it is difficult to escape the conclusion that Hannah is referring, at least partly, to Peninnah here ("her adversary" v.6), it would be rather uncharitable to suggest that she was "getting her own back!" Her mouth was not "enlarged" to gloat over Penninah, but to "rejoice" in the way that the Lord had delivered her from distress. God had vindicated her. There are important lessons for us here. See, for example, Romans 12.19-21.

B. The glory of God (vv.2-10)
This section of Hannah's psalm of thanksgiving can be divided into three sections, **(i)** The attributes of God (vv.2-3); **(ii)** The activities of God (vv.4-8); **(iii)** The assurance of God (vv.9-10).

i) The attributes of God (vv.2-3)
a) He is the holy God. "There is none holy as the Lord." It is never inappropriate to remember the holiness of God. See 1 Peter 1.14-16, with the three relevant references in Leviticus, which emphasise that God's holiness is all-embracing. See 11.45; 19.2; 20.26. Note the context in each case. At the same time, the holiness of God was a most appropriate subject at Shiloh. We have already noticed the chilling words, "and the two sons of Eli, Hophni and Phinehas, the priests of the Lord were there" (1.3). In our next study we will encounter them again. They were anything but holy. They were "sons of Belial: they knew not the Lord" (v.12). Such verses as "be ye clean...that bear the vessels of the Lord" (Is 52.11), and "holiness becometh thine house, O Lord, for ever" (Ps 93.5), were foreign to them. This reminds us that we must all "cleanse ourselves from all filthiness of the flesh and spirit, perfecting holiness in the fear of God" (2 Cor 7.1).

b) He is the unique God. "There is none beside thee." The Philistines discovered this when Dagon collapsed before the ark! (5.1-4). Notice the connection with the previous statement. "There is none holy as the Lord: **for** there is none beside thee." The worship of pagan gods was customarily accompanied by depravity. God is unique in His holiness. This divine attribute also needed emphasis at the time. Israel was idolatrous: "strange gods" were worshipped (See 7.3-4). Paul puts it like this, "We know that an idol is nothing in the world, and that there is none other God but one" (1 Cor 8.4). Notice the recurring or similar words, "I am the Lord, and there is none else, there is no God beside me" (Is 45.5,18,21,22).

c) He is the dependable God. "Neither is there any rock like our God." Hannah was evidently well aware of Deuteronomy 32, which contains the divine title "Rock" on five occasions (see vv.4,15,18,30,31). Note v.37: "And he shall say, Where are their gods, their rock in whom they trusted." The Psalms abound with references to the Lord as a "rock." The security of all who trust in Him is assured. See, for example, Psalm 62.2, "He only is my rock and my salvation; he is my defence; I shall not be greatly moved." When the Lord Jesus said to Peter, "Thou art Peter, and upon this rock I will build my church", He certainly wasn't calling *Peter* "this rock!" He was referring to *Himself* as the divine Rock of Deuteronomy 32. Notice Numbers 1.6, where "Zurishaddai" means "my Rock is the Almighty", and Numbers 3.35, where "Zuriel" means "my rock is God."

d) He is the omniscient God. "The Lord is a God of knowledge." The complete quotation is important. "Talk no more so exceedingly proudly; let not arrogancy proceed out of your mouth: **for** the Lord is a God of knowledge." This could refer to Peninnah who "provoked her sore, for to make her fret." God was listening. Psalm 73 describes people who are "corrupt, and speak wickedly concerning oppression...They set their mouth against the heavens...And they say, How doth God know? and is there knowledge in the most High?" (vv.8-11). See also Job 22.13 and Psalm 10.11. We must remember that "all things are naked and opened unto the eyes of him with whom we have to do."

e) He is the just God. "By him actions are weighed." A.McShane *(Lessons for Leaders)* puts it like this. "He is judge of all. Every action of man is weighed in His scales, and will be dealt with in perfect righteousness." When Christ reigns, He "shall not judge after the sight of his eyes, neither reprove after the hearing of his ears. But with righteousness shall he judge the poor, and reprove with equity for the meek of the earth" (Is 11.3-4). At the final judgment, men will be "judged out of those things which were written in the books, according to their works...they were judged every man according to their works" (Rev 20.12-13). Although, having trusted in Christ, we will never suffer the judgment of God against sin, we must not forget that "we must all appear before the judgment seat of Christ; that every one may receive the things done in his body, according to that he hath done, whether it be good or bad" (2 Cor 5.10). Then, "every man shall receive his own reward according to his own labour" (1 Cor 3.8). Our actions will be "weighed."

A.McShane suggests that Hannah's prayer to God reflected her knowledge of the Scriptures, and that in each case she alluded to the way in which God had revealed Himself in Israel's history. We have noted passages in Leviticus ("there is none holy as the Lord") and Deuteronomy ("neither is there any rock like our God"). This merits further study. Very clearly, Hannah was not using her imagination. Her praise and thanksgiving was based on the word of God. She did not have a complete Bible, but she used what she had. Elijah did the same. Think about 1 Kings 17.1. Read Jonah 2, and notice his quotations. Remember, too, that Hannah, Elijah and Jonah did not have a personal copy of the Scriptures! We **all** need a "working knowledge" of the Bible.

(ii) The activities of God (vv.4-8)
In this section we have six contrasts, or better, six reversals. God reverses weakness and strength (v.4); hunger and plenty (v.5); barrenness and fruitfulness (v.5); death and life (v.6); poverty and wealth (v.7); and depth and height (vv.7-8).

a) Weakness and strength. "The bows of the mighty men are broken, and they that stumbled are girded with strength" (v.4). Once again, Hannah is not making it up as she goes along! Hebrews 11.32-34 refers to the period of the Judges (plus David, Samuel and the prophets), with the comment, "Who through faith...out of weakness were made strong, waxed valiant in fight, turned to flight the armies of the aliens." Hannah would have been well aware of events like these. Some of them would have been in living memory! Now read 1 Corinthians 1.26-29. Notice, amongst other things, that God "hath chosen the weak things of the world to confound the things that are mighty." Human weakness is no problem to God, as long as we acknowledge it, and trust in Him. His "strength is made perfect in weakness." Paul adds, paradoxically, "when I am weak, then am I strong" (2 Cor 12.9-10).

b) Hunger and plenty. "They that were full have hired out themselves for bread; and they that were hungry ceased" (v.5.) Possibly, Hannah alludes here to the situation in Egypt centuries before. "Joseph's brethren were full the day they put him in the pit, but later they fell at his feet craving for bread, for they had become hungry." (A.McShane). Notice too that the hungry Egyptians became "servants unto Pharaoh" in exchange for seed, whilst "Joseph nourished his father, and his brethren, and all his father's household, with bread, according to their families" (Gen 47.12). The story of Ruth may also have been in her mind. But there is another type of hunger. The Lord Jesus said, "Blessed are they which do hunger and thirst after righteousness: for they shall be filled" (Mt 5.6).

c) Barrenness and fruitfulness. "The barren hath born seven; and she that hath many children is waxed feeble" (v.5). Whilst Hannah may have been alluding to Sarah, Rebekah and Rachel, it seems more likely that she was referring to her own experience here. To quote Ellicott's Commentary: "Here the thought of the inspired singer (the commentator evidently believed that

Hannah *sang* these words) reverts to herself, and the imagery is drawn from the story of her own life. Seven children are mentioned as the full number of the divine blessing in children (Ruth 4.15, Jer 15.9)." We know that whilst Hannah became the mother of five more children, there is no record of further children born to Peninnah. It does seem, however, that the words, "she that hath many children is waxed feeble", are more than a statement of fact. Peninnah was obviously proud of her achievements, and took every opportunity to remind Hannah of her superiority. God hates pride. There are lessons here for us all. For example, if God is blessing our work and service for Him, we must not despise those who, seemingly, are not enjoying such prosperity. Pride will rob us of divine help, and bring spiritual weakness. On the other hand, if we do not seem to be making progress, we must pray about it. Hannah did this, and proved that God hears and answers prayer.

d) Death and life. "The Lord killeth, and maketh alive: he bringeth down to the grave (*sheol*, often translated 'hell'), and bringeth up" (v.6). Once again, Hannah proves her acquaintance with Deuteronomy: "see now that I, even I, am he, and there is no god with me: *I kill, and I make alive;* I wound, and I heal: neither is there any that can deliver out of my hand" (32.39). Perhaps this is an extension of thought. The God who can reverse the course of military affairs (v.4), social affairs (v.5), and family affairs (v.5), can do anything. He is in control of death and life. Abraham believed that God was "able to raise him (Isaac) up, even from the dead" (Heb 11.19).

e) Poverty and wealth. "The Lord maketh poor, and maketh rich" (v.7). A.McShane suggests that Hannah could be alluding here to Abraham and Lot. "Lot, who had much wealth, was left destitute, and his uncle Abraham increased in riches." It is, of course, possible to be poor *and* rich at the same time, and rich *and* poor at the same time. See Revelation 2.9, and 3.17. The Lord Jesus became poor, that we might be rich (2 Cor 8. 9).

f) Depth and height. "He bringeth low, and lifteth up" (v.7). This is amplified and expanded in verse 8. "He raiseth up the poor out of the dust, and lifteth up the beggar from the dunghill, to set them among princes, and to make them inherit the throne of glory." This is quoted, almost *verbatim,* in Psalm 113.7-8. Notice the reference to "the barren woman" in verse 9. "*Dust* and the *dunghill* are figures used to denote the deepest degradation and ignominy" (Keil and Delitzsch). As A.McShane observes, "No better example of the exaltation of the lowly could be cited than that of Joseph, for was he not taken from prison to share the glory of the throne?" Quite obviously, Hannah had carefully watched God at work! The New Testament goes even further. "The Spirit itself beareth witness with our spirit, that we are the children of God: And if children, then heirs; heirs of God, and joint-heirs with Christ" (Rom 8.16-17). Read Ephesians 2.1-7. What would Hannah have made of these passages?!

The concluding words, **"For** the pillars of the earth (see also Psalm 75.3) are the Lord's, and he hath set the world upon them", emphasise that as Creator, God is quite able to elevate the lowest to the highest! After all, the existence of the earth depends on His power!

iii) The assurance of God (vv.9-11)
Hannah now turns to the future. She becomes a prophetess. Centuries later, another godly woman of the same name, Anna, was also a prophetess. See Luke 2.27. The divine programme is assured. Notice "He *will*" in v.9, and *"shall"* in v.9 and v.10 (four times). These verses assure the following.

a) The preservation of the saints. "He will keep the feet of his saints" (v.9). Compare Psalm 56.13; 116.8; 121.3). Whilst we happily, and rightly, apply this to ourselves (see, for example, 1 Peter 1. 5), there can be no doubt that it refers, in the first place, to Israel. We can trace a faithful remnant, preserved by God, throughout the Scriptures. See, for example, 1 Kings 19.18, Malachi 3.16-17, Luke 2.38. At this "present time also there is a remnant according to the election of grace", of which Paul was part. See Romans 11.1-5. In the future, during the dark days of the "great tribulation", God will have His "elect." See Matthew 24.22, "And except those days should be shortened, there should no flesh be saved: but for the elect's sake those days shall be shortened."

b) The condemnation of sinners. "The wicked shall be silent in darkness; for by strength shall no man prevail. The adversaries of the Lord shall be broken to pieces; out of heaven shall he thunder upon them: the Lord shall judge the ends of the earth" (vv.9-10). God "thundered with a great thunder...upon the Philistines" (7.10), but He will thunder universally at the end-time. See Revelation 10.3-4, etc. "Broken to pieces" takes us to Psalm 2.9 and Revelation 2.27. "The ends of the earth" reminds us that none can escape divine judgment.

c) The exaltation of the Son. "He shall give strength unto his king, and exalt the horn of his anointed" (v.10). The judgment of the wicked will be followed by the reign of the King. Whilst this was partly fulfilled in David, its ultimate fulfilment awaits the coming of "great David's greater Son." Ellicott's Commentary puts it nicely. "The words received a partial fulfilment in the splendid reigns of David and Solomon: but the pious Jew looked on the golden halo which surrounded these great reigns as but a pale reflection of the glory which would accompany King Messiah when He should appear." Then the proclamation will be made, "The kingdom of the world is become the kingdom of our Lord, and of his Christ; and he shall reign for ever and ever" (Rev 11.15 RV). The psalm begins with Hannah's exaltation ("mine horn is exalted in the Lord"), and ends with the exaltation of Christ ("exalt the horn of his anointed").

On that happy note, Elkanah returned to Ramah, leaving Samuel at Shiloh. "And the child did minister unto the Lord before Eli the priest" (v.11). This introduces our next study.

CHAPTER 2B

Samuel's Growth (2.12-36)

As noted in the previous chapter, for the purposes of our studies, we have divided 1 Samuel 2 as follows. **(1)** The prayer of Hannah (vv.1-11); **(2)** The perversity of Eli's sons (vv.12-17); **(3)** The progress of Samuel (vv.18-21); **(4)** The protest of Eli (vv.22-26); **(5)** The prophecy of judgment, (vv.27-36).

1. The Prayer of Hannah (vv.1-11)
One brief addition to what is written in the previous chapter (2A). The psalm begins with Hannah's exaltation ("mine horn is exalted in the Lord"), and ends with the exaltation of Christ ("the Lord shall give strength unto his king, and exalt the horn of his anointed"). That's real progress! Christ has pre-eminence. See Colossians 1.18. God enabled Hannah to see the ultimate glory of Israel, when God's anointed King will reign from Zion. Read Psalm 2. It is therefore with regret that we now have to consider an entirely different picture.

2. The Perversity of Eli's Sons (vv.12-17)
The outlook for Samuel looks decidedly bleak. "And Elkanah went to Ramah to his house. And the child did minister unto the Lord before Eli the priest. Now the sons of Eli were sons of Belial; they knew not the Lord." Samuel now lived among evil men. Their practices were so corrupt that "men abhorred the offering of the Lord" (v.17). Humanly speaking, Samuel was young and vulnerable. This was the boy of whom his mother said, "I will give him unto the Lord all the days of his life." But, to coin a phrase, it looked as though "he didn't stand a chance". If Nathanael had been alive, he would have said, "Can any good thing come out of Shiloh?" To which we answer, "Come and see!"

The Lord Jesus lived in a place of ill-repute, but He was never contaminated by its evil atmosphere. Job was wrong when he said, "Who can bring a clean thing out of an unclean? Not one!" (Job 14.4). God preserved Samuel amongst ceremonial and moral evil. The Lord Jesus was "holy, harmless, undefiled" in Nazareth.

This particular passage describes the ceremonial wickedness of Hophni and Phinehas. We must notice at least four things about them. **(A)** They were unregenerate (v.12); **(B)** They were totally selfish (vv.13-14); **(C)** They were intolerant (vv.15-16); **(D)** They stumbled others (v.17).

A) They were unregenerate (v.12)
"Now the sons of Eli were sons of Belial; they knew not the Lord." The word "Belial" is not the name of some pagan deity, it simply means "worthless." Hophni and Phinehas were therefore "worthless fellows." See also 1.16, 10.27. However, in the New Testament it is used as a synonym for Satan. See 2 Corinthians 6. 15, "What concord hath Christ with Belial?". Very clearly, you couldn't be "a son of Belial" and "know the Lord", in the Old Testament. The two were mutually exclusive, in the same way that Christ and Belial are mutually exclusive.

The worship of Israel was in the hands of unregenerate men. The people who were supposed to represent the people before God, were worthless. They "knew not the Lord." It is all strikingly familiar, isn't it? It happened when the Lord Jesus was here. It has happened since.

B) They were totally selfish (vv.13-14)
"And the priests' custom with the people was that, when any man offered sacrifice, the priests' servant came, while the flesh was in seething, with a fleshhook of three teeth in his hand. And he struck it into the pan, or kettle, or caldron, or pot; all that the fleshhook brought up the priest took for himself. So they did in Shiloh unto all the Israelites that came thither." The "priests' custom" was at complete variance with the word of God. God had made adequate provision for the priests. See, for example, Leviticus 7.31-36. "The breast shall be Aaron's and his sons." And the right shoulder shall ye give unto the priest for a heave-offering of the sacrifices of your peace offerings. He among the sons of Aaron...shall have the right shoulder for his part."

But Hophni and Phinehas took whatever they wanted whenever it pleased them. As A. McShane observes, "Covetousness was the plague of their hearts. They lusted after the flesh of the offerings, and were not satisfied with the portion allotted to them by the Lord." We should remember that the peace-offerings provided food for God (part of the offering was burnt on the altar), food for the priests (the breast and the right shoulder), and food for the offerer and his family. But Hophni and Phinehas totally disregarded the word of God. They were without any scruples. They took what they wanted, full stop. To put it another way, the priests fleeced the people. That's also familiar, isn't it? But worse follows.

C) They were intolerant, (vv.15-16)
"Also before they burnt the fat, the priests' servant came, and said to the man that sacrificed, Give flesh to roast for the priest; for he will not have sodden flesh of thee, but raw. And if the man said unto him, Let them not fail to burn the fat presently, and then take as much as thy soul desireth; then he would answer him, Nay; but thou shalt give it me now: and if not, I will take it by force." The fat was to be burnt on the altar. It was to be wholly devoted to God. See Leviticus 3.14-17, 7.23-25, 30-31. Without going into detail, the priests were robbing God by demanding the sacrifice before it could be offered on the altar. "He will not have sodden flesh of thee, but raw." Any protest was disregarded. The godly Israelite (like Elkanah who, presumably, suffered with everybody else), with a genuine desire to obey and please God, was threatened with force if he dared to question the priests' wishes. This is precisely what happens today. People who love the word of God are regarded as narrow, bigoted fundamentalists, whose protests deserve to be completely ignored. How dare they stand in the way of the enlightened leadership! We must not expect the religious world to applaud when we honour God.

D) They stumbled others (v.17)
"Wherefore the sin of the young men was very great before the Lord: for men abhorred the offering of the Lord." In fact, the priesthood never recovered from the damage caused by their disastrous conduct. Ellicott's Commentary puts it like this. "Religion was being brought into general disrepute through the conduct of its leading ministers." This, too, is strikingly relevant today. But we mustn't evade lessons for ourselves here. Note the following. "Give none occasion to the adversary to speak reproachfully" (1 Tim 5.14); "In all things shewing thyself a pattern of good works...that he that is of the contrary part may be ashamed, having no evil thing to say of you" (Titus 2.7-8. See also Titus 2.15). God forbid that any of us should ever bring the name of the Lord Jesus, and the word of God, into disrepute. See Romans 3.24. Unlike these wicked young men, we should "adorn the doctrine of God our Saviour in all things" (Titus 2.10).

Just think about it. Samuel was right in the middle of all this. The godly atmosphere of his home in Ramah had been exchanged for ungodliness in Shiloh. But the picture changes again. God, the Master-Jeweller, who loves to display his exquisite pieces against the darkest backgrounds, has a little gem to show us. We come then to

3. The Progress of Samuel (vv.18-21)

"But Samuel ministered before the Lord, being a child, girded with a linen ephod." We cannot possibly miss the contrast. "Wherefore the sin of the young men was very great before the Lord…**But Samuel** ministered before the Lord." At this point we ought to notice the steady progress of young Samuel. *(i)* "And the child did minister unto the Lord (compare Acts 13. 2) before Eli the priest" (2.11); *(ii)* "But Samuel ministered unto the Lord, being a child" (2.18); *(iii)* "And the child Samuel grew before the Lord" (2.21); *(iv)* "And the child Samuel grew on" (2.26); *(v)* "And the child Samuel ministered unto the Lord before Eli" (3.1); *(vi)* "And Samuel grew, and the Lord was with him, and did let none of his words fall to the ground. And all Israel knew that Samuel was established to be a prophet of the Lord" (3.19-20); *(vii)* "And the word of Samuel came to all Israel" (4.1). We will examine these references in more detail as we come to them in our studies, but we must notice two important lessons now.

Firstly, Samuel was advancing spiritually. His growth was preparatory for the vital role that God had for him. There is no need for us to say more: we must all "Grow in grace, and in the knowledge of our Lord and Saviour Jesus Christ" (2 Pet 3.18). Why not look back over the past year, and ask, "How much have *I* progressed in my Christian life?" Remember that there will be no progress in any direction unless we have progressed in our devotion to Christ.

Secondly, Samuel was progressing in difficult and unhelpful circumstances. We are glad to notice that he was encouraged by Eli, but Shiloh merited a government health warning. Don't use your circumstances as an excuse for spiritual failure. Remember Samuel! Older Christians should not wring their hands and say, "Young Christians today have far greater difficulties and temptations than we had." Remember Samuel! He wore "a linen ephod", the symbol of purity (it was made from white cloth), and he "kept himself pure" (1 Tim 5.22). He didn't "twiddle his thumbs" either. Samuel "ministered before the Lord." Whilst we do not have many details, he was obviously busy in service for God, which is more than can be said for some Christians!

Samuel was out of Hannah's sight, but he was not out of Hannah's mind. He got a new coat every year: a larger coat every year. She expected him to grow! His clothes reflected his growth. Do people see developments in our spiritual dress? "Meditate upon these things; give thyself wholly to them; that thy profiting (progress) may appear to all", (1 Tim 4.15). For the clothes we ought to be wearing, see Colossians 3.12-14. Notice too, that the devotion of Elkanah and his family did not stop. The "yearly sacrifice" continued. It's nice to see quiet consistency amongst God's people, isn't it! Their devotion contrasts vividly with the contempt exhibited by Hophni and Phinehas. It's also nice to see that God is no man's debtor. The interest on the loan was paid, as we have already noticed, at the rate of 500%!

"And the child grew before the Lord." Keil and Delitzsch explain it like this: "Near to Him (at the sanctuary), and under His protection and blessing." But the picture changes yet again, and we now listen to

4. The Protest of Eli (vv.22-26)
Hophni and Phinehas were "sons of Belial" morally as well as ceremonially. "Now Eli was very old, and heard all that his sons did unto all Israel (ceremonially: see v.14); and how they lay with the women that assembled at the door of the tabernacle of the congregation (morally)." In the first case, the priests deliberately failed to honour God. In the second place, they were guilty of gross immorality. The lesson is clear: if we do not give God His rightful place in our lives, we become morally vulnerable. Compare Romans 1.18-32.

Eli remonstrated with his sons and warned them, but that was all. A.McShane rightly assesses the situation as follows. "His words were unheeded, as we might expect, for nothing short of deposing them from the priesthood would have met the demands of the case. Doubtless the old man hoped for improvement, for he did not relish the thought that his house would no longer continue in office, and that priests of another line would serve the tabernacle." When immorality invaded the assembly at Corinth, Paul gave clear instructions. "Therefore put away from among yourselves that wicked person." Read 1 Corinthians 5 in this connection. Notice, "Know ye not that a little leaven leaveneth the whole lump?" (v.6). Immorality affects the whole assembly, not just the guilty parties. So does false teaching: see Galatians 5. 9. It would have been decidedly unpleasant for Eli to expel his sons from the priesthood, and it is equally unpleasant to exclude believers from fellowship on either moral or doctrinal grounds. But the assembly is a place where God is to be honoured, and where the testimony is to be jealously preserved. This transcends even family considerations. If David had corrected Adonijah in his childhood and youth, he might never have "exalted himself, saying, I will be king." But "his father had not displeased him at any time in saying, Why hast thou done so?" (1 Kings 1.5-6).

The section ends with another contrast. "They hearkened not unto the voice of their father, because the Lord would **slay** them. And the child Samuel grew on, and was in **favour** both with the Lord, and also with men." This sounds familiar, doesn't it? Luke describes the boyhood and youth of the Lord Jesus in the same way. "And Jesus increased in wisdom and stature, and in favour with God and man" (Lk 1.52).

But Eli's mild rebuke was not the end of the matter. God now intervenes. He is a "God of knowledge, and by him actions are weighed", (v.3). He knew all about the arrogance (v.16) of Hophni and Phinehas. There is nothing mild in what now follows.

5. The Prophecy of Judgment (vv.27-36)
We must now listen to the solemn message of the "man of God." Amongst other things, a "man of God" must have the word of God. His message can be summarised as follows. **(A)** The privileges of Levi (vv.27-28); **(B)** The preference of Eli (v.29); **(C)** The prediction of judgment (vv.30-34); **(D)** The priest who would come (vv.35-36).

A) *The privileges of Levi (vv.27-28)*
"Thus saith the Lord, Did I plainly appear unto the house of thy father, when they were in Egypt in Pharaoh's house? And did I choose him out of all the tribes of Israel to be my priest, to offer upon mine altar, to burn incense, to wear an ephod before me? and did I give unto the house of thy father all the offerings made by fire of the children of Israel?" This is quite self-explanatory. See, for example, Exodus 4.14-16, 28.1, Deuteronomy 18. 1. Whilst God bestowed great responsibilities on Aaron and his sons, He also provided for them through the "offerings made by fire of the children of Israel". Now read 1 Corinthians 9. 7-14. Note the words, "Do you not know that they which minister about holy things live of the things of the temple? and *they which wait at the altar are partakers with the altar?* Even so hath God ordained that they which preach the gospel should live of the gospel" (vv.13-14). God commissions His servants, and provides for them. Let's add

something else: what a privilege to be chosen by God to serve Him! But what an awesome responsibility!

B) The preference of Eli (v.29)
"Wherefore kick ye at my sacrifice and at mine offering, which I have commanded in my habitation; and honour thy sons above me, to make yourselves fat with the chiefest of all the offerings of Israel my people?" This is also quite self-explanatory. The priesthood had abused its privileges. The expression "chiefest of all the offerings of Israel" means "the first of every sacrificial gift of Israel" (Keil and Delitzsch). The priests took that part of the offerings which belonged to God. Centuries later, He had to say, "Will a man rob God? Yet ye have robbed me" (Mal 3.8). Whilst the circumstances were slightly different, the result was the same. God did not have first place in the lives of His people. But are **we** giving Him first place? Do **we** give Him our best?

Whilst Eli was not personally guilty in the same way as his sons, he was held responsible for their evil conduct. See also 3. 13. This makes sobering reading for assembly elders. "A bishop (overseer) must be blameless, as the **steward** of God" (Tit 1.7). He is responsible for the flock, and should therefore take steps to ensure that God's word is taught and obeyed. This is no easy task, and can sometimes bring unpopularity. The work can be particularly difficult when God's interests clash with family interests. Eli failed here, and so have others.

C) The prediction of judgment (vv.30-34)
i) The principle of judgment. "Them that honour me I will honour, and they that despise me shall be lightly esteemed" (v.30). On a technical note, it does seem that we must distinguish between "thy house" (the family of Eli) and "the house of thy father" (the whole priesthood, as in (v.27). Since "the priest's office shall be theirs (Aaron and his sons) for a perpetual statute" (Ex 29.9), this verse does not mean that the priesthood would cease (see vv.35), but that Eli's "laxity cost him the priesthood, and he is told that he had forfeited what the Lord intended him to enjoy in that favoured position." (A.McShane). Are **we** prepared to honour God? Or does He have to say, "If then I be a father, where is mine honour?" (Mal 1.6). Lip service will not do. See Matthew 15.8.

ii) The nature of judgment. "Behold, the days come, that I will cut off thine arm, and the arm of thy father's house, that there shall not be an old man in thine house" (v.31). The "arm" signifies power and strength. See, for example Job 22.9, Psalm 37.17. Eli had spared his sons, but God would not spare him, or his family. Eli had "sown the wind" and would "reap the whirlwind" (Hos 8.7). The early death of Eli's successors is emphasised in (vv.31-33). Eli lived long enough to witness the triumph of the Philistines, and the capture of the ark (v.32). The family of Eli would not be entirely destroyed (v.33), but the surviving priest would "look upon the decay with his eyes, and pine away with grief in consequence." (Keil and Delitzsch). The words, "to consume *thine* eyes, and to grieve *thine* heart", evidently refer, not to Eli personally, but to his family. For surviving priests of Eli's family, see 14.3; 22.20. Ultimately, Solomon dismissed Abiathar (descended from Ithamar through Eli) and gave the high priesthood to Zadok (descended from Eleazar), "that he might fulfil the word of the Lord, which he spake concerning the house of Eli in Shiloh." See 1 Kings 2.26-27,35. Eli left a sad legacy to his family. What kind of legacy are **we** going to leave for the next generation? For the best possible legacy, read 2 Timothy 2.2.

iii) The sign of judgment. "And this shall be a sign unto thee, that shall come upon thy two sons, on Hophni and Phinehas; in one day they shall die both of them." No comment is necessary. See 4.11. There can be no doubt about the fulfilment of any message which is prefaced by, "Thus saith the Lord" (v.27).

(D) The priest who would come (vv.35-36)
"And I will raise me up a faithful priest, that shall do according to that which is in mine heart and in my mind: and I will build him a sure house; and he shall walk before mine anointed for ever." Who is this "faithful priest?" It has been suggested that this refers to Samuel. After all, he took the place of Eli at the head of the nation, and acted not only as a prophet, but also as a priest. See, for example, 7.9-10,17. It was Samuel who anointed both Saul and David, and his grandson, Heman, "the king's seer in the words of God", was placed by David over the choir in "the house of God." See 1 Chronicles 6.33. 25.4-5. However, Samuel's descendants did not follow their father into the priesthood, and it is therefore difficult to say that God gave him "a sure house" as a priest.

The alternative is Zadok. As we have seen, he became high priest in the reign of Solomon, when the priesthood reverted to the family of Eleazar. Ahimelech and Zadok were joint priests previously. See 2 Samuel 8.17 etc). We can therefore say that he "walked before God's anointed", that is, before Solomon. Zadok actually anointed Solomon! But this prophecy points beyond Solomon. It does say, "And he shall walk before **mine anointed for ever!**", that is, the Lord Jesus. Ezekiel 40-48 describes the millennial temple and its environs. The priests then will be "the sons of Zadok among the sons of Levi, which come near to the Lord to minister unto him" (40.46). See also 43.19, 44.15, 48.11. (The last two of these references evidently look back to 2 Samuel 15.24-29). The "anointed" must therefore be the Lord Jesus, Who will "have dominion also from sea to sea, and from the river unto the ends of the earth" (Ps 72.8). Hannah saw His glory when she said, "He shall give strength unto his king, and exalt the horn of his **anointed**" (v.10).

The prophecy concludes by describing the utter humiliation of the house of Eli. "And it shall come to pass, that every one that is left in thine house shall come and crouch to him for a piece of silver and a morsel of bread, and shall say, Put me, I pray thee, into one of the priests' offices, that I may eat a piece of bread." No doubt this was fulfilled in the lifetime of Zadok. The very family which demanded the best part of the offerings (vv.12-16) is reduced to begging! "Whatsoever a man soweth, that shall he also reap" (Gal 6.7).

CHAPTER 3

Samuel's call (3.1-21)

We have already noticed the steady progress of young Samuel. He must have been very young indeed when his parents brought him to Shiloh, but he never looked back. *(i)* "And the child did minister unto the Lord before Eli the priest" (2.11); *(ii)* "But Samuel ministered unto the Lord, being a child" (2.18); *(iii)* "And the child Samuel grew before the Lord" (2.21); *(iv)* "And the child Samuel grew on" (2.26); *(v)* "And the child Samuel ministered unto the Lord before Eli" (3.1); *(vi)* "And Samuel grew, and the Lord was with him, and did let none of his words fall to the ground. And all Israel…knew that Samuel was established to be a prophet of the Lord" (3.19-20); *(vii)* "And the word of Samuel came to all Israel" (4.1). Let's remember that this progress was made against a background of failure in **priestly ministry** (2.12-17), failure in **priestly purity** (2.22), and failure in **priestly authority** (2.29). Are **we** growing "in grace, and in the knowledge of our Lord and Saviour Jesus Christ?" Don't make your circumstances an excuse for slow progress or no progress. Remember Samuel!

Samuel had been **"*lent*** to the Lord" (1.28), he **"*ministered*** before the Lord" (2.18), and he **"*grew*** before the Lord" (2.21). Now he hears the voice of the Lord. "The Lord called Samuel…and the Lord called yet again, Samuel…and the Lord called Samuel again the third time…and the Lord came, and stood, and called as at other times, Samuel, Samuel" (vv.4,6,8,10). Samuel learned at least four things in this chapter. *(1)* He learned to recognise the voice of God (vv.1-10); *(2)* He learned to appreciate the holiness of God (vv.11-14); *(3)* He learned to communicate the message of God (vv.15-18); *(4)* He learned to trust the word of God (vv.19-21). This chapter describes a milestone in Samuel's life. Thus far, he had come to know a great deal ***about*** the Lord. Now he began to ***know*** the Lord, and nothing was ever the same again! We are not told at what age God spoke to Samuel. He is described as a "child" at the time (v.8), but we should remember that the word "child" is used in a wide sense in the Old Testament. He was obviously a growing lad. See 2.21 & 26.

1. He learned to recognise the voice of God (vv.1-10)
The first paragraph of the chapter can be divided as follows. **(A)** Israel and the voice of God (v.1). **(B)** Samuel and the voice of God (vv.2-10).

A) Israel and the voice of God (v.1)
"And the child Samuel ministered unto the Lord before Eli. And the word of the Lord was precious in those days; there was no open vision." The word "precious" means "rare" and the words "there was no open vision" are literally, "a vision was not spread." See JND. "And the word of Jehovah was rare in those days; a vision was not frequent." Very simply, but very sadly, God was not speaking to His people. We don't have to look far for the reason. The word of God was flouted, not only by the priests, as we have seen, but in the worship of "strange gods" (7.3). See Psalm 78.55-66, which refers to this period. Disobedience will rob us of the voice of God. There is no record that God communicated with Abraham whilst he was in Egypt. When we read God's word, we should expect to hear His voice, but we cannot expect Him to speak to us if we are not prepared to obey Him. Disobedience is **sin.** Samuel himself makes this clear in 15.22-23.

A.McShane suggests that it was because "the word of Jehovah was rare in those days" (JND) that Eli was so slow in realising that God had spoken to Samuel. People just didn't expect to hear God's voice.

B) Samuel and the voice of God (vv.2-10)
i) The circumstances of the call, (vv.2-3). It was **"at that time."** The spiritual and moral life of the nation, and in consequence, national life in its entirety, had reached rock bottom. But God was determined, in His sovereignty, to bless His people, and it all began when a boy heard His voice at Shiloh. J.N.Darby's translation might help us to get the details more clearly. "And it came to pass at that time, when Eli lay in his place (now his eyes began to grow dim, he could not see), and the lamp of God had not yet gone out, and Samuel lay in the temple of Jehovah where the ark of God was, that Jehovah called to Samuel." The words, "ere the lamp of God went out in the temple of the Lord", simply mean that God spoke to Samuel during the night. The seven-branched lampstand ("the lamp of God") burned "from evening to morning before the Lord." See Exodus 27.20-21 and Leviticus 24.3.

The reference to Eli's physical eyesight reminds us that spiritual eyesight is vital. See, for example, 2 Peter 1.9, "But he that lacketh these things (they are listed in vv.5-7) is blind, and cannot see afar off." If you can't see the necessity for spiritual progress ("add to your faith"), then you are blind. See also Revelation 3.17, "Thou sayest, I am rich, and increased with goods, and have need of nothing; and knowest not that thou art wretched, and miserable, and poor, and blind, and naked." If you are completely occupied with material progress, then you are blind. How's **your** eyesight?

ii) The individuality of the call. Samuel heard his name! God spoke to him personally. See, particularly (v.6), "And the Lord called yet again, Samuel", and (v.10), "And the Lord came, and stood, and called as at other times, Samuel, Samuel." God does speak to us individually, doesn't He? Haven't **you** heard Him say, through His word, "This is the way, walk ye in it?" (Is 30.21). Perhaps it has been His "still small voice" saying, "What doest thou here?" (1 Kings 12.19-20).

iii) The persistence of the call. God spoke to Samuel four times that night. This exceeded Elihu's expectation. "God speaketh once, yea twice, yet man perceiveth it not" (Job 33.14). But God did not become impatient. After all, Samuel was still young (vv.1,8) and "did not yet know the Lord, neither was the word of the Lord yet revealed unto him." God dealt with Samuel gently and tenderly. We must notice that on each occasion, Samuel **did** respond, even if he did get it wrong three times! It would have been another matter entirely if Samuel had been a mature grown man, and had deliberately shut his ears to the voice of God. We all have good reason to thank God for His patience and grace, but we must not trade on His understanding and compassion.

God wanted Samuel to **know** Him, which is more than knowing **about** Him. He came to know God at an early age. Once again, A.McShane has some valuable comments here; "Whatever care Hannah bestowed upon her child, Samuel, whatever training she gave him, and whatever clothing she provided for him, there was one thing she could not do, and that was to impart to him the knowledge of the Lord. This he must have for himself."

iv) The help with the call. Whatever we may say about Eli, he did recognise that God was speaking to Samuel. He "perceived that the Lord had called the child." Good advice followed. "Go, lie down: and it shall be, if he call thee, that thou shalt say, Speak, Lord; for thy servant heareth." The old man was ready and willing to help the lad, which reminds us that older Christians should be ready to help younger Christians, and younger Christians should be prepared to accept the advice and guidance of older Christians.

v) The response to the call. "And the Lord came, and stood, and called as at other times, Samuel, Samuel. Then Samuel answered, Speak; for thy servant heareth." We know that he was told to say, "Speak, **Lord;** for thy servant heareth." But he was not reprimanded. After all, he was still very young! Notice too that "the Lord **came,** and **stood,** and **called** as at other times." We can therefore understand his omission. It's surprising that he said anything at all! Whilst we are told how God appeared to His servants on other occasions (see, for example Genesis 18.1-2 etc, Joshua 5.13-15), we are not told in what way the Lord came, stood, and revealed Himself here.

There can be no better prayer before reading the scriptures than, "Speak, Lord; for thy servant heareth." There should be a desire to **hear His voice** ("speak"), a desire to **recognise His authority (**"Lord"), and a desire to **do His will** ("thy servant heareth").

> Oh, give me Samuel's ear!
> The open ear, O Lord,
> Alive and quick to hear
> Each whisper of Thy word;
> Like him to answer at Thy call,
> And to obey Thee first of all.

Samuel certainly learned to recognise the voice of God. He evidently enjoyed very close communion with God. See, for example, 9.15-16, "Now the Lord had told Samuel *in his ear* a day before Saul came, saying, tomorrow about this time I will send thee a man out of the land of Benjamin, and thou shalt anoint him to be captain over my people Israel." Samuel was obviously very well attuned to the voice of God! God was able to have "a word in his ear!" It is so important to hear and obey God's voice. See 1 Samuel 22.15.

2. He learned to appreciate the holiness of God (vv.11-14)
God did not go behind Eli's back. The "man of God" had already notified Eli that judgment on his family was imminent. "I have told him that I will judge his house for ever" (v.13. See 2.27-36). It is therefore significant that whilst it was a "man of God" who spoke to Eli, it was God Himself who spoke to

Samuel on the same subject. The two messages were substantially the same, but the message to Samuel was evidently part of his training. In any case, it seems unlikely that Samuel was aware that God had already passed sentence on the house of Eli. Amongst other things, Samuel learned, first hand from God Himself, that sin is immensely serious, and must be judged. We know that this is true for unsaved people, but we must not forget that our unconfessed sin will be judged by God. This does not involve loss of salvation, but it certainly involves loss of fellowship with God. We should notice.

A) The certainty of coming judgment (vv.11-12)
"Behold, I will do a thing in Israel, at which both the ears of everyone that heareth it shall tingle. In that day I will perform against Eli all things which I have spoken concerning his house. when I begin, I will also make an end." There can be no doubt that the particular calamity which would cause "the ears of everyone that heareth it shall tingle", was the capture of the ark of the covenant. This was the crowning disaster in the battle with the Philistines. See 4.18. For "tingling ears", see also 2 Kings 21.12, Jeremiah 19. 3.

God was preparing Samuel for the disaster that lay ahead for Israel, in the same way that he prepared Abraham for the overthrow of Sodom and Gomorrah. "Shall I hide from Abraham that thing which I do?" (Gen 18.17). Let's remember too that He has shown "unto his servants things which must shortly come to pass" (Rev 1.1). Samuel would not be taken by surprise when disaster fell. But more than that, he would know that everything was in the hand of God. We can remain confident that God is in absolute control of even the most disastrous events. Nothing can thwart His purpose. "When I begin, I will also make an end."

B) The reason for coming judgment (v.13)
"For I have told him that I will judge his house for ever for the iniquity that he knoweth; because his sons made themselves vile, and he restrained them not." (v.13). God is not arbitrary in judgment. "We are sure that the judgment of God is according to truth against them which commit such things" (Rom 2.2). This is why, at the final judgment, John saw "the dead, small and great, stand before God; and the books were opened: and another book was opened, which is the book of life: and the dead were judged out of those things which were written in books, according to their works" (Rev 20.12-15).

Chapter 3

Eli was well aware that his sons were guilty of gross spiritual and moral misconduct. They had "made themselves vile", but their weak and indulgent father, who was both high priest and judge (4.18), failed to remove them from office. It is always disastrous when things go wrong, and good men remain silent. Leaders amongst God's people will have to give an account of their stewardship at the judgment seat of Christ.

Perhaps this part of the message prepared Samuel in another way. Years later, when "Samuel was old", he made his sons "judges over Israel", but they "walked not in his way, but turned aside after lucre, and took bribes, and perverted judgment" (8.1-6). We know nothing more about them, and we do not know how Samuel addressed the situation. Perhaps he remembered what happened at Shiloh. Whatever the facts, we must make sure that we learn from our own mistakes, and from the mistakes of other people.

C) The permanence of coming judgment (v.14)
"And therefore have I sworn unto the house of Eli, that the iniquity of Eli's house shall not be purged with sacrifice nor offering for ever." As we have already seen, the priesthood ultimately passed from Abiathar (descended from Ithamar through Eli) to Zadok (descended from Eleazar), in the reign of Solomon. The millennial priests will be the "sons of Zadok." The house of Eli will never be reinstated. It will be permanently disgraced. "The iniquity of Eli's house shall not be purged with sacrifice nor offering for ever." Let's say again that whilst we cannot lose our salvation, there is the dreadful possibility that we could "be ashamed before him at his coming" (1 Jn 2.28). Bad workmanship will incur loss." See 1 Corinthians 3.15.

3. He learned to communicate the message of God (vv.15-18)
"And Samuel lay until the morning, and opened the doors of the house of the Lord. And Samuel feared to shew Eli the vision." On a technical note, it is clear that some kind of structure must have been erected at Shiloh in connection with the tabernacle. We have already noticed that Eli "sat upon a seat by a post of the temple of the Lord". Now Samuel opens "the doors of the house of the Lord." We have no further information about this structure, but we do know that one of Samuel's tasks was to act as a doorkeeper. This reminds us of Psalm 84.10, although the word "doorkeeper" here actually means "someone who stands on the threshhold", and does not necessarily mean a doorkeeper. There was nothing particularly glamorous about opening "the doors of the house of the Lord", but it was a

beginning, and "he that is faithful in that which is least is faithful also in much." Samuel didn't burst upon Israel like a meteor. He made quiet steady progress, and worked humbly for God. That's a good basis for promotion!

We are not at all surprised that "Samuel feared to shew Eli the vision." But Eli was insistent. "What is the thing that the Lord hath said unto thee? I pray thee hide it not from me. God do so to thee, and more also, if thou hide anything from me of all the things that he said unto thee. And Samuel told him every whit, and hid nothing from him." Notice Eli's acceptance of God's word. He knew that God had acted righteously, and made no protest.

So Samuel learned another lesson that was to stand him in good stead in his coming ministry. In New Testament terms, he learned to "preach the word" and to "be instant in season, out of season" (2 Tim 4.2). On occasions, his ministry would be most unpalatable, but he was a splendid example of a true prophet. "The prophet that hath a dream, let him tell a dream; and he that hath my word, let him speak my word faithfully" (Jer 23.28). Paul was able to say, "I have not shunned to declare unto you all the counsel of God" (Acts 20.27). God's word can be most unpopular, even, sometimes, alas, amongst God's people. Now, finally:

4. He learned to trust the Word of God (vv.19-21)
Samuel's public ministry had begun. "And Samuel (no longer "the child Samuel") grew, and the Lord was with him, and did let none of his words fall to the ground." Whilst this *could* mean that Samuel did not let any part of **God's** word fall to the ground, it is more likely that it means that God did not let any part of **Samuel's** words fall to the ground. God fulfilled the prophetic witness of Samuel. This is supported by what follows. "And all Israel from Dan even to Beer-sheba knew that Samuel was established to be a prophet of the Lord." They knew, because Samuel met the test described in Deuteronomy 18.21-22; His word "came to pass". See 4.1. "And what Samuel said **happened** to all Israel" (JND, and AV. Margin). It is significant that this statement follows the words, "And the Lord appeared again in Shiloh: for the Lord revealed himself to Shiloh by the word of the Lord" (3.21). Quite obviously, Samuel only communicated what God had told him, and it is therefore not surprising that his predictions were completely fulfilled!

The fact that God "did let none of them fall to the ground", reminds us that God honours His word. We therefore have every encouragement to preach and teach the word of God. See Jeremiah 1.12, "I am watchful over my word to perform it" (Jer 1.12 JND). See Isaiah 55.10. 11, "My word…shall not return unto me void; but it shall accomplish that which I please, and it shall prosper in the thing whereto I sent it."

The words, "And what Samuel said **happened** to all Israel", bring us to the next section in the book, chapters 4-6, which describe the events predicted by Samuel.

CHAPTER 4

The Capture of the Ark (4.1-22)

Samuel's training, which began in his childhood, resulted in his recognition by all Israel from Dan (in the north) to Beersheba (in the south) that he "was established to be a prophet of the Lord" (2.20). Bearing in mind that "when the word of the prophet shall come to pass, then shall the prophet be known, that the Lord hath truly sent him" (Jer 28.9), we now read, "And what Samuel said happened to all Israel" (4.1 JND): so there was no doubt that Samuel had been "truly sent" by the Lord.

This solemn chapter records the fulfilment of God's word through Samuel, hence the introduction: "And the word of Samuel came (margin "came to pass") to all Israel." There is no further record of Samuel's ministry for at least twenty years. As we shall see, the ark was in Philistine territory for seven months (v.6), and twenty years elapsed after that before we hear Samuel's voice again: see 7.1-3.

We must now ponder the events in this chapter which made "both the ears (not just one ear!) of every one that heareth it to tingle." The chapter can be divided as follows. *(1)* The defeat of Israel (vv.1-2); *(2)* The decision to use the ark (vv.3-5); *(3)* The determination of the Philistines (vv.6-9); *(4)* The disaster for Israel (vv.10-11); *(5)* The death of Eli (vv.12-18); *(6)* The departure of the glory (vv.19-22).

1. The defeat of Israel (vv.1-2)

"Now Israel went out against the Philistines to battle, and pitched beside Eben-ezer (the name was actually given to the place some twenty years later: see 7.12) and the Philistines pitched in Aphek...and when they joined battle, Israel was smitten before the Philistines: and they slew of the army in the field about four thousand men." It seems that Israel took the initiative and challenged their enemies, but they were defeated in battle. The elders were quite right when they said, "Wherefore hath the **Lord** smitten us today before the Philistines?" (v.3). The explanation is clear: in the first place, they just didn't ask God for help and guidance, and secondly, how could they be victorious when there was such corruption in national life? The reason for their defeat had been spelt out long before it happened. "But it shall come to pass, if thou wilt not hearken unto the voice of the Lord thy God, to observe to do all his commandments and statutes which I command thee this day; that all these curses shall come upon thee...The Lord shall cause thee to be **smitten before thine enemies:** thou shalt go out one way against them, and flee seven ways before them: and shalt be removed into all the kingdoms of the earth" (Deut 28.15,25). (Israel has certainly been "removed into all the kingdoms of the earth!"). The lesson is clear for us **all,** let alone Israel; **disobedience will bring defeat.** When things go wrong in our lives, and we are unable to defeat the world, the flesh and the devil, it is a sure signal that something is wrong in our relationship with God. Israel's disobedience at this point is spelt out in detail in Psalm 78.55-64. Note particularly, at this juncture, the words, "They provoked him to anger with their high places, and moved him to jealousy with their graven images. When God heard this, he was wroth, and greatly abhorred Israel."

2. The decision to use the Ark (vv.3-5)

"The elders of Israel said...let us fetch the ark of the covenant of the Lord out of Shiloh unto us, that, when **it** cometh among us, **it** may save us out of the hand of our enemies." Once again, God was not consulted. The leadership completely misread the situation. They were probably thinking of the "grand battle hymn" of Israel, "And it came to pass, when the ark set forward, that Moses said, Rise up, Lord, and let thine enemies be scattered; and let them that hate thee flee before thee" (Num 10.35). But in those days God was with His people. Ellicott's Commentary is worth quoting here. "It was a curious decision, this baseless hope of the elders, that the unseen God was inseparably connected with that strange and beautiful symbol of His presence."

Woe betide any local assembly, when the elders either disregard the word of God, or are insufficiently acquainted with its teaching. It has been rightly said that an assembly seldom, if ever, rises above the level of its spiritual guides. It has been pointed out that in 1 & 2 Samuel, the "elders of Israel" were invariably wrong. See, for example 1 Samuel 8.4 and 2 Samuel 17.4. Notice too that it is always a recipe for disaster to say "Let us." Compare Genesis 11.3. It is not surprising that following the counsel of the **"elders**

1 Samuel

of Israel", the **"people** sent to Shiloh, that they might bring from thence the ark of the covenant of the Lord of hosts." We need not be surprised, either, that in the ensuing battle, God allowed the ark to be taken by the Philistines. Israel treated it like a lucky mascot. "When **it** cometh among us, **it** may save us." The previous defeat (vv.1-2) had not brought Israel before God in sorrow and repentance. They had not addressed the cause of their defeat. The presence of the ark at Eben-ezer was purely cosmetic. There was no consciousness of the claims of "the Lord of hosts, which dwelleth between the cherubims" (v.4). It was "a form of godliness, but denying the power thereof" (2 Tim 3.5).

The lesson is brought home even more when we compare this passage with 2 Samuel 15.25. David was without the ark, but he had the presence of God. Israel, here, had the ark, but they did not have the presence of God.

This is very searching. If there is no spiritual reality, and no sincere repentance because of sin, we can pronounce the name of Christ *ad infinitum,* but it will avail nothing. As A.McShane rightly observes, "the mere quotation of Matthew 18.20 does not assure us of His presence, if the conditions are not in accordance with His will." As we shall see, God had certainly not ceased to dwell "between the cherubims", but the conditions amongst His people precluded His help and blessing against the Philistines. Let us be warned. We must not treat Christ in the same way.

The arrival of the ark in the camp was greeted with "a great shout, so that the earth rang again." The transfer of the ark from the tabernacle at Shiloh to the camp at Eben-ezer raises some interesting questions. For example, did Eli endeavour to prevent this happening, and why did Hophni and Phinehas survive when they entered the "holiest of all" to obtain the ark? The two priests certainly did not survive for long! Quite obviously, God had either withdrawn His presence, or did not intervene because He intended to teach Israel a lesson they would not easily forget. After all, "judgement must begin at the house of God" (1 Pet 4.17, citing Ezek 9.6). Israel could shout until they were hoarse, but God was not on their side. Some professing Christians make a lot of noise, often incoherent, accompanied by stamping, dancing and wild gesticulations (just like the prophets of Baal, 1 Kings 18.26-28), but we must not think for one moment that this is a sign of God's presence. "To this man will I look, even to him that is poor and of a contrite spirit, and trembleth at my word" (Is 66.2).

3. The Determination of the Philistines (vv.6-9)
We shall say more about the Philistines in connection with events in Chapter 7, but we should notice two things about them here.

A) Their fear
The Philistines were disconcerted by the arrival of the ark in the camp of Israel. "They said, God *(Elohim)* is come into the camp. And they said, Woe unto us! for there hath not been such a thing heretofore. Woe unto us! who shall deliver us out of the hand of these mighty Gods? These are the Gods that smote the Egyptians with all the plagues in the wilderness" (vv.7-8).

In the first place, it was a **wrong** assumption. The Philistines expected God to be in the camp, in the same way that people expect us to maintain high standards, but God was **not** there. At least, He was not there to lead His people to victory. In the second place, it was a **correct** statement. He **was** a God of immense power, and quite capable of delivering His people. Alas, through their disobedience, Israel created the impression that the God who had so wonderfully delivered them from Egypt was insufficient to deliver them from the Philistines. What impression of God do **we** give to other people?

Notice too that the Philistines used the plural. "these mighty Gods...the Gods that smote the Egyptians." Keil and Delitzsch may be right in saying that "the Philistines spoke of the God of Israel in the plural, as heathen who knew only of *gods,* and not of one Almighty God", but it is interesting that Philistines did call Him *"Elohim",* which is a plural word! They also "understood that the ark of the Lord *(Jehovah)* was come into the camp." Perhaps the "heathen" world knew far more about the true God than we give them credit for! Put another way, the "heathen" world **then** was far more intelligent than the "heathen" world **now,** and for that matter, more intelligent than the so-called "Christian" world!

B) Their fortitude
"Be strong, and quit yourselves like men, O ye Philistines, that ye may be not servants unto the Hebrews, as they have been to you: quit yourselves like men, and fight." The Philistines did not know the weakness of Israel, but our spiritual opponents, who **are** well-aware of our strength and resources, are **still** prepared to fight against us. Our enemies do not "throw in the towel" and leave the ring in defeat. The strength of the opposition is described by Paul, "We wrestle not against flesh and blood, but against

principalities, against powers, against the rulers of the darkness of this world, against spiritual wickedness in high places" (Eph 6.12). We can rightly say, "If God be for us, who can be against us?", but be prepared for a fight! The enemy will continue the battle with dogged determination.

4) The disaster for Israel (vv.10-11)
What a disaster! "And the Philistines fought, and Israel was smitten, and they fled every man to his tent: and there was a very great slaughter; for there fell of Israel thirty thousand footmen. And the ark of God was taken; and the two sons of Eli, Hophni and Phinehas, were slain."

A) *The army was smitten*
"There fell of Israel thirty thousand footmen." The survivors "fled every man to his tent." It was a total rout. Israel was now defenceless. Psalm 78 gives more details. "He gave his people over also unto the sword; and was wroth with his inheritance. The fire consumed their young men; and their maidens were not given to marriage" (vv.62-63). Bearing in mind that this defeat was attributable, amongst other things, to "the high places" and "graven images" in Israel (v.58), we learn that disobedience will rob us of victory, and destroy our power to fight. The lesson of the first defeat is repeated, and it needs constant repetition. God was true to his word to Eli through "the man of God". "Thou shalt see an enemy in my habitation, in all the wealth which God shall give Israel" (1 Sam 2.32).

B) *The ark was captured*
"The ark of God was taken." See, again, Psalm 78, "He forsook the tabernacle of Shiloh, the tent which he placed among men; and delivered his strength into captivity, and his glory into the enemy's hand" (vv.60-61). See also Jeremiah 7.12-15. It was this, above everything else, that would make "both the ears of every one that heareth it to tingle." The ark taken by the Philistines! It so appalled a dying mother that she called her newborn son Ichabod, saying, "The glory is departed from Israel: for the ark of God is taken" (v.22). God forbid that we should permit anything in **our** lives that could rob us of the presence of Christ, the true Ark. We must not think, however, that the capture of the ark meant that God was now subject to Philistine power! Events in the next two chapters prove that God is perfectly able to look after His own interests without the help of His people!

C) *The priests were slain*
"The two sons of Eli, Hophni and Phinehas, were slain." See, yet again,

Psalm 78. "Their priests fell by the sword; and their widows made no lamentation" (v.64). We will defer comment on the "widows" until later. Whilst Hophni and Phinehas were "sons of Belial", we must remember that disobedience will rob **us** of effective priesthood. God fulfilled his intention to slay Hophni and Phinehas (2.25), and their death was the promised sign to Eli that his descendants would be stricken by untimely death, and ultimately be replaced by another priestly family. See 2.33-36. The death of Hophni and Phinehas emphasises that God will judge sin, and every promise to do so will be completely and exactly fulfilled.

> Though the mills of God grind slowly,
> Yet they grind exceeding small.
> Though with patience He stands waiting,
> With exactness grinds He all.

5. The death of Eli (vv.12-18)

This paragraph needs little comment. It is quite self-explanatory. Above everything else, it does emphasise Eli's deep concern about the ark of the covenant. We find him "upon a seat by the wayside watching: for his heart trembled for the ark of God." Whilst his two sons had evidently complied without protest with the wishes of the people, led by "the elders of Israel", and carried the ark from Shiloh to Eben-ezer (see v.4), their father was quite different. He was certainly weak, especially when it came to disciplining his own family, but He was deeply concerned for the glory of God. Hophni and Phinehas were "sons of Belial; they knew not the Lord." Eli's grave concern is emphasised by the way in which he reacted to the awful news from the battlefield. *(a)* "Israel is fled before the Philistines." That was bad enough. *(b)* "There hath been a great slaughter among the people, and thy two sons also, Hophni and Phinehas, are dead." That was even worse. *(c)* "And the ark of God is taken." That was the final straw. "And it came to pass, when he made mention of the ark of God, that he fell from off the seat backward by the side of the gate, and his neck brake, and he died: for he was an old man and heavy. And he had judged Israel forty years." It is often said that Eli's heart broke before his neck.

Eli died in utter disgrace. His failure to implement and maintain the claims of God over Israel resulted in national humiliation and the capture of the ark of the covenant. A.McShane captures the torment of Eli. "How could he live, and the ark not in its place, and what future was there for the Tabernacle if its greatest treasure was missing?" The death of Eli reminds us that "If any man defile the temple of God, him shall God destroy" (1 Cor 3.17). It had already happened at Corinth. See 1 Corinthians 11.28-30.

6. The departure of the Glory (vv.19-22)

Eli's daughter-in-law, the wife of Phinehas, evidently shared his concern for the ark. Notice the order in which she heard the news. "And his daughter in law, Phinehas' wife, was with child, near to be delivered: and when she heard the tidings *(a)* that the ark of God was taken, and *(b)* that her father in law and *(c)* her husband were dead, she bowed herself and travailed; for her pains came upon her." As she died, she referred to the same three events in the same order. "And about the time of her death the women that stood by her said unto her, Fear not; for thou hast born a son. But she answered not, neither did she regard it. And she named the child I-cha-bod (meaning, 'no glory', or 'Alas, the glory'), saying, The glory is departed from Israel because *(a)* the ark of God was taken, and *(b)* because of her father in law and *(c)* her husband. And she said, The glory is departed from Israel: for the ark of God is taken." The capture of the ark took precedence over the death of her father in law and her husband. In fact, her husband is mentioned last!

Her last words, twice repeated, reveal that her deepest distress was caused by the capture of the ark and its implications. "And she named the child I-cha-bod (he is mentioned again in 14.3), saying, **The glory is departed from Israel**...And she said, **The glory is departed from Israel**: for the ark of God is taken." As Keil and Delizsch observe, "The repetition of these words shows how deeply the wife of the godless Phinehas had taken to heart the carrying off of the ark, and how in her estimation the glory of Israel had departed with it." There can be little doubt that she valued the ark, and all that it represented, more than her husband. In great weakness, and faced with imminent death (v.20), she thought only of the ark. Let's remember that spirituality is not the prerogative of the brothers!

How much do **we** value the Lord Jesus, of whom the ark is such a beautiful picture, and how much do **we** value the testimony that each assembly should bear for Him. Both Ephesus and Laodicea, the first and last of the seven churches addressed by the Lord Jesus in Revelation 2-3, faced the possibility of extinction, because they had lost their passion for Christ. The Lord Jesus warned Ephesus that he would "remove thy candlestick out of his place, except thou repent", and Laodicea that He would "spue thee out of my mouth."

It would be tragic if it had to be said of our assembly, "The glory is departed."

CHAPTERS 5-6

The Return of the Ark (5.1-6.21)

There are two occasions in the Old Testament when ears "tingled." In both cases, Israel faced disaster from which there was no apparent recovery. The first occasion was defeat at the hands of the Philistines: "And the Lord said to Samuel, Behold, I will do a thing in Israel, at which both the ears of everyone that heareth it shall **tingle.**" The second occasion was captivity at the hand of the Babylonians. "And the Lord spake by his servants the prophets (including Jeremiah see 19 3), saying...Behold, I am bringing such evil upon Jerusalem and Judah, that whosoever heareth of it, both his ears shall **tingle"** (2 Kings 21.1-12).

In both cases, the "glory departed." As she died, the wife of Phinehas named her child "Ichabod, saying, The glory is **departed** from Israel...for the ark of God is taken."(1 Sam 4.21). Centuries later, shortly before Jerusalem fell to Nebuchadnezzar, Ezekiel watched the departure of the glory of the Lord. "Then the glory of the Lord **departed** from off the threshold of the house...And the glory of the Lord went up from the midst of the city, and stood upon the mountain which is on the east side of the city" (Ezek 10.18; 11.23).

But this was not the end. In both cases, the glory returned. While the ark, taken by the Philistines, returned seven months later, the word "glory" does not appear again in the Old Testament (apart from 1 Samuel 6.5, where it is used in a different connection) until "the glory of the Lord...filled the house of the Lord" at the dedication of the temple. See 1 Kings 8.11. The glory that was withdrawn prior to the Babylonian captivity will return when Christ returns to reign. Ezekiel saw the return of "the glory of the Lord" (43.2). Significantly, Christ will return to the mount of Olives (Zech 14.4) from which the "glory of the Lord" departed in Ezekiel 12.

1 Samuel

We must now trace events leading to the return of the ark by the Philistines. These are covered in 1 Samuel 5-6, which can be entitled **(1)** The ark amongst the Philistines, Chapter 5, and **(2)** The ark returned to Israel, Chapter 6.

1. The Ark amongst the Philistines (5.1-12)

There are twelve direct references to the ark in this chapter. On six occasions it is called "the ark of the God of Israel" (v.7; v.8-three times; v.10; v.11). On four occasions it is called "the ark of God" (vv.1,2, and v.10 twice). On two occasions it is called "the ark of the Lord" (vv.3,4). Notice that the Philistines always called it, "the ark of the God of Israel." The narrator always calls it "the ark of God" when the Philistines moved it from place to place. But it is called "the ark of the Lord (Jehovah)" when presiding over the downfall of Dagon. Interesting, isn't it? Food for thought! The ark has other names in the Bible. The subject will repay careful study!

There are clear similarities between events at Ashdod, Gath and Ekron. *(i)* The "hand of the Lord" was on all three cities. Ashdod (v.6); Gath (v.9); Ekron (v.11). His hand was "heavy upon them" in Ashdod. His hand was "very heavy" at Ekron. *(ii)* The population was decimated in all three cities. God "destroyed them" at Ashdod (v.6). He was against them "with a very great destruction" at Gath; He inflicted them with "a deadly destruction" at Ekron (v.11). *(iii)* The survivors suffered in the same way in all three cities. At Ashdod, God "smote them with emerods" (v.6). At Gath, "He smote the men of the city, both small and great, and they had emerods in their secret parts" (v.9). At Ekron "the men that died not were smitten with the emerods" (v.12). This all proves that "the triumphing of the wicked is short" (Job 20 5).

There are no prizes for analysing this chapter! *(A)* The ark at Ashdod (vv.1-7); *(B)* The ark at Gath (vv.8-9); *(C)* The ark at Ekron (vv.10-12). Centuries later, the evangelist Philip preached at Ashdod "But Philip was found at Azotus (the Greek form of Ashdod) and passing through he preached in all the cities, till he came to Caesarea" (Acts 8.40).

A) The Ark at Ashdod (vv.1-7)

"And the Philistines took the ark of God, and brought it from Eben-ezer unto Ashdod. When the Philistines took the ark of God, they brought it into the house of Dagon, and set it by Dagon." By placing the ark in "the house of Dagon", the Philistines were proclaiming the superiority of their god over the God of Israel. Sadly, it happened again when Saul's head was "fastened in Dagon's temple" (1 Chron 10.10). The Babylonians did the same. See Daniel 1 2, Nebuchadnezzar carried "vessels of the house of God" to Shinar, where he placed them in "the treasure house of **his** god" (Dan 1.2). Belshazzar found out to his cost, that this did not pay (see Daniel 5), and so did the Philistines! The capture of the ark only served to emphasise the power of God. It resulted in destruction for Dagon, and destruction for the people. The men of Ashdod cried, "his hand is sore upon us, and upon Dagon our god" (v.6).

i) Destruction for Dagon (vv.2-5)
While some commentators have concluded that "Dagon" derives from *"dagan"*, meaning corn, and was therefore the grain-god, the "true derivation is from *"dag"*, a fish, which represents the sea from which the Philistines drew their wealth and power" (Ellicott's Commentary). We are told that the idol had a human head and hands, and the body of a fish.

The Philistines found Dagon on his face "before the ark of the Lord" on the first morning (v.3), and in pieces "before the ark of the Lord" on the second morning (v.4). This simply proves that "an idol is nothing in the world, and that there is none other God but one" (1 Cor 8.4). It also proves that God means exactly what He says "I am the Lord: that is my name: and my glory will I **not** give to another, neither my praise to graven images" (Is 42.8). The Philistines worshipped a "god that cannot save" (Is 45.20). Dagon certainly didn't save them when Samson pulled down the temple at Gaza! See Judges 16.23-30.

Although Keil and Delitzsch think otherwise, the refusal of the priests and worshippers of Dagon to "tread on the threshold *(miptan)* of Dagon in Ashdod unto this day" (v.5), does seem the best explanation of Zephaniah 1 9, "In the same day also will I punish all those that leap on (JND "over") the threshold *(miptan)*, which fill their master's houses with violence and deceit." The word *"miptan"* means the "threshold of a sanctuary." If Zephaniah 1.9 does refer to 1 Samuel 5.5, then it just demonstrates the depths to which Judah had sunk in the days of Zephaniah. The "fear of the Lord" had given place to the fear of idols.

ii) Destruction for the people (vv.6-7)
"But the hand of the Lord was heavy upon them of Ashdod, and he destroyed them, and smote them with emerods, even Asdod and the coasts thereof."

People at Ashdod died under "the hand of the Lord", and the survivors were afflicted with "emerods". Two different words are translated "emerods" in chapters 5-6. Most of the references may be rendered "tumour", but chapter 6 vv.11,17) are a little more specific, and evidently refer to what we call "haemorrhoids." It is not difficult to see affinity between the words "emerods" and "haemorrhoids."

We should remember that whilst there wasn't a Hebrew in sight at Ashdod, God was perfectly able to look after His own interests without their help! The ark prevailed! The people who thought the God of Israel was inferior to Dagon soon discovered, within hours, that they had made a dreadful mistake. This reminds us that at the end-time, the whole world will unite against Christ (see Revelation 19.19 etc), only to be utterly defeated. Christ, the true ark, will prevail! Notice that at the end-time, under the first vial, a "noisome and grievous sore" will afflict "the men which had the mark of the beast, and...them which worshipped his image" (Rev 16.2).

We are not surprised to read that the men of Ashdod determined to get rid of the ark without delay, which brings us to

B) The ark at Gath (vv.8-9)
The story was repeated "The hand of the Lord was against the city with a very great destruction and he smote the men of the city, both small and great, and they had emerods in their secret parts." The presence of the ark at Gath was an intolerable liability, and "therefore they sent the ark of God to Ekron."

C) The ark at Ekron (vv.10-12)
Bad news travels fast. "The Ekronites cried out saying, They have brought about the ark of the God of Israel to us, to slay us and our people." We can imagine the panic! Enough was enough. There was only one thing to do - send the ark back to Israel. "So they sent and gathered together all the lords of the Philistines, and said, Send away the ark of the God of Israel, and let it go again to his own place, that it slay us not, and our people for there was a deadly destruction throughout all the city; the hand of God was very heavy there. And the men that died not were smitten with the emerods the cry of the city went up to heaven." Ekron was evidently plagued with even more severity than Ashdod and Gath. "The longer the Philistines resisted and refused to recognise the chastening hand of the living God...the more severely would they necessarily be punished, that they might be brought at last to see that the God of Israel...was the omnipotent God, who was

able to destroy His foes" (Keil & Delitzsch). No attempt was made to carry the ark to either of the two remaining Philistine cities. We can be quite sure that Gaza and Askelon just didn't want to know!

2. The ark returned to Israel (6.1-21)

There are ten direct references to the ark in this chapter. On one occasion it is called "the ark of the God of Israel" (v.3). On eight occasions it is called "the ark of the Lord" (vv.1, 2, 8, 11, 15, 18, 19, 21). On one occasion it is called simply, "the ark" (v.13). The Philistines called it, again, "the ark of the God of Israel (v.3), but they **also** called it "the ark of the Lord" (vv.2,8). Now that *is* interesting! They used the covenant name. We can divide this chapter into two sections. **(A)** How the ark was returned (vv.1-12), and **(B)** How the ark was received (vv.13-21).

A) How the ark was returned (vv.1-12)

We should notice *(i)* The trespass offering (vv.1-6) *(ii)* The transportation, (vv.7-8) *(iii)* The test (vv.7-12).

i) The trespass offering (vv.1-6)

After seven months of misery, the Philistines "called for the priests and the diviners, saying, What shall we do with the ark of the Lord? Tell us wherewith we shall send it to his place." The "priests and diviners" recommended that a "trespass offering" should accompany the ark. On each occasion, the expression "trespass offering" translates *"asham"*, which is the word used in Leviticus 6.6 and Numbers 5.7 etc. for payment of compensation where property had been misappropriated. The "trespass offering" was "Five golden emerods, and five golden mice, according to the number of the lords of the Philistines; for one plague was on you all, and on your lords (v.4)." We now learn that the Philistines had to contend with mice as well as emerods: "Wherefore ye shall make images of your emerods, and images of your mice that mar the land." The presentation of the golden emerods and golden mice was evidently an acknowledgement that the God of Israel had inflicted them with the plagues. Hence the words, "And ye shall give glory to the God of Israel peradventure he will lighten his hand from off you, and from off your gods, and from off your land." (The Philistines actually sent back far more than five golden mice. See v.18). Notice that their **desire for deliverance** was accompanied by the **danger of delay** "Wherefore then do ye harden your hearts, as the Egyptians and Pharaoh hardened their hearts? When he had wrought wonderfully among them, did they not let the people go, and they departed?"

A.McShane is worth quoting at length here "Is it not strange that they were conscious of their trespass, and confessed it clearly. Yet the people, who professed to know the Lord and were linked with His name, made no confession when disaster befell them at the battle of Aphek. Can it be that the uncircumcised heathen knew more of the claims of God than the enlightened Israelites?" Like so many people today, the Philistines did not understand that sin could only be dealt with by shed blood. But Israel offered no trespass offering at all! We should also notice that the Philistines "called for the priests and diviners" to give them guidance, but Israel did not seek the counsel of "the living and true God" before the battle of Aphek.

On a technical note, the words "then ye shall be healed, and it shall be known to you why his hand is not removed from you" (v.3), simply mean that if, as a result of returning the ark plus the trespass offerings, they are healed, there will then be no doubt why they had suffered so much with the emerods and mice.

ii) The transportation (vv.7-8)
"Now therefore make a new cart, and take two milch kine on which there hath come no yoke, and tie the kine to the cart, and bring their calves home from them." Something like a hundred years later, David decided to remove the ark from "the house of Abinadab that was in Gibeah" and carry it to Jerusalem. Compare 1 Samuel 7.1,2 and 2 Samuel 6.1-3. It was transported, not by the "the sons of Kohath" who were to carry the ark personally "upon their shoulders" (Num 7.9), but on "a new cart!" It seems almost incredible that God's people should set aside His instructions for the carriage of the ark in favour of a Philistine expedient! They remembered what the Philistines did, but failed to remember the word of God. Sadly, Christendom is full of Philistine expedients. It is often anything but the word of God. People who know what the Bible teaches are especially responsible to God. That's why the Philistines were not smitten by God when they put the ark on their "new cart".

iii) The test (vv.9-12)
These verses are quite self-explanatory. Contrary to their natural instincts, the two cows ignored their calves, and without any human compulsion, "took the straight way to the way of Beth-shemesh, and went along the highway, lowing (as if protesting) as they went, and turned not aside to the right hand or to the left; and the lords of the Philistines went after them unto the border of Beth-shemesh." (Beth-shemesh was about twenty miles

from Ekron "as the crow flies"). There was now no doubt that the plagues had been inflicted on the Philistines by God. In their own words, it was not "a chance that happened to us" (v.9). The two "milch kine" were driven by divine power. It was the same power that turned the colt "whereon never man sat" into the placid animal on which the Lord Jesus rode into Jerusalem.

(B) How the ark was received (vv.13-21)
We should notice *(i)* The worship when the ark was treated rightly (vv.13-18) and *(ii)* The wrath when the ark was treated wrongly (vv.19-21).

i) The worship (vv.13-18)
a) There was rejoicing. "And they of Beth-shemesh were reaping their wheat harvest in the valley and they lifted up their eyes, and saw the ark, and **rejoiced to see it."** So the ark returned to Israel at harvest time, which reminds us that the Lord Jesus, who is "the firstfruits of them that slept" (1 Cor 15.20), will come again to gather all His people, whether dead ("asleep") or alive at the time. What a harvest that will be! The people were busy when the ark returned, reminding us of Luke 19.13, "Occupy till I come." In the meantime, we can rejoice with the disciples in the "upper room" who were "glad when they saw the Lord." The men of Beth-shemesh "saw...and rejoiced." At the moment, we "see him not", but we "rejoice with joy unspeakable and full of glory" (1 Pet 1.8).

b) There was reverence. "And the **Levites** took down the ark of the Lord." See Numbers 4.5, 7.9; 2 Samuel 15 24 etc. Only sanctified men could carry the ark. Holy things must be handled by holy people. Beth-shemesh was a Levitical city. See Joshua 21.16.

c) There was sacrifice. "They clave the wood of the cart, and offered the kine a burnt-offering unto the Lord...and the men of Beth-shemesh offered burnt-offerings and sacrificed sacrifices *(zebach)* the same day unto the Lord." The two sacrifices named were voluntary "sweet-savour offerings." The burnt-offering was wholly for God, reminding us of the complete devotion of the Lord Jesus to God. It was offered in worship. The word *"zebach"* is used in connection with the peace offering, which stresses fellowship with God through Christ.

d) There was no delay. "The men of Beth-shemesh offered burnt-offerings and sacrificed sacrifices **the same day** unto the Lord." Do we worship as willingly and enthusiastically?

1 Samuel

All this was observed by the "five lords of the Philistines" (v.16). What kind of impression do **we** give to other people? Do they see whole-hearted devotion to Christ?

ii) The wrath (vv.19-21)
"And He smote the men of Beth-shemesh, because they had looked into **the ark of the Lord**, even He smote of the people fifty thousand (omitted by JND) and threescore and ten men" (vv.19-20). In order to look into the ark, the mercy seat had to be removed! That is a sobering thought for a start. A.McShane in "Lessons for Leaders" writes "The due reverence observed at its arrival was soon discarded, and the men of Beth-Shemesh, who should have known better, ventured to lift its lid. Their curiosity cost them their lives...Irreverence has never been, and will never be tolerated by God...No cloud of glory or outward evidence of the Lord's presence was seen at Beth-shemesh, but the dead bodies around the ark testified that He had not vacated his throne, nor reduced the standard of his holiness." There are many people today, religious leaders included, who think they can say what they like and do what they like about Christ. Their fate will be no less than the men of Beth-shemesh. However, we must **all** beware of over-familiarity in our fellowship with God.

The chapter concludes with the appeal to Kirjath-jearim (meaning "the city of woods" see Psalm 132.6). "And the men of Beth-shemesh said, Who is able to stand before this holy Lord God? and to whom shall he go up from us. And they sent messengers to the inhabitants of Kirjath-jearim, saying, The Philistines have brought again the ark of the Lord; come ye down, and fetch it up to you." Whilst the "men of Beth-Shemesh...**looked into** the ark", Eleazer was "sanctified to **keep** the ark of the Lord" at Kirjath-jearim.

The hymn-writer answers the question, "Who is able to stand before this holy Lord God?" as follows

> There is a way for man to rise
> To that sublime abode;
> An Offering and a Sacrifice,
> A Holy Spirit's energies,
> An Advocate with God.

CHAPTER 7

The Philistines Defeated (7.1-17)

We can divide this chapter as follows.**(1)** Introduction (vv.1-2); **(2)** Instruction (vv.3-6); **(3)** Invasion (vv.7); **(4)** Intercession (vv.8-9); **(5)** Intervention (vv.10-14); **(6)** Itinerancy (vv.15-17).

1. Introduction (vv.1-2)
After the disaster at Beth-shemesh, "the men of Kirjath-jearim came, and fetched up the ark of the Lord, and brought it into the house of Abinadab in the hill, and sanctified Eleazar his son to keep the ark of the Lord." Presumably, Abinadab and Eleazar were Levites, but there is no supporting evidence. Kirjath-jearim means "the city of woods", and Psalm 132, which refers to David's desire to move the ark to Jerusalem, evidently refers to the location of the ark here. "I will not give sleep to mine eyes, or slumber to mine eyelids, until I find out a place for the Lord, an habitation for the mighty God of Jacob. Lo, we heard of it at Ephratah: we found it in the fields of the wood" (vv.4-6). It remained in the house of Abinadab for twenty years, which refers to the time that elapsed before "all the house of Israel lamented after the Lord." However, the ark remained at Kirjath-jearim long after this, and was not removed until the early part of David's reign, as described in Psalm 132. See 2 Samuel 6.3: "And they set the ark of God on a new cart, and brought it out of the house of Abinadab that was in Gibeah." Gibeah means "the hill", so Abinadab hadn't moved house!

After twenty years (the words, "the time was long", are literally, "the days were many"), "all the house of Israel lamented after the Lord." As Keil and Delitzsch observe, the words of Samuel that follow, "If ye do return unto the Lord with all your heart", "assume that the turning of the people to the Lord their God had already inwardly commenced." This is reminiscent of the days of the Judges, when Israel "cried unto the Lord" (see 3.9; 3.15; 4.1 etc) because of enemy oppression. In fact, v.3 makes it quite clear that "all the house of Israel lamented after the Lord" because of Philistine oppression. Now, after twenty years silence, we hear the voice of Samuel again. This does not imply, of course, that he had been inactive, but the change of heart amongst God's people indicated that the time had come for him to assume leadership.

2. Instruction (vv.3-6)
In this paragraph we must notice that Samuel did three things **(i)** He taught the people, (vv.3-4); He spoke to them about the Lord, (v.3); **(ii)** He prayed for the people, (vv.5-6). He spoke to the Lord about them, (v.5); **(iii)** He judged the people, (v.6).

i) *Samuel taught the people (vv.3-4)*
"And Samuel spake unto all the house of Israel, saying, If ye do return unto the Lord with all your hearts, then put away the strange gods and Ashtaroth from among you, and prepare your hearts unto the Lord, and serve him only: and he will deliver you out of the hand of the Philistines." Samuel's appeal contains important teaching for us:

a) It was addressed to *"**all** the house of Israel."* Notice that *"**all** the house of Israel lamented after the Lord…Samuel spake unto **all** the house of Israel…Gather **all** Israel to Mizpeh, and I will pray for you unto the Lord."* The entire nation mourned before God, the entire nation was instructed by Samuel, and the entire nation gathered for prayer. It speaks for itself, doesn't it?

b) It involved the *"hearts"* of the people." "If ye do return unto the Lord with all your *hearts*…prepare your *hearts* unto the Lord." The word "heart"` is used as the figure of inward life. Little, if anything, would be accomplished if Israel just "put away the strange gods." It would be "a form of godliness, but denying the power thereof." Their hearts must be right with God. Only then could they deal with idolatry effectively. Half-heartedness was not sufficient either. *"Return unto the Lord with all your hearts, and serve him only."* See Psalm 119.58,69. Note 1 Peter 3.15, "Sanctify the Lord God in your *hearts*." (For a definition of the word "heart", read and ponder the first three references to it in the Bible; Genesis 6.5,6; 8.21).

c) It was a call to repentance. "Put away the strange gods and Ashtaroth (the goddess of the Phoenicians and Zidonians) from among you." Repentance is a thorough change of mind about sin. It means that we see sin in the same way as God Himself. He hates sin. It is abhorrent to Him. Idolatry is particularly abhorrent to Him. It is the transgression of the first and second commandments: "Thou shalt have no other gods before me. Thou shalt not make unto thee any graven image, or any likeness of anything...Thou shalt not bow down thyself to them, nor serve them" (Ex 20.1-5). The New Testament warns us against idolatry. See Colossians 3.5, 1 John 5.21. Christians sometimes need to repent. See, for example, Revelation 2.5. ("Baalim and Ashtaroth" (v.4), are plural words: in the singular it is Baal and Astarte).

This is strikingly different to what happened in Chapter 4. Then, there was no sorrow for sin, and the ark, which was treated simply as a lucky mascot, was carried into the camp at Eben-ezer on the shoulders of polluted priests. Its arrival was accompanied by a roar of applause, rather than the noise of sorrow and weeping for sin. The entire procedure was purely cosmetic. There was no spiritual reality, and it all resulted in disaster. But look now at the promised results of repentance, and whole-hearted devotion to God. "Prepare your hearts unto the Lord, and serve him only: and he **will deliver you** out of the hand of the Philistines" (v.3). God honours reality. It begins in the heart.

ii) Samuel prayed for the people (vv.5-6)
"And Samuel said, Gather all Israel to Mizpeh, and I will pray for you unto the Lord. And they gathered together to Mizpeh, and drew water, and poured it out before the Lord, and fasted on that day, and said there, We have sinned against the Lord." Notice three things.

a) "They...drew water, and poured it out before the Lord." Quite obviously, this was symbolic. Perhaps it was a symbol of their own weakness. We use the expression "as weak as water." Read, in this connection, 2 Samuel 14.14 ("for we must needs die, and are as water spilt on the ground, which cannot be gathered up again") and Genesis 49.4 ("unstable as water, thou shalt not excel"). Perhaps it was a symbol of outpoured grief. See Lamentations 2.19, "Arise, cry out in the night.in the beginning of the watches pour out thine heart like water before the face of the Lord." See also Psalm 22.14. Amongst other things, prayer is an expression of our own weakness, and dependence on God.

b) "They...fasted on that day." Abstention from food enables people to wait without distraction upon God. Leaving aside the biological reason for fasting (it sharpens the mind and heightens our mental powers), fasting is basically self-denial. Quite obviously, there is nothing sinful about food or drink (depending, of course, on **what** you drink), which reminds us that devotion to the Lord does involve self-discipline, and the exclusion or limitation of perfectly legitimate things in our lives. Are **we** prepared to make personal sacrifices in order to spend time in prayer, study of the scriptures, and service for God?

c) "They...said there, We have sinned against the Lord." So there was confession of sin. See 1 John 1.9, "If we confess our sins, he is faithful and just to forgive us our sins, and to cleanse us from all unrighteousness."

iii) Samuel judged the people (v.6)
"And Samuel judged the children of Israel in Mizpeh." That is, under his guidance, counsel, and direction, they made an end of their sinful practices, and were restored to a proper relationship with God. The nation was cleansed, and fit for divine blessing. There can be no blessing, or victory, if we persist in sin. "If we would judge ourselves, we should not be judged" (1 Cor 11.31). Mizpeh means "watch-tower". We need to examine ourselves.

3. Invasion (v.7)
Spiritual progress always attracts the enemy. It poses a threat to Satan's interests, and he will do everything possible to reduce God's people to weakness and subservience. "And when the Philistines heard that the children of Israel were gathered together to Mizpeh, the lords of the Philistines went up against Israel. And when the children of Israel heard it, they were afraid of the Philistines." It is remarkable, but not altogether surprising, how often progress is immediately tested. Hezekiah's sweeping and successful reforms were followed by an Assyrian invasion. See 2 Chronicles 32. 2, **"After these things,** and the establishment thereof, Sennacherib king of Assyria came, and entered into Judah, and encamped against the fenced cities." The reconstruction of the walls of Jerusalem under Nehemiah, was followed by backsliding. If your spiritual life is healthy, be particularly careful and prayerful. You are in the direct line of attack!

The time has come to say a little more about the Philistines. They were descended from Ham (Genesis 10.14; compare 1 Chronicles 1.12), and according to some authorities, came originally from Crete (Caphtor). See Deuteronomy 2.23, Jeremiah 47.4, Amos 9.7. We meet them in Genesis 21.32 and in 26.1 etc., and it seems that they were located in close proximity to Egypt. See Exodus 13.17. They were obviously a warlike people at this time, let alone later. They evidently moved north and settled on the Mediterranean coast. Israel's failure to dispossess them was a costly error. Its repercussions lasted for centuries. Even today, the "Gaza strip" is frequently in the news, and Palestine is a corruption of Philistine!

We should notice how the Philistines operated, and learn from their tactics. Notice, for example, the following: **(a) They filled wells.** See Genesis 26.15, "For all the wells which his (Isaac's) father's servants had digged: the Philistines had stopped them, and filled them with earth." **(b) They prevented ascent.** See 1 Samuel 10.5, "After that thou shalt come to the hill of God, where there is a garrison of the Philistines." **(c) They monopolised weapons.** See 1 Samuel 13.19, "Now there was no smith found throughout all the land of Israel: for the Philistines said, Lest the Hebrews make them swords or spears." **(d) They despatched spoilers.** See 1 Samuel 13.17, "And the spoilers came out of the camp of the Philistines in three companies." **(e) They exercised lordship.** See Judges 15.11. "Knowest thou not that the Philistines are rulers over us?" (The men of Judah to Samson). The satanically led "principalities and powers" will endeavour to do exactly the same to us. Give this some serious thought! Is it happening to *you*?

4. Intercession (vv.8-9)
"And the children of Israel said unto Samuel, Cease not to cry unto the Lord our God for us, that he will save us out of the hand of the Philistines. And Samuel took a sucking lamb, and offered it for a burnt-offering wholly unto the Lord: and Samuel cried unto the Lord for Israel; and the Lord heard him." Let's look at these two important verses as follows *(i)* How Israel spoke to Samuel (v.8), and *(ii)* How Samuel spoke to the Lord (v.9). Notice here that Samuel acts as a priest.

i) How Israel spoke to Samuel (v.8)
God's people were deeply conscious of their inadequacy, but they recognised Samuel was a man in touch with God, and could represent them before Him. Later generations also knew this to be the case. See Psalm 99.6, and Jeremiah 15.1. James reminds us that "the effectual fervent prayer of a righteous man availeth much" (Jas 5.16). Samuel's priestly ministry reminds us that we have a "great high priest" who has "entered heaven itself, now to appear in the presence of God for us." We should now notice:

a) The urgency of their request. "Cease not to **cry** unto the Lord our God for us." They were in earnest. Their national survival was at stake. Twenty years before, the Philistines had proved utterly superior in battle, and had evidently retained their mastery over Israel. Emerods and mice had not brought a long term change in their attitude to God's people. No wonder they were "afraid of the Philistines." But at least they recognised their peril. So often, we fail to even realise that danger exists. The spiritual forces which oppose us vary their tactics, but their overall objective is to rob us of spiritual power and effectiveness. Notice, too, that their sense of urgency prompted them to request on-going prayer. **"Cease not** to cry unto the Lord our God for us." See Colossians 4.2.

b) *The basis of their request.* Their cry was based on a proper relationship with the Lord. They had "put away Baalim and Ashtaroth, and served the Lord only." Hence their request, "cease not to cry unto the Lord **our** God for us, that he will save us." Twenty years before they said, "Let us fetch the ark of the covenant of the Lord out of Shiloh unto us, that when **it** cometh among us, **it** may save us out of the hand of our enemies", 4.3. But now it is **"the Lord our God**...**he** will save us."

c) *The specific nature of their request.* There is nothing like danger to focus our prayers! **"Save us** out of the hand of the Philistines. They had certainly got their priorities right! The early church did the same. "And now, Lord, behold their threatenings: and grant unto thy servants, that with all boldness they may speak thy word" (Acts 4.29).

ii) How Samuel spoke to the Lord (v.9)
Samuel displayed the same urgency: he "cried unto the Lord", and we must carefully notice the basis on which "the Lord heard him." Samuel's intercession rested on the excellence of the sacrifice he offered. "And Samuel took a sucking lamb, and offered it for a burnt-offering wholly unto the Lord." In the case of the sin-offering, the **sin of the offerer** was transferred to the offering, but in the case of the burnt-offering, the **excellence of the offering** was transferred to the offerer. It reminds us that we are "accepted in the beloved" (Eph 1.6). Like **our** prayers, Samuel's intercession was accepted because of the worthiness of Christ. Let's remember that the value of His death extended backwards through time, as well as forward to our own generation, and beyond. We are not therefore surprised to read, "And the Lord heard him." When we pray "in the name of our Lord Jesus Christ", we are stating the ground on which God hears and answers our prayers. It is not some kind of suitable postscript to our prayers.

All this reminds us that "the weapons of our warfare are not carnal, but mighty through God to the pulling down of strongholds" (2 Cor 10.4). This brings us to:

5. Intervention (vv.10-14)

"And as Samuel was offering up the burnt-offering, the Philistines drew near to battle against Israel: but the Lord thundered with a great thunder on that day before the Philistines, and discomfited them; and they were smitten before Israel. And the men of Israel went out of Mizpeh, and pursued the Philistines, and smote them, until they came under Beth-car." Centuries before, God "cast down great stones from heaven upon them (the southern Canaanite kings)...they were more which died with hailstones then they whom the children of Israel slew with the sword" (Josh 10.11). Israel's God was "the Lord of hosts" (1.3), "Who governs all the powers of heaven, both visible and invisible, as He rules in heaven and earth." In the Old Testament, He used hail (Josh 10.11), thunder (1 Sam 7.10) and stars (Jud 5.20) to defeat the enemies of His people. On other occasions, He used angels. See, for example, 2 Chronicles 32.21. The final intervention in world affairs will be quite different. He will intervene personally and directly: "And I saw heaven opened, and behold a white horse; and he that sat upon him was called Faithful and True, and in righteousness he doth judge and make war" (Rev 19.11-2).

Notice the sequel to divine intervention. *(a) **Remembrance of God's help** (v.12).* "Then Samuel took a stone...and called the name of it Eben-ezer, saying, Hitherto hath the Lord helped us." There was thanksgiving to God. *(b) **Repression of the enemy (v.13).*** "So the Philistines were subdued, and they came no more into the coast of Israel: and the hand of the Lord was against the Philistines all the days of Samuel." *(c) **Restoration of territory (v.14).*** "And the cities which the Philistines had taken from Israel were restored to Israel, from Ekron even unto Gath; and the coasts thereof did Israel deliver out of the hands of the Philistines." The Amorites were the most powerful of the Canaanite tribes. The peace with Israel was probably recognition by the Amorites of Israel's new strength. These were the results of renewed devotion to God. It gave Israel victory over their enemies, and on-going strength. It will yield the same results for us too. These three things were accompanied by *(d) **Regularity of ministry (vv.15-17).*** We will, however, make this our final major point, and call it.

6. Itinerancy (vv.15-17)

Samuel was an itinerant preacher. Some people would call him a "circuit preacher!" "And Samuel judged Israel all the days of his life. And he went from year to year in circuit to Bethel, and Gilgal, and Mizpeh, and judged Israel in all those places. And his return was to Ramah; for there was his house; and there he judged Israel; and there he built an altar unto the Lord." All four places were fairly close together in the south of the land. There are at least three things to notice here.

i) *The duration of Samuel's ministry*

He "judged Israel all the days of his life." What a marvellous testimony! It is remarkable particularly because we do not have a detailed record of his work after the defeat of the Philistines at Mizpeh, and events leading to the anointing of Saul. But he "judged Israel all the days of his life!" His record was "on high." We must emulate Samuel, and serve God faithfully, whether or not our service is noted on earth. There are many believers who do a great deal humbly and quietly. "The day shall declare it."

ii) *The circuit of Samuel's ministry*

His annual "circuit" took him to Bethel, Gilgal, and Mizpeh. These are all places that we should visit regularly!

a) We should visit **Bethel,** and listen to Jacob: "Surely the Lord is in this place; and I knew it not. And he was afraid, and said, How dreadful is this place! This is none other but the house of God, and this is the gate of heaven" (Gen 28.16-17). There wasn't a brick in sight, but it was "the house of God!" It was a sacred place. God was there. Now read 1 Timothy 3.15. The "house of God" is still a sacred place! Remember, the "house of God" today is the "people, not the steeple!" (David Newell).

b) We should visit **Gilgal.** It was there that circumcision was reinstituted. See Joshua 5.1-9. Paul sums up its significance in Philippians 3."We are the circumcision, which worship God in the spirit, and rejoice in Christ Jesus, and have **no confidence in the flesh."** Circumcision was a sign of no confidence in self, and complete confidence in God. Hence the removal of part of the literal flesh. We need to be constantly reminded that "without faith it is impossible to please him: for he that cometh to God must believe that he is, and that he is the rewarder of them that diligently seek him" (Heb 11.6). We ought to spend considerable time at Gilgal.

c) We should visit **Mizpeh.** As we have seen, Mizpeh was the place of victory over the enemy. But it was a divinely-achieved victory. "The Lord thundered with a great thunder on that day upon the Philistines." This just reminds us that "greater is he that is in you, than he that is in the world" (1 Jn 4.4). It also reminds us of 1 Corinthians 1.29. We must never forget that victory can only be accomplished by divine power. Let's raise our "Ebenezer!"

iii) The base of Samuel's ministry

Samuel was based at home! "And his return was to Ramah; for ***there*** was his house; and ***there*** he judged Israel; and ***there*** he built an altar unto the Lord." So he lived at Ramah, he served at Ramah, and he worshipped at Ramah. Ramah means "the high place." Our "high place" is heaven itself, and we must "seek those things which are above", and set our "affections on things above" (Col 3.1-2). Sadly, we shall see in Chapter 8 that godliness does not run in the blood.

CHAPTER 8

"Give us a king" (8.1-22)

We now reach the second major division of 1 Samuel. As we noticed in our introduction, the book can be divided into three sections with reference to its three principal characters. In chapters 1-7, **Samuel** is prominent. In chapters 8-15, **Saul** is prominent. In chapters 16-31, **David** is prominent. Quite clearly, the three sections overlap. "Samuel lives well on into the reign of Saul, and also sees David rise to prominence; while Saul continues his reign until David is thirty years old." J.Sidlow Baxter *(Explore the Book)*. However, the three sections do focus our attention on Samuel, David, and Saul, respectively.

But 1 Samuel 8 does more than prepare the way for Saul. It introduces a completely new chapter in Israel's history. Saul was the first king of Israel, and the reigns of Saul, David and Solomon, each lasting for forty years, comprise the "United Kingdom Period", in which the twelve tribes of Israel were united under one king. However, the anointing of Saul was far more than a change in visible government. It marked the end of theocracy, under which Israel had been ruled directly by their unseen heavenly King, and the beginning of the monarchy, under which they were subject to visible earthly rule. It was a retrograde step; "They have rejected me, that I should **not reign** over them" (v.7). It is most interesting to notice what God says about this elsewhere.

i) Nothing catches God by surprise. See Deuteronomy 17.14-15. "When thou art come unto the land which the Lord thy God giveth thee...and shalt say, I will set a **king** over me, **like as all the nations that are round about me**; thou shalt in any wise set him king over thee, whom the Lord thy God shall choose." God anticipated their demand for a king, and the very language they would use!

Chapter 8

ii) Nothing can stop God's original intention. See Hosea 13.10-11. *"I* will be *thy king:* where is any other that may save thee in all thy cities? and thy judges of whom thou saidst, Give me a king and princes? I gave thee a king in mine anger, and took him away in my wrath."

The chapter can be divided as follows; *(1)* The desire for a king, (vv.1-6); *(2)* The demands of the king (vv.7-18); *(3)* The determination for a king (vv.19-22).

1. The Desire for a King (vv.1-6)
There were two reasons behind Israel's desire for a king; *(A)* Internal corruption, and *(B)* external conformity.

A) Internal corruption
"And it came to pass, when Samuel was old, that he made his sons judges over Israel. Now the name of his firstborn was Joel; and the name of his second, Abiah: they were judges in Beer-sheba. And his sons walked not in his ways, but turned aside after lucre, and took bribes, and perverted judgment." We should notice three things here:

i) The appointment of his sons. The priesthood had already failed. Since the ark was not returned to Shiloh, we can only assume that the place had been abandoned, in which case, what had happened to the tabernacle? (What conclusions do you reach in view of 2 Samuel 6.17, 7.2, 1 Kings 1.39, 2.28-30, 1 Kings 8.4?). The ark was in Kirjath-jearim. Samuel had certainly arrested the downward trend in Israel, and "as long as he laboured in the word (7.15-17), backed by noble example, he was a blessing to the people." But now "we detect an error of fleshly anxiety in the light of "old age" which had far-reaching results. Samuel "made his sons judges over Israel", which was the Lord's prerogative alone, Judges 2.18." C.E.Hocking. *("Key men in Sacred History", Precious Seed)*. God had chosen the men to lead Israel (see Numbers 1.4-16), and, through the Holy Spirit, He chooses the men to lead in the assembly today (see Acts 20.28). Things inevitably go wrong when human appointments supersede God's appointments. Eli's two sons **lost their right** to function as priests. Samuel's two sons had **no right** to function as judges. Keil and Delitzsch suggest that Samuel did not appoint his sons to succeed him, but to support him, and that this is confirmed by their location in Beersheba, which was on the southern border of Canaan.

ii) The names of his sons. Unlike the sons of Eli, Samuel's sons had fine names. **Joel** means "Jehovah is God." In the words of Thomas Newberry, **"Jehovah"** is "a combination in marvellous perfection of the three periods of existence in one word, the future, the present, and the past. First, *"yehi"*, "he will be", long tense; second, *"hove"*, "being", participle; third, *"hahyah"*, "he was", short tense used in the past." In the New Testament, God speaks in the same way; "Grace be unto you, and peace, from him which is, and which was, and which is to come", Revelation 1.4. **"El"** signifies "strong", "first." "It is the title which shows God to be the Mighty One, the First Great Cause of all" (Thomas Newberry). **Abiah** means "whose Father is Jehovah."

Fine names indeed! But Jehovah was **not** Joel's God. In fact, Joel was anything but strong. He was decidedly weak. Jehovah was **not** Abiah's Father! He displayed no family likeness whatever. Both sons failed to live in the good of their names. But what about **us?** James speaks about "that worthy name by which ye are called" (Jas 2.7). We say that we are Christians, but do people see Christ in us?

iii) The conduct of his sons. In New Testament language, Joel and Abiah were guilty of "partiality", 1 Timothy 5.21. See Proverbs 29.4, "The king by judgment establisheth the land: but he that receiveth gifts overthroweth it." Joel and Abiah did not meet the criteria of Deuteronomy 16.18-19. "Judges and officers shalt thou make thee in all thy gates...and they shall judge the people with just judgement. Thou shalt not wrest judgement; thou shalt not respect persons, neither take a gift: for a gift doth blind the eyes of the wise, and pervert the words of the righteous." Psalm 15 is compulsory reading on this subject. We must be careful that we do not sacrifice the demands of God's word on the altar of family relationships, or personal friendships. We must not jettison principle in favour of sentiment.

All this led "the elders of Israel" to say, "Behold, thou art old, and thy sons walk not in thy ways." The people soon recognised the failure of the two judges, in the same way that an assembly will soon recognise unspirituality in its leadership. Samuel's "ways" could be summed up as follows. *(a)* he was accustomed to hearing the voice of God, *(b)* he was accustomed to declaring the truth of God, and *(c)* he was accustomed to judging the people of God. We could say of Samuel, and men and women like him, "whose faith follow", Hebrews 13.7. Paul, who must be included in this category, was able to say to the assembly at Corinth, "Timotheus...shall bring you into remembrance of my ways which be in Christ", (1 Cor 4.17). Sadly, the very men who should have maintained God's interests as the unseen King of Israel actually brought His reign into disrepute. It just emphasises the necessity for us to "adorn the doctrine of God our Saviour in all things", (Tit 2.10). This led to the second reason for their desire for a king:

B) *External conformity*

"Now make us a king to judge us **like all the nations**." They had the answer to the problem of Samuel's advancing years, and the failure of his sons! The outlook was bleak, and therefore, they argued, the solution lay in new arrangements. After all, if Samuel could make his sons judges, he could just as easily appoint a king! A monarchy with proper succession was a much better arrangement than the uncertainty created by the appointment of unworthy people like Joel and Abiah, and a settled constitution would ensure that the demands of God's word were fully met by sound legal practice. It all sounds very plausible. It worked very well elsewhere. Hence the demand, "make us a king to judge us like all the nations."

To sum up, Israel had not learned the lesson that "it is better to trust in the Lord than to put confidence in man. It is better to trust in the Lord than to put confidence in princes" (Ps 118.8-9). They were saying that human arrangements are much more dependable than faith in God! Let's be clear about this: living by faith does not appeal to unspiritual people. In the same way, the New Testament principles of gathering are not attractive to Christendom. There is little or no general appeal about the Lordship of Christ, the sole sufficiency of the word of God, the sovereignty of the Holy Spirit, and the priesthood of all believers. The simple pattern of New Testament church life is replaced by division between clergy and laity, by centralisation, by synods. In fact, by anything but the word of God.

Uniformity is the order of the day. Whatever happens, we must not be different. People today do not want the God who put "a difference between the Egyptians and Israel" (Ex 11.7). Individually and corporately, we are not to be "conformed to this world." Sadly, God's people increasingly ape the world in outlook, speech, dress, pursuits and conduct. But more than that, they ape the world in its craze for entertainment and music, all in the cause of "livening up the church and making it more attractive to modern young people." Sober, edifying Bible teaching, and spiritual worship, are "old hat." Let's be "like all the nations!"

In all this, Israel had conveniently forgotten its own history. God had not failed them in the past. They had only to remember their deliverance from Egypt, passage through the wilderness en route to Canaan, and conquest of the land. Samuel drives this very lesson home in 12.6-11. Then, in more recent times, what about that stone between Mizpeh and Shen? Hadn't the nation entreated Samuel to pray for them: "Cease not to cry unto the Lord...that he will save us?" Hadn't God answered his prayer and "thundered with a great thunder?" That stone was there to commemorate it all. Samuel "called the name of it Eben-ezer, saying, Hitherto hath the Lord helped us." But Israel had obviously been paying attention to what was happening around them, with the result that they had become sold on the idea that other people's methods were better. Samuel calls this "wickedness", and the people themselves call it "evil" in 12.16-19.

Leaders do grow old, and, sadly, leaders can be unspiritual, but this does not mean that we should lose confidence in God, and cease to cry to Him for help, preservation and guidance. Men certainly fail, but God will never fail. It is all too easy to blame our failure on our methods, rather than our sin and unspirituality. The old saying is so true, We look for better **methods,** but God looks for better **men.**"

Samuel evidently took their request personally. He apparently regarded it as a vote of "no confidence" in him. Hence the reassurance, "they have not rejected thee, but they have rejected me, that I should not reign over them", (v.7). But Samuel did take his displeasure (v.6) "to the Lord in prayer." He did not remonstrate with "the elders of Israel." There was no "war of words." Like Hezekiah, centuries later, Samuel "spread it before the Lord", and the Lord put him in a position to reply.

2. The demands of the King (vv.7-18)
God answered Samuel's prayer in two ways. **(A)** He strengthened Samuel, (vv.7-8), and **(B)** He warned Israel, (vv.9-18). As A.McShane points out, "there are occasions when even the best of men cannot stop what they feel to be wrong, but faithfulness to God and His truth compels them to so speak, that no doubts can be left in the minds of wrong-doers about the seriousness of their crimes." See 12.23.

A) God strengthened Samuel, (vv.7-8)
"And the Lord said unto Samuel, Hearken unto the voice of the people in all that they say unto thee: for they have not rejected thee, but they have rejected me, that I should not reign over them. According to all the works

which they have done since the day that I brought them up out of Egypt even unto this day, wherewith they have forsaken me, and served other gods, so do they also unto thee." There are some important lessons in these verses:

i) Samuel was to accede to their request. At first glance, this is rather surprising. Some commentators have deduced from this that it was the will of God for Israel to have a king, although this was not the right time and, in any case, their motives were wrong. This is certainly not the case in 10.19 and 11.17! It seems more feasible to suggest that God allowed His people to have a king to prove that human arrangements, however attractive and logical, are only second best. As a result of their choice, Israel would suffer. "And ye shall cry out in that day because of your king which ye shall have chosen you; and the Lord will not hear you in that day", (v.18. Compare Psalm 106.14-15.Israel "lusted exceedingly (for flesh to eat) in the wilderness, and tempted God in the desert. and he gave them their request; **but** sent leanness into their soul." The nation even suffered under Solomon. See 1 Kings 12.4. Let's make it **our** aim to go for God's best in our lives. Remember Isaiah 55.8-9, "For as the heavens are higher than the earth, so are my ways higher than your ways, and my thoughts than your thoughts." Aim high! There was, however, another reason for allowing Israel to have a king. See 9.16

ii) Samuel learned that there was a cost in serving God. It meant sharing the reproach of His will and His word. "They have not rejected thee, but they have rejected me that I should not reign over them." The Lord Jesus made this lesson clear: "Remember the word that I said unto you, The servant is not greater than his lord. If they have persecuted me, they will also persecute you; if they have kept my saying, they will keep your's also" (Jn 15.20-21). If you intend to serve God, expect trouble from the world, and in particular, trouble from the religious world.

iii) Samuel learned that God understood his position. This is the other side of the coin. Bear this in mind as you read it again: "They have not rejected thee, but they have rejected me that I should not reign over them." In rejecting Samuel, Israel rejected God Himself. Saul of Tarsus learned this lesson on the Damascus road. See Acts 9.4. When we are under pressure, it is heartening to know that "we have not an high priest which cannot be touched with the feeling of our infirmities; but was in all points tempted like as we are, yet without sin" (Heb 4.15).

iv) Samuel learned to be longsuffering. God had "suffered their manners in the wilderness" for forty years (Acts 13.18), and it hadn't ended there. It continued "even unto this day." Now it was Samuel's turn! "So do they also unto thee."

(B) God warned Israel, (vv.9-18)
"Now therefore hearken unto their voice: howbeit yet protest solemnly unto them, and shew them the manner of the king that shall reign over them. And Samuel told all the words of the Lord unto the people that asked of him a king. And he said, This will be the manner of the king that shall reign over you." C.E.Hocking sums it up as follows: "In his grace and mercy, God made them aware of the consequence of their choice. The change would prove for the worse, not the better. The outward majesty of the royal state would be matched by the despot's will. Absolute submission would be demanded by "the king that shall reign over you." In this connection, we must notice the repeated expression, "He will take", (vv.11,13,14,15,16,17). It was "taking" rather than "giving." Compare Luke 12.32. (Note: it would be a profitable study to contrast the **demands of** the king with the blessings and benefits **bestowed** by God. For example, "he will take your sons", but God has given His Son, and we are made "sons of God"). The appointment of a king would bring bondage. He would make appointments, against which there could be little protest, and create a vast organisation. As A.McShane observes, "the simple dwelling and living habits of Samuel would not be acceptable to the monarch of the nation, and would not be in keeping with the stately palaces of the surrounding kings. If they wanted to be like the nations, they would have to pay the high price entailed by their demand." In this connection, it is significant that Israel's great leaders of the past, such as Moses and Joshua, lived amongst the people and shared their simple lifestyle. This is the pattern for leadership today amongst God's people. See 1 Peter 5.1-3. Compare Acts 20.28, "Take heed therefore to yourselves, and to all the flock, **wherein** the Holy Spirit hath set you as overseers" (JND).

A.McShane points out that the court of Israel's king would be a replica of the courts of Egypt. We have only to read the Bible narratives for confirmation. Chariots and horses, claims on the land, servants and slaves, all remind us of Egypt. It is equally obvious that Christendom has copied the world, and continues to do so. God faithfully warned Israel of the consequences of making "a king…like all the nations", and it is, equally, a warning to us as well. But the warning was all to no avail:

3. The determination for a King (vv.19-22)

"Nevertheless the people refused to obey the voice of Samuel; and they said, Nay; but we will have a king over us; that we may be like all the nations; and that our king may judge us, and go out before us, and fight our battles." The expressions, "the people **refused** to obey" and "we **will** have a king over us", strike a chilling note. See 1 Samuel 15.22-23. We must look at the implications of their reasons for desiring a king:

i) It meant loss of separation. "That we may be like all the nations." They had already made this clear, see (v.5). It was a far cry from the way Balaam described them: "Lo, the people shall dwell alone, and shall not be reckoned among the nations" (Num 23.9). It is always regrettable when "the wisdom of men" and "the wisdom of this world" (1 Cor. 2.5-6) becomes the wisdom of God's people. Remember, we are not to be "conformed to this world."

ii) It meant devaluation of priesthood. "That our king may judge us." See Deuteronomy 17.8-12. When there was a matter too difficult for local settlement, the parties concerned were to go "to the place which the Lord thy God shall choose; and thou shalt come unto the priests the Levites, and unto the judge that shall be in those days, and enquire; and they shall shew thee the sentence of judgement." The priest is described as a man "that standeth to minister there before the Lord thy God." It was God's purpose that His mind and will should be conveyed by priestly men. See Malachi 2.7. This is precisely what will happen in the Millennium. See Ezekiel 44.24. But today, religious leaders debate and decide without even mentioning the name of God! When was the last time that the leaders of the so-called Established Church in this country opened their Bibles, prayed for divine guidance, took note of God's will, and thundered "Thus saith the scripture?"

iii) It meant displacement of faith. "That our king may...go out before us." They wanted a visible head. Godly kings made it clear that the people should look beyond them for leadership. Jehoshaphat is an example: "We have no might against this great company that cometh against us; neither know we what to do: but **our eyes are upon thee.** And all Judah stood **before the Lord**", 2 Chronicles 20.12-13.

iv) It meant diminished responsibility. "That our king may...fight our battles." Once again, this represented a transfer of faith from the Lord to the king. It is all very different from their last encounter with the Philistines, when "the children of Israel said to Samuel, Cease not to cry unto **the Lord** for us, that **he** will save us out of the hand of the Philistines" (7.8). While, obviously, the people did not expect their king to ride out alone against the enemy, they were more than happy to let him take the responsibility. Some Christians are rather like that. Why should we concern ourselves? After all, what do we have leaders for? It's all down to the "oversight" isn't it? But shouldn't we **all** be "valiant for the truth?", Jeremiah 9.3. Aren't we **all** deeply involved in the spiritual conflict described in Ephesians 6.10-12? Shouldn't we **all** "stand up and be counted?"

In the final analysis, the king would only be as good as his own character. It was a poor exchange for the Lord who says, "I am the Lord, I change not" (Mal 3.6). "And Samuel heard all the words of the people, and he rehearsed them in the ears of the Lord. and the Lord said to Samuel, Hearken unto their voice, and make them a king. And Samuel said unto the men of Israel, Go ye every man unto his city." We now wait to see what happens next.

CHAPTER 9

"Behold the man whom I spake to thee of!" (9.1-27)

Israel's desire for a king was marked by determination on their part, and displeasure on God's part. Having been shown "the manner of the king" who would reign over them, Israel remained quite determined in their intention. "And they said, Nay; but we *will* have a king over us; that we also may be like all the nations; that our king may judge us, and go out before us, and fight our battles" (8.19-20). God's displeasure was clearly expressed, not only at the time, but centuries later. "I gave thee a king in mine anger, and took him away in my wrath" (Hosea 13.10-11). God acceded to their request, if only to prove their folly in rejecting Him. "They have rejected me, that I should not reign over them" (8.7). We now meet the king that God gave them in His anger. This does not mean that God deliberately impeded his appointment, or that He made life as difficult as possible for him. The king was given the best possible start, but his ultimate failure emphasises that it is perilous to substitute human arrangements for the will of God.

We can divide the chapter as follows. *(1)* The son of Kish (vv.1-2); *(2)* The search for the asses (vv.3-5); *(3)* The stature of Samuel (vv.6-13); *(4)* The sovereignty of God (vv.14-17); *(5)* The surprises for Saul (vv.18-24); *(6)* The stoppage on the journey (vv.25-27). Notice how Saul's servant describes Samuel in v.6. Among other things, he is called the "man of God" four times in vv.6-10. Notice the sovereignty of God in vv.14-17. The timing was perfect, down to the very time Samuel left his house in v.14! This promises to be another interesting chapter, and that's an understatement!

1. The Son of Kish (vv.1-2)
The chapter commences with the descent of the future king (v.1), and a description of the future king (v.2).

A) His descent (v.1)
"Now there was a man of Benjamin, whose name was Kish, the son of

Abiel, the son of Zeror, the son of Bechorath, the son of Aphiah, a Benjamite, a mighty man of power." Perhaps the genealogy is intended to reinforce that Saul, the son of Kish, met the criteria demanded in Deuteronomy 17.15, "Thou shalt in any wise set him king over thee, whom the Lord thy God shall choose: one from among thy brethren shalt thou set king over thee: thou mayest not set a stranger over thee, which is not thy brother." The expression, "a mighty man of power", is identical to "mighty man of wealth" in Ruth 2.1, and signifies, according to Keil and Delitzsch, "not a brave man, but a man of property."

B) His description (v.2)
"And he had a son, whose name was Saul, a choice young man, and a goodly: and there was not among the children of Israel a goodlier person than he: from his shoulders and upward he was higher than any of the people." Saul means "asked for", and the name occurs as a verb in connection with the birth of Samuel. See 1.17 & 27. "Saul" seems a very appropriate name for the man that Israel had asked for! Bearing in mind that Saul had a grown-up son (Jonathan: see 13. 2) it has been estimated that he was about forty or forty-five years old. It is therefore encouraging to everybody in their "forties" to read that he was "a choice **young** man!" Timothy was probably approaching his "forties" when Paul wrote, "Let no man despise thy youth." A young man ceased to be a "youth" when he was ineligible to join the army, and that was at age forty! All of which reminds us that responsibility in the service of God is not the exclusive privilege of "greyheads!" "It is good for a man that he bare the yoke in his youth" (Lam 3.27). 1 Samuel 8 begins with "old" Samuel. 1 Samuel 9 begins with "young" Saul!

The description of Saul emphasises that he looked the part! He was, every inch, a king, and there were plenty of inches! From his shoulders and upward he was higher than any of the people." Very impressive! He was just the right candidate for the job. After all, Israel didn't seem too concerned about the spiritual qualifications of their king. God gave them what they wanted. As ever, "man looketh on the outward appearance." Sadly this impressive young man would say, some thirty-five years later, "I have played the fool." Centuries later we read about another Benjamite. He also started life with the same name, but he didn't look like Saul, the son of Kish. In fact some people said that his "bodily presence is weak, and his speech contemptible." But Saul of Tarsus, who became Paul the apostle, was able to say, "I have fought a good fight, I have finished my course, I have kept the faith." Spiritual stature is vastly more important than physical stature! (In different ways, both men fulfilled Genesis 49. 27).

2. The Search for the Asses (vv.3-5)
When we first meet Saul, he is looking for lost asses. When we first meet David, he is keeping sheep. For Saul, it was a fruitless search. "They found them not...there they were not...they found them not." It has been said that although Saul had all the outward features of a good captain, he failed miserably with straying animals, and that this, allegorically, describes the end before the beginning. "Saul's search for the lost asses, a telling picture of stubborn and self-willed Israel, was fruitless, despite the lengths to which he went to find them." (C.E.Hocking). Whilst this is true, we have to add that Saul's failure to find the missing animals was predetermined by God. This is made very clear in v.16. "Tomorrow about this time, *I* will send thee a man out of the land of Benjamin, and thou shalt anoint him to be captain over my people Israel." The search brought Saul to the unnamed city at the same time as Samuel! It reminds us of events during the second missionary journey, when Paul and his colleagues were "forbidden of the Holy Ghost to preach the word in Asia." and "after they were come to Mysia, they assayed to go into Bythinia: but the Spirit suffered them not" (Acts 16.6-7). God shut both doors because he wanted his servants elsewhere, and through this, the gospel came to Europe! (see vv.8-12). We learn from Saul's failure to find the missing asses that our disappointments are as much part of the divine plan as our successes. God has our good, and His glory, in mind in the trials and triumphs of life.

3. The Stature of Samuel (vv.6-13)
Samuel had a splendid testimony! We can look at this paragraph as follows *(A)* The character of Samuel (v.6); *(B)* The gift for Samuel (vv.7-10) *(C)* The presence of Samuel (vv.11-13).

A) The character of Samuel (v.6)
"And he (Saul's servant) said unto him, Behold now, there is in this city a man of God, and he is an honourable man; all that he saith cometh surely to pass: now let us go thither; peradvanture he can show us our way that we should go." Keil and Delitzsch argue at great length that the city in question was *not* Ramah, Samuel's home town. "Let every man be fully persuaded in his own mind!" It is much more interesting to notice that Saul's servant knew a great deal more than his master about Samuel! In fact, we get the impression that Saul knew nothing at all about him! This

could mean that Samuel kept a low profile. After all, he was "old" (8.1), although he evidently lived for as much as another thirty years! (See 25.1). It could mean that Saul had not been particularly interested in Samuel or his ministry. It is clear, however, that "Saul was shown that day, though it is likely that he never learned the lesson, that the simple peasant may have more light than his position might imply" (A.McShane). We must remember that "God hath chosen the foolish things of the world to confound the wise; and God hath chosen the weak things of the world to confound the things which are mighty." We must never despise the help of any child of God.

i) Samuel's relationship with God. He was "a man of God." The expression occurs in vv.6, 7, 8, & 10. It is used of Elijah (e.g. 1 Kings 17.24) and Elisha (e.g. 2 Kings 4.16). In the New Testament, it is used of Timothy (see 1 Tim 6.11). "A man of God" is, of course, equally "a child of God" and "a son of God", but the expression emphasises his spiritual growth and maturity. He displays the character of God.

ii) Samuel's relationship with others. He was "an honourable man." That is, he was held in honour. It was unchallenged. "Behold, here I am: witness against me before the Lord, and before his anointed: whose ox have I taken? or whose ass have I taken?...or of whose hand have I received any bribe to blind my eyes therewith?...And they said, Thou hast not defrauded us, nor oppressed us, neither hast thou taken ought of any man's hand"(12.3-5).

iii) Samuel's relationship with his ministry. "All that he saith cometh surely to pass." His reliability as a prophet was recognised (See 4.1), "And what Samuel had said happened to all Israel" (JND). He was known as a man with the word of God. In this connection, we should also notice that Samuel is called a "seer." This means what it says: "one who sees." In the New Testament, we have "overseers." (It is usually translated "bishops", but *episkopos* means "one who watches or looks over"). So Samuel was a man with divinely-given vision. That's why his ministry was reliable. Note the connection between seers and prophets in v.9. We do not have prophets today, because the Scriptures are complete, but we do have teachers who draw our attention to what God has said in His word.

B) The gift for Samuel (vv. 7-10)
"What shall we bring the man?" Saul, the future king of Israel, was evidently broke! (Perhaps his wealthy father wasn't too generous!). His servant had

"the fourth part of a shekel of silver", and that did not amount to very much! Just think about it: the man with nothing was about to be anointed king of Israel! This reminds us of another King who came with nothing. He wasn't even greeted with a feast. He was "laid...in a manger; because there was no room for them in the inn."

We mustn't think that Saul and his servant expected to pay Samuel a fee for guidance! As Ellicott's Commentary points out, "the custom of offering gifts was in many cases an act of respectful homage to a superior rather than a mere fee." Well, what can **we** offer?

> What can I bring Thee my Saviour
> In return for Thy great love to me,
> For redemption so full and so precious,
> By the blood shed on Calvary's tree?
> What can I offer Thee, Saviour
> When the whole of creation is Thine,
> Take my heart, my life, and my all, dear Lord
> To be fashioned by Thy love divine.

C) The presence of Samuel (vv.11-13)

Samuel was not only in residence, but had arrived that very day. Not only so, he was evidently host at the feast following the sacrifice which, in all probability, was a peace offering (see Leviticus 7.15 etc). He invited Saul and his servant to join him at the feast (v.19), indicated where they were to sit (v.22), and had already given instructions to the cook (vv.23-24). We get the impression that a man who could cater for "about thirty persons" did not need "the fourth part of a shekel of silver!" As we will see next, the timing and arrangements were perfect. Do notice the practice of asking a blessing on meals (see v.13): "In everything give thanks."

But there is, perhaps, a little problem here. What about "the high place?" This does seem to be the first time that a "high place" is mentioned in connection with the worship of the Lord. We know that "high places" were usually associated with idolatry. See, for example 1 Kings 11.7, where Solomon built "an high place for Chemosh, the abomination of Moab, in the hill that is before Jerusalem." We know that God's people were to worship only at "the place which the Lord your God shall choose out of all your tribes to put his name there... thither shall ye bring your burnt-offerings, and your sacrifices...and there ye shall eat before the Lord your God" (Deut

12.5-7: see also vv.11-14). We do have to remember, however, that at this time, Shiloh had been forsaken (see Psalm 78.60), and that Jerusalem did not become "the place of the name" until the reign of David. In such distressing times, there was provision for God's people to approach Him with sacrifice and offering. Compare 6.14; 7.17.

4. The Sovereignty of God (vv.14-17)
God's sovereignty does not necessarily involve the miraculous. He exercises His sovereignty in ordinary events. These verses illustrate two ways in which God achieves His purposes.

A) He achieves His purpose when people ARE NOT aware of it
As far as Saul was concerned, his father's asses were missing, and they were just about to enter a city where there was someone who could evidently help them. Contrary to their expectations, they met that very man in the city gate! Compare v.14 with v.17. It was certainly not a coincidence that Samuel left his house at precisely the moment Saul and his servant were making their way to the "high place." God had sent Saul to Samuel. "Tomorrow about this time *I* will send thee a man out of the land of Benjamin." How often God overrules our circumstances without us knowing! But we can look back afterwards, and sing:

> All the way my Saviour leads me,
> What have I to ask beside.

B) He achieves His purpose when people ARE aware of it
When Samuel left his house, he knew exactly what was going to happen. God had told him the day before! But more than that, God confirmed it on the spot. "And when Samuel saw Saul, the Lord said unto him, Behold the man whom I spake to thee of! this same shall reign over my people." (v.17) God can overrule our circumstances without us knowing, and He can also make His will very clear to us. We have the first illustrated in Saul, and the second in Samuel.

The intimacy of Samuel's fellowship with God is very clear from the way in which God was able to speak to Him in such a personal way. "Now the Lord had told Samuel in his ear a day before Saul come...Behold the man whom I spake to thee of!" The lad who learned to recognise the voice of God in Shiloh, did not need a spiritual "hearing aid" in later years! God was able to say, "A word in your ear, Samuel." We are told that this is, literally, "had uncovered the ear of Samuel", and that it refers to the action of pushing aside the head-dress in order to whisper in someone's ear. Compare the "tingling" ears of the people in 3.11 with Samuel's ear here! The ear of the Lord Jesus was always open to the voice of God (see Isaiah 50.4). We should also notice the mercy of God towards Israel. Yes, they were wrong in desiring a king, but God was willing to help them in their distress. "Thou shalt anoint him to be captain over **my** people Israel: that he may save **my** people out of the hand of the Philistines: for I have looked upon **my** people, because their cry is come unto me." (Compare Ex 2.23-25). God was "touched with the feeling of their infirmities" (see Heb 4.15). His love for them is emphasised by the repeated expression, **"my** people."

5. The Surprises for Saul (vv.18-24).
Saul must have been surprised to learn **(A)** That Samuel knew all about him (vv.19-20); **(B)** That he had an illustrious future (vv.21-22); **(C)** That he was the honoured guest at the feast (vv.22-24). It must have left him quite shell-shocked!

A) His concerns were known to Samuel (vv.19-20)
Saul was left in no doubt that Samuel really was "the seer!" "Go up before me unto the high place; for ye shall eat with me today, and tomorrow I will let thee go, and will tell thee all that is in thine heart. And as for thine asses that were lost three days ago, set not thy mind on them; for they are found." Since Samuel relieved Saul's anxiety by telling him that the asses had been found, the expression, "all that is in thine heart", appears to be a general statement. Samuel knew all about Saul. The fact that Samuel had proved himself to be "a seer" gave credence to what follows. If he knew all about the asses, and about Saul himself, then Saul had every reason to believe what followed. Saul's attention is suddenly transferred from asses to higher things.

B) His illustrious future (vv.21-22)
"And on whom is all the desire of Israel? Is it not on thee, and on all thy father's house?" Left to ourselves, with only our Authorised Version, we would have no difficulty in interpreting this statement! We would say that it meant, "Saul, you are the man that Israel is looking for to be king!" However, the Hebrew students tell us that it actually means "And to whom does all that is worth desiring in Israel belong? Is it not to thee, and all thy father's house?" It has been translated, "And for whom is all that is desirable in Israel? Is it not for you, and for all your father's house? (RSV). In other

words, Saul would preside over all Israel, and so fulfil Samuel's prediction (8.11-17). We, too, have a wonderful future. Unlike Saul's earthly inheritance as king of Israel, we have "an inheritance incorruptible, and undefiled, and that fadeth not away, reserved in **heaven"** (1 Peter 1.4).

Like Gideon (Judges 6.15), Saul protested his unworthiness of such a prospect. He was "little in his own sight" (15.17). "There was no vulgar elation at the prospect which lay before him, no hurried grasping at the splendid prize which the seer had told him the God of his fathers had destined for him." (Ellicott's Commentary). What a pity that he didn't stay that way! God hates pride (see 1 Pet 5.5-6).

C) His honoured place at the feast (vv.22-24).
"And Samuel took Saul and his servant, and brought them into the parlour (chamber), and made them sit in the chiefest place among them that were bidden, which were about thirty persons." Our privileged position is even greater. God has "quickened us together with Christ...and hath raised us up together, and made us sit together in heavenly places in Christ Jesus" (Eph 2.5-6). Saul and his servant were not unexpected guests. Samuel had previously told the cook to have something special ready. "Bring the portion which I gave thee, of which I said unto thee, Set it by thee. And the cook took up the shoulder...and set it before Saul. And Samuel said, Behold, that which is left (reserved)!...for unto this time hath it been kept for thee since I said, I have invited the people": more evidence that Samuel was "the seer!" But if this was amazing, it is even more staggering to discover that we were "chosen...in him (Christ) before the foundation of the world"! (Eph1.4). The presence of Saul's servant at the feast reminds us of the Saviour's words, "If any man serve me, let him follow me; and where I am, there shall also my servant be: if any man serve me, him will my Father honour" (Jn 12.26).

6. The Stoppage on the Journey (vv.25-27)
These verses speak for themselves. It is interesting to notice where Samuel and Saul spoke together, both after the feast, and the following morning. It was "upon the top of the house." They were not distracted by anything happening at ground level. We all need to get above the clamour of this world. God makes His will known in this atmosphere: see, for example, (Acts 10. 9).

It is also instructive to notice that Samuel bore no grudge against the man who was replacing him. As A.McShane observes "There was neither bitterness, envy, nor jealousy in the old man's heart. If Saul failed in his stewardship, and we all know that he did, he could never blame his ruin on spiteful treatment meted out to him by the man of God."

We now wait to see what Samuel meant in saying, "Stand thou still a while, that I may shew thee the word of God". There can be nothing more important than listening to the word of God! We all need to "stand still", and listen to His voice.

CHAPTER 10

"God save the King" (10.1-27)

Israel's request for a king had been granted, and this chapter describes his consecration by Samuel, together with his presentation to the people. While it is often said that Saul was "the people's choice", it is equally true that God chose him (See 10.24). God gave them the man they wanted. He certainly looked the part. He was "a choice young man, and a goodly: and there was not among the children of Israel a goodlier person than he: from his shoulders and upward he was higher than any of the people" (9.2). Just the man to "judge them, go out before them, and to fight their battles!" (8.20).

We left Samuel and Saul standing together at "the end of the city", and now discover what Samuel meant when he said, "Stand thou still a while, that I may shew thee the word of God." The chapter can be divided as follows. *(1)* The anointing of Saul (v.1); *(2)* The confirmation to Saul (vv.2-13); *(3)* The humility of Saul (vv.14-16); *(4)* The presentation of Saul (vv.17-27).

1. The Anointing of Saul (v.1)
"Then Samuel took a vial of oil, and poured it upon his head, and kissed him, and said, Is it not because the Lord hath anointed thee to be captain over his inheritance?" We should notice.

i) *The anointing of Saul.*
This marks a new departure. Up to this point, only priests had been anointed (see Ex 28.41 etc.). We should add that the tabernacle and its vessels were anointed (Ex 40.9-11), and so were parts of the meal and peace offerings. Saul is later called "his (the Lord's) anointed" (12.3,5). See also 1 Samuel 24.6 etc. Saul's anointing by Samuel symbolised his anointing by God. "Is it not because **the Lord** hath anointed thee to be captain over his inheritance?" It indicated *(a)* that Saul had been consecrated, or set

apart, by God as king. Saul was marked out in this way. It indicated *(b)* that Saul would enjoy divine help in discharging his duties as king, for oil in Scripture is an emblem of the Holy Spirit (See Is 61.1; Acts 10.38; 2 Cor 1.21-22.)

Prophets (1 Kings 19.16), priests and kings were all anointed, indicating that God had set them apart for those particular functions. The title "Christ" means "the anointed one". He is prophet, priest and king! We, too, have been anointed by God (see 2 Cor 1.21-22 above). We have "an unction (*chrisma*, anointing) from the Holy One...the anointing which ye have received of him abideth in you" (Jn 2.20,27). The fact that the Holy Spirit indwells us indicates, among other things, that God has set us apart to serve Him, and given us the power and ability to do so.

ii) The kissing of Saul.
This could certainly have been a sign of affection, but it seems more likely that it was an expression of Samuel's recognition of the new king. In this way, Samuel paid homage or reverence to the Lord's anointed. See Psalm 2.11-12, "Serve the Lord with fear, and rejoice with trembling. Kiss the Son, lest he be angry, and ye perish from the way." This reminds us of 1 Thessalonians 5.12, "Know them which labour among you, and are over you in the Lord, and admonish you, and...esteem them very highly in love for their work's sake."

iii) The work of Saul.
The Lord had anointed him "to be captain (*nagid*, "leader, one before") over his inheritance." Israel remained **God's** people. They were "his inheritance." Saul was a steward: he was to act on God's behalf. Exactly the same is said about elders in the New Testament. See here Titus 1.7, 1 Peter 5.1-3...note JND here: "Not as lording it over your possessions".

2. The Confirmation for Saul (vv.2-13)
The comments of Keil and Delitzsch make an excellent introduction to this section. "To confirm the consecration of Saul as king over Israel...Samuel gave him three more signs which would occur on his journey home, and would be a pledge to him that Jehovah would accompany his undertakings with His divine help, and practically accredit him as His anointed". We will look at this section, with its three signs, as follows. *(A)* The significance of the signs for Saul (vv.2-6); *(B)* The effect of the signs on Saul (vv.7-8); *(C)* The reaction of the people to Saul (vv.9-13).

1 Samuel

A) The significance of the signs (vv.2-6)

Speaking generally, the three signs were proof to Saul that God had chosen him to be king, and that Samuel had acted as a true prophet of the Lord in communicating with him. But each sign emphasises a different aspect of his calling.

i) The first sign emphasises the position of the king. "Thou shalt find two men by Rachel's sepulchre (Rachel was the mother of Benjamin, from whom Saul was descended) in the border of Benjamin at Zelzah; and they will say unto thee, The asses which thou wentest to seek are found: and, lo, thy father hath left the care of the asses, and sorroweth for you, saying, What shall I do for my son?" (v.2). (The "two men" who stood by the sepulchre in which the body of the Lord Jesus had been laid, had an infinitely better message than the two men who stood by Rachel's sepulchre! See Luke 24.1-8). As commentators have pointed out, locating the asses relieved Saul of further anxiety over their disappearance. "This showed him that henceforth in his new life he was to dismiss all lower cares, and give himself alone to higher and more important matters" (Ellicott's Commentary). While we all ought to give priority to the Lord's work, this is particularly a requirement in leaders. "No man that warreth (no man on active service) entangleth himself with the affairs of this life; that he may please him who hath chosen him to be a soldier" (2 Tim 2.4). Notice that Paul does not say "engageth himself", but "entangleth himself!" But how would Saul survive?

ii) The second sign emphasises the provision for the king. "Then thou shalt go on forward from thence, and thou shalt come to the plain ("oak", JND) of Tabor, and there shall meet thee three men going up to God to Bethel, one carrying three kids, and another carrying three loaves of bread, and another carrying a bottle of wine: and they will salute thee, and give thee two loaves of bread; which thou shalt receive of their hands" (vv.3-4). The three men were obviously en route to Bethel to sacrifice to God. Saul would be provisioned out of the sacrifice intended for God Himself. The "Lord's anointed" therefore learned the lesson that his needs would be supplied. This reminds us of the Lord's teaching in Matthew 6. 25-34, culminating with the words, "But seek ye first the kingdom of God, and his righteousness; and all these things shall be added unto you".

It's worth remembering, too, that our contributions to the Lord's work are, first and foremost, to the Lord Himself. While servants of God benefit from our stewardship, we give to the **Lord.** Saul was fed from loaves which were to be offered to God.

iii) The third sign emphasises the power of the king. "After that thou shalt come to the hill of God, where is a garrison of the Philistines. and it shall come to pass, when thou art come thither to the city, that thou shalt meet a company of prophets coming down from the high place with a psaltery (a type of lyre with ten strings), and a tabret (a tambourine. called a "timbrel" in Exodus 15.20) and a pipe, and a harp (a stringed instrument like the "psaltery", but larger), before them; and they shall prophesy. And the Spirit of the Lord shall come upon thee, and thou shalt prophesy with them, and thou shalt be turned into another man" (vv.5-6). The power of the Holy Spirit (v.6) was God's answer to the power of the Philistines (v.5). See 1 John 4.4.

The competent authorities tell us that "the hill of God" is, literally, *"Gibeah of God"*, and since people there evidently knew Saul and his father (see vv.11), it was evidently Saul's home town, known also as "Gibeah of Saul": see 10.26, 11.4, Is 10.29 etc). It must be of some significance that there was "a garrison (or military post) of the Philistines" there. We all know that the enemy invades sacred places. However, a citizen of that very place had been chosen to lead Israel against them! It is also of interest to notice the connection between music and prophecy. The "company of prophets" were evidently engaged in praise and worship, and it was in this atmosphere that they received and communicated the word of God. Compare Acts 13.1-2. Finally, we should notice that it was in this atmosphere that Saul received divine power, and was equipped by God for the work before him. Whatever we understand by the expression, "turned into another man" as applied to Saul (we should probably not regard the change in Saul as regeneration in the Christian sense), it is very clear in the New Testament that there is a vast change in the lives of men and women who are indwelt by the Holy Spirit. In fact, if there is no change, we can assume that there has been no regeneration at all. "By their fruits ye shall know them."

B) The effect of the signs (vv.7-8)
The fulfilment of these three predictions was to have a twofold effect on Saul. *(i)* He was told what he could do (v.7), and *(ii)* He was told where he should go (v.8).

i) What he could do. "And let it be, when these signs are come unto thee, that thou shalt do as occasion serve thee; for God is with thee" (v.7). Keil and Delitzsch put it like this. "The occurrences of the signs mentioned was to assure him of the certainty that God would assist him in all that he undertook as king". The first "occasion" was the Ammonite siege of Jabesh-gilead (see chapter 11). But this did not mean that Saul could do exactly as he liked. His movements were to be regulated by the word of God. This follows:

ii) Where he should go. "And thou shalt go down before me to Gilgal; and, behold, I will come down unto thee, to offer burnt-offerings, and to sacrifice sacrifices of peace-offerings: **seven days** shalt thou tarry, till I come to thee, and shew thee what thou shalt do" (v.8). While in chapter 11 the nation gathered at Gilgal and "there they sacrificed sacrifices of peace-offerings before the Lord: and there Saul and all the men of Israel rejoiced greatly" (vv.14-15), Samuel was evidently referring to events in Chapter 13. "And the people were called together after Saul to Gilgal…As for Saul, he was yet in Gilgal, and all the people followed him trembling. And he tarried **seven days**, according to **the set time that Samuel had appointed"** (vv.4,7-8). Chapter 13 marks the beginning of the campaign against the Philistines. Saul had been chosen for this purpose (see 9.16). A battle loomed. The Philistines assembled a vast army, and "the men of Israel saw that they were in a strait." Samuel, the "prophet of the Lord" foresaw this, and promised guidance for Saul against overwhelming odds. Sadly, as we shall see, Saul's impatience lost him the kingdom. The important thing to notice now is that whilst Saul could expect divine help as king of Israel, his liberty in this way was not licence to do as he pleased. He was subject to the word of God. Samuel makes this very clear here. "Thou **shalt** go down before me to Gilgal…seven days **shalt** thou tarry, till I come to thee". See Galatians 5.13: "For, brethren, ye have been called unto liberty; only use not liberty for an occasion to the flesh."

C) The reaction to the signs (vv.9-13)
"And it came to pass. when all that knew him beforetime saw that, behold, he prophesied among the prophets, then the people said one to another, What is this that is come unto the son of Kish? Is Saul also among the prophets?" This presupposes that Saul's previous life was altogether different! This is not surprising. After all, the Holy Spirit does transform people's lives, doesn't he? People should see this, shouldn't they? Do they see this in **our** lives? (see 2 Cor 5.17). In some cases, the change is particularly dramatic. (see 1 Peter 4.3-4). One citizen of Gibeah took issue

with the statement, "Is Saul also among the prophets?" (see v.12). "And one of the same place answered and said, But who is **their** father? Therefore it became a proverb, Is Saul also among the prophets." This thoughtful gentleman simply observed that since "the prophets," with whom Saul was now associated, did not possess the gift of prophecy by inheritance (their gift didn't run in the family), but as a gift from the Lord, it was equally possible for the Lord to give Saul the same gift in the same way. If Amos had been alive at the time, he would have given a hearty "Amen!" (see Amos 7.14-15). This reminds us that ability to serve God does not "run in the blood". Preaching and teaching fathers do not necessarily produce preaching and teaching sons. The Holy Spirit divides to "every man severally as **he** will" (1 Cor 12.11).

3. The Humility of Saul (vv.14-16)
Enter Saul's uncle. He is not named here, but it was probably Ner; see 14. 50-51. We will see quite a lot of "Abner, the son of Ner, Saul's uncle", in due course. Presumably Saul's uncle connected the transformation of Saul with his interview with Samuel. Hence the question, "Tell me, I pray thee, what Samuel said unto you." Saul's answer reflects his early humility. "When thou wast little in thine own sight, wast thou not made head of the tribes of Israel, and the Lord anointed thee king over Israel?" (15.17). We noticed this in 9.21, now we have it again. "And Saul said unto his uncle, He told us plainly that the asses were found. But of the matter of the kingdom, whereof Samuel spake, he told him not". Saul did not "trumpet" his God-given appointment. Compare 2 Corinthians 12. 1-4. Paul waited for fourteen years before he told other people about his visit to paradise, and only spoke about it then under pressing circumstances. Most of us wouldn't have been able to wait to publicise the experience! God "requires" us to walk humbly with Him. See Micah 6.8.

4. The Presentation of Saul (vv.17-27)
While Saul made no mention "of the matter of the kingdom", Samuel took steps to present him to the nation. "And Samuel called the people together unto the Lord to Mizpeh". It was at Mizpeh that Samuel prayed, and "the Lord thundered with a great thunder...upon the Philistines, and discomfited them" (7.10). Perhaps the selection of Mizpeh, the site of a former victory over the Philistines, was a sign of further victory over them in battle. Sadly, through his disobedience, Saul was ultimately slain by the Philistines. We should notice the following.

1 Samuel

A) Remonstration (vv.18-19)
"Thus saith the Lord God of Israel, I brought up Israel out of Egypt, and delivered you out of the hand of the Egyptians, and out of the hand of all kingdoms...and ye have this day rejected your God, who himself saved you out of all your adversities and your tribulations; and ye have said unto him, Nay, but set a king over us." God not only asked His people to trust Him. He had **proved** that they could trust Him. Joshua made that clear. "Ye know in all your hearts and in all your souls, that not one thing hath failed of all the good things which the Lord your God spake concerning you; all are come to pass unto you, and not one thing hath failed thereof" (Josh 23.14). But all the available evidence could not change their minds: they still preferred to trust a visible human leader, rather than the invisible but unfailing God.

Their determination to have a king did not deter Samuel from teaching them "the good and the right way" (12.23). Samuel remained faithful to the word and will of God. He uses striking and significant language. "ye have this day rejected **your God,** who **himself** saved you out of all your adversities and your tribulations; and ye have said **unto him,** Nay, but set a king over us." Failure to trust God is a personal affront to Him.

B) Revelation (vv.20-22)
The name of the king was revealed by a process of elimination. This raises an obvious question. Why didn't Samuel simply proclaim Saul king, and therefore obviate what was probably a lengthy process? That would have been much simpler! But Samuel was a wise man. He wanted to make it clear that the **Lord** had chosen Saul. Hence the expressions, "the tribe of Benjamin was **taken**...the family of Matri was **taken**...Saul the son of Kish was **taken**." When Saul could not be found, "they enquired of the **Lord** further...and the **Lord** answered". We are not told precisely how Israel discovered, *(a)* that the king would be a Benjamite, *(b)* that he would come from the family of Matri and *(c)* that it would be Saul the son of Kish. There can be no doubt, however, that God made all this clear through the Urim and Thummim. See Exodus 28.30. Read Numbers 27.18-21 in this connection. The important thing to notice here is that Saul was not chosen as the result of any bias, favouritism, or even sound judgement on the part of Samuel. He was chosen by God. This is important when it comes to the government and guidance of local assemblies. It is not a question of democratic choice, but rather divine choice. See Acts 20.28.

C) Recognition (vv.23-25)

"And they ran and fetched him thence: and when he stood among the people, he was higher than any of the people from his shoulders and upward (see 9.2). And Samuel said to all the people, See ye him whom the Lord hath chosen, that there is none like him among all the people? And all the people shouted, and said, God save the king." We are told that this was literally, "Let the king live!" The emphasis upon his appearance is significant. With some exceptions (see v.27), the nation heartily approved the choice of Saul. He created the right impression. After all, a giant king was needed to fight the giant Philistines! It is interesting, however, to compare this with the choice of David, whom Samuel described as "a man after his (God's) own heart", (13.14). Eliab, David's oldest brother, looked a most likely candidate to Samuel. But God thought otherwise. "Look not on his countenance, or on the height of his stature; because I have refused him: for the Lord seeth not as man seeth; for man looketh on the outward appearance, but the Lord looketh on the heart" (16.7). First impressions are not necessarily correct. See 1 Timothy 5.24-25.

"The manner of the kingdom" (v.27), which could read, "the law of the kingdom", does not evidently refer to the right of the king as described in 8.11-17, but to the way in which the kingdom was to be governed. Ellicott's Commentary describes "the manner of the kingdom" as "the divinely established rights and duties of the God-appointed king" together with "the limitations of his power". The king could not do as he pleased. Details are not given here, but it does seem likely that Samuel based his document on Deuteronomy 17.14-20. Among other things, the king must "write him a copy of this law in a book out of that which is before the priests and the Levites", and "read therein all the days of his life." But read the entire passage. It is most interesting. The king was subject to the word of God as much as his subjects. We are not told exactly where the document was placed, but the words, "laid...it up before the Lord" strongly suggest that it was put alongside the ark which was then at Kirjath-jearim (7.1).

D) Response (vv.26-27)
i) The response of Saul. He went home, and resumed work on the family farm! See 11.5. This raises a number of interesting questions. Did he really expect life to continue as before? Or was he just waiting to see what was going to happen? Or did he find all the publicity distasteful? Or was he just attempting to "opt out?" Keil and Delitzsch suggest that he was waiting

for "higher instructions to act, before he entered upon the government". See chapter 11.

ii) **The response of the people.** Some were people "whose hearts God had touched." They formed his escort, and wished to show their readiness to serve him. This reminds us of Psalm 110.3, "Thy people shall be willing in the day of thy power." Are we ready and willing to be identified with the King *now*? Remember, it involves bearing His reproach. He is rejected at present, but the "crowning day" is coming! But there were some who said, "How shall this man save us? and they despised him, and brought him no presents." They are called "the children of Belial", meaning "worthless persons". Ellicott's Commentary suggests that they "despised him because in no way had he made his mark, either in the arts of war or peace...it is evident that Saul was a man of no special culture." But this is just the kind of man that God delights to use. See 1 Corinthians 1.26-31. Wisely, Saul said nothing. It would not be long before "the children of Belial" discovered that "this man" **could** save them!

There are many people today who say of the Lord Jesus, "How shall this man save us?" We should be so glad that He has saved **us**, and that we belong to those "whose hearts God has touched".

CHAPTER 11

"Victory at Jabesh-Gilead" (11.1-15)

The children of Israel had demanded a king to "judge us, and go out before us, and fight our battles" (8.20). They now had the king they wanted, but not everybody was satisfied. "The children of Belial said, How shall this man save us? And they despised him, and brought no present." They doubted him, despised him, and denied him, but it wasn't long before "the children of Belial" discovered that "this man" **was** able to save Israel from her enemies. King Saul's reign began with a striking victory over Nahash, the Ammonite. It was achieved in the power of the Spirit of God (v.6), reminding us that

> Every virtue we possess,
> And every victory won,
> And every thought of holiness,
> Are His alone.

The chapter can be divided as follows: *(1)* The threat from Nahash (vv.1-3); *(2)* The leadership of Saul (vv.4-8); *(3)* The promise of help (vv.9-11); *(4)* The restraint of Saul (vv.12-13); *(5)* The renewal of the kingdom (vv.14-15).

1. The Threat from Nahash (vv.1-3)

"Then Nahash the Ammonite came up, and camped against Jabesh-Gilead: and all the men of Jabesh said unto Nahash, Make a covenant with us, and we will serve thee." Jabesh-Gilead lay to the east of the River Jordan. It was located in territory which once belonged to the children of Ammon, and this was not the first time that they had attempted to regain the area. Some sixty to seventy years before, they invaded Gilead, and were defeated by Jephthah. See Judges 10.17–11.33. The siege of Jabesh-Gilead was evidently the latest event in a campaign by Nahash against Israel. See 12.12.

1 Samuel

It is worth remembering that if Abraham had obeyed God completely in Ur of the Chaldees, his descendants would not have been troubled by either the Ammonites or the Moabites. "Now the Lord had said unto Abram, Get thee out of thy country, and from thy kindred, and from thy father"s house, unto a land that I will shew thee." But "Abram departed, as the Lord had spoken unto him; and **Lot** went with him" (Gen 12.1-4). As a result, Ammon and Moab were born in the most deplorable circumstances. See Genesis 19.30-38. We must remember that failure to completely obey God's word can store up trouble for other people, as well as ourselves.

Amongst other things, we should notice that the threat from Nahash involved *(A)* The sight of God's people (v.2); *(B)* The shame of God's people (v.2); *(C)* The salvation of God's people (v.3).

A) *Their sight (v.2)*
"And all the men of Jabesh said unto Nahash, Make a covenant with us, and we will serve thee. And Nahash the Ammonite answered them, On this condition will I make a covenant with you, that I may thrust out your right eyes." The word "right" often carries the idea of honour, and to lose the right eye would involve a terrible loss of prestige. (The Lord Jesus referred to the "right eye" and the "right hand" Mt 5.29-30). "Anxious to avoid open conflict with the enemy, the men of Jabesh propose terms of surrender. They even suggest becoming servants of Nahash, thus ignoring entirely the claim that God had on them as His redeemed people, and forgetting the glorious victory of their own Jephthah on a former occasion." (Peter J. Pell, *"Bible Class Notes - 1 Samuel)*. Nahash means "serpent", and this reminds us that Satan will do all in his power to disable us spiritually. Ineffective Christians give him no trouble. He doesn't bother too much about them! Compromise with Nahash would have blinded the men of Jasbesh-Gilead, and compromise will do the same for us. "Fortunately, the enemy showed himself in his true colours. Sin is a hard master, and it is best to discover it before we are under its power" (P.J.Pell).

B) *Their shame (v.2)*
"On this condition will I make a covenant with you, that I may thrust out all your right eyes, and lay it for a **reproach** upon all Israel." Compare 17.26. Nahash intended to bring shame on God's people. He evidently did not expect Israel to rally in support of their beleaguered brethren in Jabesh-Gilead, otherwise he would not have given them seven days" grace! We know that events proved Nahash wrong, but it does raise important issues

for us. Cain asked the question, "Am I my brother's keeper?" Paul illustrates the New Testament answer by referring to the interdependence of the human body: "God hath tempered the body together...that there should be no schism in the body; but that the members should have the **same care** one for another" (1 Cor 12.24-27). But **do** we care for one another? It is shameful to refuse help to fellow-believers in need.

C) Their salvation (v.3)
"Give us seven days" respite, that we may send messengers unto all the coasts of Israel: and then, if there be no man to save us, we will come out to thee." Don't expect "seven days respite" from Satan! The men of Jabesh evidently did not look for divine help. "If there is no **man** to save us, we will come out to thee." They had not "cried unto the Lord" (Jud 3.9 etc). In fact, they also seem to have forgotten that they had a king! The messengers were sent "unto all the coasts of Israel", not specifically to Gibeah of Saul. Sadly, the word of God was either forgotten or ignored. They didn't seem to remember the closing words of Moses: "The eternal God is thy refuge, and underneath are the everlasting arms: and he shall thrust out the enemy from before thee; and shall say, Destroy them" (Deut 33.27). Do **we** turn to God, not only in the crises of life, but at **all** times?

2. The Leadership of Saul (vv.4-8)
At first glance, the appearance of Saul does not look too promising. The king, who was supposed to fight Israel's battles (8.20), arrives home after a hard day's work in the fields to find the city in great distress. But Saul becomes "the man of the hour", and fully answers the derisory question, "How shall this man save us?" (10.27). We must notice **(A)** The power of his leadership (vv.6-7); **(B)** The attitude under his leadership (v.7); **(C)** The support for his leadership (vv.7-8).

A) The power of his leadership, (vv.6-7)
The people "lifted up their voices and wept" (v.4), but Saul acted. It's all too easy to bemoan the difficulties and disappointments, and do nothing at all about it! Some commentators criticise Saul for the way in which he united Israel against Nahash, but the passage does say, "And the Spirit of God came upon Saul when he heard these tidings", and we can only conclude that he acted with divine power and authority. Ellicott's Commentary puts it like this: "The Holy Spirit...endued him with extraordinary wisdom, valour, and power for the great and difficult work which lay before him." Compare Judges 3.10, 6.34, and 11.29. When

the battle was over, Saul was careful to give glory to God: "Today the **Lord** hath wrought salvation in Israel" (v.13).

Saul's anger has been criticised, but, surely, it was anger at the intimidation of God's people by Nahash. After all, if the Ammonites had carried out their threat, it would have been a "reproach to all Israel." The apostle Paul displayed the same spirit when he wrote: "Who is weak, and I am not weak? Who is offended (stumbled), and I burn not?" (2 Cor 11.29).

It is to Saul's credit that he did not act without acknowledging Samuel, which proves that although he was king, Saul "still recognised the authority which Samuel possessed in Israel as the prophet of Jehovah", Keil and Delitzsch. Saul, at this stage in his life, was not marked by self-confidence and self-sufficiency.

B) The attitude under his leadership (v.7)
"And the fear of the Lord fell on the people." Not "the fear of Saul", or even "the fear of Samuel", but "the fear of the Lord." Generally speaking, this refers, not so much to fear of punishment, but to reverential awe. The "fear of the Lord" is a desire to do nothing that will displease Him. "The fear of the Lord is to hate evil" (Prov 8.13). On this occasion, however, "the fear of the Lord" may have a stronger meaning. Hence the RV rendering, "And the dread of the Lord (margin, "a terror from the Lord") fell on the people."

C) The support for his leadership (vv.7-8)
"They came out with one consent." The whole nation, Israel and Judah, were represented at Bezek, to the west of the River Jordan. "And when he numbered them in Bezek, the children of Israel were three hundred thousand, and the men of Judah thirty thousand." We are to "keep the unity of the Spirit in the bond of peace" (Eph 4.3). The assembly at Philippi was urged to "stand fast in one spirit, with one mind, striving together for the faith of the gospel" (1.27). The early church was of "one accord" (Acts 2. 1; 2.46; 4.24; 5.12-13 etc). It has been said that "there is nothing worse than a bunch of irreconcilable people preaching a gospel of reconciliation!"

Israel's united support for Jabesh-Gilead is all the more striking when we remember that Jabesh-Gilead failed to support Israel against the Benjamites. See Judges 21.8. There was no "give as good as you get" attitude here! That's worth remembering, isn't it?!

3. The Promise of Help (vv.9-11)
This paragraph is self-explanatory. Notice **(A)** The promise made (vv.9-10) and **(B)** The promise fulfilled (v.11).

A) The promise made (vv.9-10)
"And they said unto the messengers that came, Thus shall ye say unto the men of Jabesh-Gilead, Tomorrow, by that time the sun be hot, ye shall have help. And the messengers came and shewed it to the men of Jabesh; and they were glad." In fact, they never forgot the help of Saul. See 31.11-13. It seems that the inhabitants of Jabesh decided that they could contribute to their deliverance by putting the Ammonites off their guard! See v.10.

B) The promise fulfilled (v.11)
Perhaps Saul remembered how Gideon defeated the Midianites. He "put the people in three companies; and they came into the midst of the host in the morning watch, and slew the Ammonites until the heat of the day." Compare Judges 7.16. The "morning watch" was between 2 a.m. and 6 a.m. According to Ellicott's Commentary, "the Jews anciently divided the night from 6 p.m. to 6 a.m. into three watches. The subsequent division into four watches was borrowed from the Romans."

On a practical note, Saul fulfilled his promise, and we too should be people of our word. See Acts 11.29, "And the disciples, every man according to his ability, **determined** to send relief unto the brethren which dwelt in Judaea. Which they **did**, and sent it to the elders by the hands (hand) of Barnabas and Saul." Yes, another Saul brought help!

4. The Restraint of Saul (vv.12-13)
This is a very nice piece. "And the people said unto **Samuel,** Who is he that said, Shall Saul reign over us? Bring the men, that we may put them to death. And **Saul** said, There shall not a man be put to death this day: for today the Lord hath wrought salvation in Israel." Notice that the people spoke to Samuel, but Saul answered them! We would call this bad manners, but Saul's reply is most commendable. He certainly didn't take the opportunity to "get his own back! See Romans 12.17-21, "Recompense no man evil for evil...avenge not yourselves...be not overcome of evil, but overcome evil with good." Commentators quote Seb. Schmidt here: "Since Jehovah had shown such clemency on that day, that He overlooked their sins, and had given them a glorious victory, it was only right that they should follow His example, and forgive their neighbour's sins without bloodshed!"

1 Samuel

Sadly, Saul did not always show such clemency. "Oh that Saul had ever remembered the God Who had wrought salvation in Israel! The cruel and sacrilegious massacre at Nob (22.18-19), or the horrors of that night at Endor, and of the day that followed at Mt. Gilboa, would never have been recorded." (Peter J.Pell).

5. The Renewal of the Kingdom (vv.14-15)
"Then said Samuel to the people, Come, and let us go to Gilgal, and renew the kingdom there." Saul had been anointed king by Samuel (10.1), and proclaimed king at Mizpeh (10.24), but he had now proved that he was worthy to be king. His wisdom and ability were beyond doubt. "And all the people went to Gilgal; and there they made Saul king before the Lord in Gilgal. We must notice **(A)** Where the kingdom was renewed (v.14), and **(B)** What the renewal of the kingdom involved (v.15).

A) Where it was renewed, (v.14)
Samuel led the people to Gilgal to remind them of their relationship with God. It was there that the Israelites were circumcised "the second time." See Joshua 5.1-9. The rite of circumcision had not been practised in the wilderness because Israel's very presence there was evidence of their unbelief. See Hebrews 3.18-19. But in faith and obedience, Israel had crossed the Jordan, and entered the land. Like their father, Abraham, they had believed God, and circumcision, the sign of faith, was reinstituted at Gilgal which was the first place of encampment in Canaan. Samuel therefore called them to Gilgal in order to remind them that they must continue to believe and obey God. Circumcision signified no confidence in self (Gilgal means "a rolling away"), and complete confidence in God. Paul summarises the significance for us in Philippians 3.3, "For we are the circumcision, which worship God in the spirit, and rejoice in Christ Jesus, and have no confidence in the flesh." Paul takes the subject a little further in Colossians 2.11-12 where he links "the circumcision made without hands" with the death of the Lord Jesus. Israel went to Gilgal to be reminded of their relationship with God, but we go to Calvary. This brings us to

B) What was involved (v.15)
Three things took place at Gilgal, and the same three things, in principle, should take place as we remember the death of the Lord Jesus Christ.

i) They recognised their king. "**There** they made Saul king before the Lord in Gilgal." They acknowledged his rule and authority. As "the circumcision" who "have no confidence in the flesh", we should gladly submit to the authority of the Lord Jesus in our lives. We know that the Lord Jesus is the "**King** of Israel" and "**King** of nations." He is never described as "King" of the church. He is **Lord** and **Head** of the church. But even so, we must bow to His rule. Perhaps **we** need to "renew the kingdom." It means that we must "present our bodies a living sacrifice, holy, acceptable unto God, which is our reasonable service." It means that we must recognise that we are "not our own." It means that we "should not henceforth live unto ourselves, but unto him which died for us, and rose again."

ii) They enjoyed fellowship with God. "**There** they sacrificed sacrifices of peace offerings before the Lord." Quite clearly the "peace offerings" were offered here "for a thanksgiving" (Lev 7.12). The outstanding feature of the peace offering was its provision for God, for the priest, and for the offerer and his family. As "the circumcision" who "have no confidence in the flesh", we enjoy fellowship with God in our enjoyment of Christ and in our thanksgiving for Him.

iii) They rejoiced together. "**There** Saul and all the men of Israel rejoiced together." As "the circumcision" who "have no confidence in the flesh", we are the most joyful people in the world. "Then were the disciples glad when they saw the Lord." "Whom having not seen, we love; in whom, though now we see him not, yet believing, we rejoice with joy unspeakable and full of glory." The threefold occurrence of "there" reminds us of Psalm 133: "Behold, how good and how pleasant it is for brethren to dwell together in unity...**there** the Lord commanded the blessing, even life for evermore."

"Thus ended the brightest day in all the reign of Saul. Had he and Israel continued in the good of Gilgal, their joy would have remained" (Peter J.Pell). Now that is a lesson for us all!

CHAPTER 12

Samuel's last speech to Israel (12.1-25)

No, this isn't the last **appearance** of Samuel, but it is his last **public address** to the nation. It represents a watershed in Israel's history. With this speech, Samuel terminates the rule of the judges, which involved both civil and military leadership, and passes responsibility for rule to the monarchy. In the words of A.McShane, "Here Samuel, the last of the judges, bows out as civil leader, and from now onward acts only as a prophet." It was the close of a period covering four hundred and fifty years. See Acts 13.20. Saul, following his victory over the Ammonites at Jabesh-Gilead, was now firmly established as Israel's first king. It was time for Samuel to give his parting message.

This chapter can be divided into four paragraphs as follows: *(1)* Samuel's righteousness (vv.1-5); *(2)* Samuel's reasoning (vv.6-15); *(3)* Samuel's request (vv.16-19); *(4)* Samuel's reassurance (vv.20-25).

1. Samuel's Righteousness (vv.1-5)

The first thing we should do is to take an "overview" of these verses, and combine it with an "overview" of the next paragraph. In this section, Samuel proves to them that they could not say that **he** was guilty of misrule, and therefore a change was necessary. In the next section, (vv.6-15), Samuel proves that they could not say that the **Lord** had failed them, and therefore they needed good human leadership. Any doubts about Samuel's arguments were destroyed when the Lord "sent thunder and rain", causing the people to say, "We have added unto all our sins this evil, to ask us a king" (v.19). Two statements stand out as we begin to read the chapter:

A) "The king walketh before you" (v.2)

This is exactly what they wanted: "And Samuel said unto all Israel, Behold, I have hearkened unto your voice in all that ye said unto me, and have made a king over you. And now, behold, the king walketh before you." Well, he had certainly made a good start! Everything looked promising. We must remember, however, that "even though a scheme succeeds, this is in no way proof that it is right...Success can easily be deceptive. The spiritual man may, at times, have to allow the passage of time to prove him right in his judgement" (A.McShane).

B) "I have walked before you" (vv.2-5)

"Now, behold, the king walketh before you: and I am old and grayheaded; and, behold, my sons are with you: and I have walked before you from my childhood." Samuel had a consistent "track-record" which stretched from "childhood" to old age. He "judged Israel all the days of his life" (7.15). (Although he describes himself as "old and grayheaded", he lived for around another thirty years!) He probably refers to his sons as proof of his age and maturity. He certainly couldn't refer to them as his worthy successors! See 8.1-5. They "took bribes and perverted judgement", whereas their father was able to say, "Of whose hand have I received any bribe to blind mine eyes therewith?" In the words of Ellicott's Commentary, "The old judge must have been very confident of his own spotless integrity to venture upon such a solemn challenge."

The following verses illustrate Paul's advice to Timothy: "Take heed unto **thyself,** and unto the doctrine; continue in them: for in doing this thou shalt both save thyself, and them that hear thee" (1 Tim 4.16). This is vitally important. Timothy was to be an example of his own teaching. This is exactly what Paul did himself: see 2 Timothy 3.10. He was to give attention to himself, as well as his teaching. The Lord Jesus censured the scribes and Pharisees for their inconsistency: "The scribes and Pharisees sit in Moses' seat: all therefore whatsoever they bid you observe, that observe and do; but do ye not after their works: for they **say**, and **do not**" (Mt 23.1-3). The Lord Jesus had the moral right to censure them in this way because there was no inconsistency whatever with Him. "The former treatise (Luke's Gospel) have I made, O Theophilus, of all that Jesus began both to **do** and **teach**" (Acts 1.1). It could not be reported of Him that "He said, and did not." This raises a most important question:

What we **say** may be right, but are **we** right?

There should be no discrepancy between our profession and our practice, between our belief and our behaviour, between our confession and our conduct.

We should notice the striking similarity between Samuel's appeal to Israel, and Paul's appeal to the Ephesian elders at Miletus. **Samuel:** "Behold, here I am: witness against me before the Lord, and before his anointed: whose ox have I taken? or whose ass have I taken? or whom have I defrauded? whom have I oppressed? or of whose hand have I received any bribe to blind mine eyes therewith? and I will restore it to you" (v.3) **Paul:** "I have coveted no man's silver, or gold, or apparel. Yea, ye yourselves know, that these hands have ministered unto my necessities, and to them that were with me" (Acts 20.33-34). The similarity between the two servants of God is even clearer in their appeal to both God and men as witnesses of their integrity. **Samuel:** "And they said Thou hast not defrauded us, nor oppressed us, neither hast thou taken ought of any man's hand. And he said unto them, The **Lord** is witness against you, and **his anointed** is witness this day, that **ye** have not found ought in my hand" (v.5). **Paul:** "For our exhortation was not of deceit, nor of uncleanness, nor in guile...for neither at any time used we flattering words, as **ye** know, nor a cloke of covetousness; **God** is witness...**Ye** are witnesses, and **God** also, how holily and justly and unblameably we behaved ourselves among you that believe" (1 Thess 2. 3-10). It has been nicely said that "God saw what they saw." Paul was able to say, "And herein do I exercise myself, to have always a conscience void of offence toward God, and toward men" (Acts 24.16). We must behave in a way that ensures that "the name of God and (his) doctrine be not blasphemed".

2. Samuel's Reasoning (vv.6-15)
This paragraph heading comes straight out of the text! "Now therefore stand still, that I may **reason** with you before the Lord of all the righteous acts of the Lord, which he did to you and to your fathers." We will look at the section as follows: **(A)** Their fathers (vv.6-11); **(B)** Their folly (vv.12-13); **(C)** Their future (vv.14-15).

A) Their fathers (vv.6-11)
The competent authorities tell us that verses 5 & 6 should be read together. "And he said unto them, The Lord is witness against you, and his anointed is witness this day, that ye have not found ought in my hand. And they answered, *He is* witness." To which Samuel replied: *"It is* the Lord that advanced Moses and Aaron, and that brought your fathers up out of the land of Egypt." The God who bore witness to Samuel's integrity was the same God who had delivered Israel from Egypt under the leadership of Moses and Aaron. By this means, Samuel reminded the people that God

had **never failed them.** He did not fail them at the beginning of their national history, and he had not failed them since. They had proved His faithfulness in the lifetime of Samuel himself. Samuel calls this "the righteous acts of the Lord, which he did to you and to your fathers." The following verses amplify this. Samuel begins, again, with Moses and Aaron (v.8), and ends with himself (v.11).

These verses are far more than a "potted" history of Israel. Samuel refers to their history in order to make an important point. In fact, he emphasises the point twice: "Your fathers **cried unto the Lord**, then **the Lord sent** Moses and Aaron" (v.8). "They **cried unto the Lord**...and **the Lord sent** Jerubbaal, and Bedan, and Jephthah, and Samuel" (vv.10-11).

i) God had not failed His people when they cried to Him under cruel bondage **in Egypt.** "I have surely seen the affliction of my people which are in Egypt, and have heard their cry by reason of their taskmasters; for I know their sorrows; and am come down to deliver them out of the hand of the Egyptians" (Ex 3.7-8).

ii) God had not failed His people when they cried to Him under bondage to their enemies **in Canaan,** even though they deserved captivity. Although "they forgat the Lord their God", and suffered the consequences, He still heard their cry, "We have sinned...but now deliver us out of the hand of our enemies, and we will serve thee." Samuel emphasises not only the faithfulness of God, but the patience of God. He refers indirectly to deliverance under Ehud (who defeated the Moabites), and directly to deliverance under "Jerubbaal, and Bedan, and Jehpthah, and Samuel." (Jerubbaal is, of course, Gideon: see Judges 6.32. The reference to Bedan is not quite so clear, but most commentators come down in favour of Barak. All four are mentioned in Hebrews 11.32. As Keil and Delitzsch observe, "it is extremely improbable that Samuel should have mentioned a judge here, who had been passed over in the book of Judges on account of his comparative insignificance".

Samuel ends this part of his address with a conclusion: "The Lord...delivered you out of the hand of your enemies on every side, and ye dwelled safe." There was no need to look elsewhere. Israel's history proved that God could deliver and preserve them. But there was within the nation "an evil heart of unbelief" (Heb 3.12). So:

1 Samuel

B) Their folly (vv.12-13)

All the evidence of God's saving and preserving power counted for nothing when Nahash appeared on the scene. Israel preferred to "walk by sight" rather than by faith. See 2 Corinthians 5.9. Samuel could no longer say, "Ye cried unto the Lord." They cried for a king! "And when ye saw that Nahash the king of the children of Ammon came against you, ye said unto me, Nay; but a king shall reign over us; when the Lord your God was your king." We gather from this that Nahash must have invaded the eastern part of Israel (Trans-jordan) immediately before Israel requested a king. The siege of Jabesh-Gilead, which ended with defeat for Ammon, was therefore the last of a series of forays against Israel.

To request a king when God had proved His ability to lead them to victory, was therefore illogical and defamatory. There is a note of irony in Samuel's words: "Now therefore behold the king **ye** have chosen, and whom **ye** have desired!" But at the same time, Samuel emphasises the grace of God, for that same king had been divinely-appointed: "And, behold, the Lord hath set a king over you." God gave them the king they desired, but just think of what would have happened if **they** had selected their own king! Where did this leave Israel? How would God treat them now? After all, they had rejected Him. Notice what follows.

C) Their future (vv.14-15)

A.McShane catches the spirit of these verses nicely: "Now that all was fixed, and there was no going back on the appointment of Saul, we might well think that there was no hope for the future. But the prophet shows us otherwise, for obedience will still be blessed in spite of past failures. However, the promise is not without warning, for departure from God will be followed by His wrath, as had happened in former days." Although it was far from ideal, God had allowed them to have a king. But that guaranteed nothing. The future welfare of the nation depended on their relationship with God. Samuel spells out the alternatives clearly:

i) "If ye will fear the Lord, and serve him, and **obey** his voice, and not rebel against the commandment of the Lord, then shall both **ye** and also **the king** that reigneth over you continue following (or, "be after") the Lord your God." According to competent authorities, the words, "If ye will fear the Lord", have the meaning, "O that ye would only serve the Lord."

ii) "But if ye will **not obey** the voice of the Lord, but rebel against the commandment of the Lord, then shall the hand of the Lord be against you, as it was against your fathers."

It is important to remember that we began our Christian life by **obeying God.** The gospel is "made known to all nations for the **obedience** of faith", (Rom 16.26). It can be said of us, as it was said of the Christians at Rome, "But God be thanked, that ye were the servants of sin, but ye **obeyed** from the heart that form of doctrine which was delivered you" (Rom 6.17). It is equally important to remember that we continue our Christian lives by obeying God. "Wherefore gird up the loins of your mind…as **obedient** children, not fashioning yourselves according to the former lusts in your ignorance" (1 Pet 1.13-14).

3. Samuel's Request (vv.16-19)

While Samuel had promised that on-going obedience on the part of both king and people would secure divine help and blessing, this did not mean that their rejection of the unseen God in favour of a visible king was just a technical triviality. Israel was guilty of grave sin, and Samuel took the opportunity to emphasise the seriousness of their conduct. When things go wrong, faithful men ought to appeal to the word of God, and bring its teaching to bear upon the situation. All too often, things go wrong, and good men stay silent. But not Samuel!

Up to this point, the nation remained silent. In fact, there is no evidence thus far that Israel had heeded anything that Samuel had said about their desire for a king. On the contrary, they had persisted in their demand. "The people refused to obey the voice of Samuel; and they said, Nay; but we **will** have a king over us" (8.19). Samuel's reasoning, both here and elsewhere (see 8.10-18), failed to wring from them a confession of their sin, but the storm succeeded where Samuel's remonstration failed. He called on God to "send thunder and rain; that ye may perceive and see that your wickedness is great", and as a result, the people cried to Samuel, "Pray for thy servants unto the Lord thy God (no longer "our God", 7.8), that we die not: for we have added unto all our sins this evil, to ask us a king."

On a technical note "wheat harvest occurs in Palestine (this is a quote from Keil & Delitzsch) between the middle of May and the middle of June, and during this time it scarcely ever rains." The thunder and rain were therefore rightly recognised as divine intervention.

Although the storm had the desired effect, and the people now knew beyond doubt that Samuel had been right to censure their desire for a king, it is rather sad that their confession was brought about by a storm rather than the scriptures. Ellicott's Commentary makes the significant observation that "the terrible storm of rain accompanied by thunder...struck the people naturally with great fear, and **for the moment** they thoroughly repented of the past, and entreated Samuel...to intercede for them." This reminds us that we should be people whose convictions are firmly based on the word of God. Although, in this case, God clearly spoke to Israel through the storm, circumstances are not necessarily the best guide, or even the right guide. We must be governed and guided by "what saith the Scripture?"

4. Samuel's Reassurance (vv.20-25)
It must have been most reassuring to hear Samuel say, "Fear not!" Two reasons follow. They were not to fear **(A)** because of the Lord's faithfulness (vv.20-22), and **(B)** because of Samuels' faithfulness (vv.23-25).

A) The faithfulness of God (vv.20-22)
"The Lord will not forsake his people for his great name's sake: because it hath pleased the Lord to make you his people." This was the ground on which Joshua cried to God after the defeat at Ai. "The Canaanites and all the inhabitants of the land shall hear of it, and shall environ us round, and cut off our name from the earth: and what wilt thou do unto **thy great name?**" (Josh 7.9). Moses used the same argument after the debacle at Kadesh-Barnea. See Numbers 14.11-16. This will be the ground on which God will restore and bless His people in the future. "Thus saith the Lord: I do not this for your sakes, O house of Israel, but for **mine holy name's sake,** which ye have profaned among the heathen, whither ye went" (Ezek 36.21-23): read the entire chapter. God will be faithful to the covenant made with the patriarchs.

But the current enjoyment of God's faithfulness to Israel depended on Israel's faithfulness to God. Compare 2 Chronicles 15.1-2, "The Lord is with you, while ye be with him; and if ye seek him, he will be found of you; but if ye forsake him, he will forsake you." That couldn't be clearer, could it?! Samuel spelt this out clearly by stressing the alternatives: "Fear not: ye have done all this wickedness: yet turn not aside from following the Lord, but serve the Lord with all your heart. And turn ye not aside: for then should ye go after vain things, which cannot profit nor deliver; for they are vain." Samuel refers here to idolatry. Compare Isaiah 44.9, "They that make a graven image are all of them **vanity**; and their delectable things shall **not profit**." See also Jeremiah 2.11 ("that which doth not profit"), and 10.8 ("the stock is a doctrine of vanities"). This is not the first time that Samuel called for whole-hearted allegiance to God. See 7.3. Devotion to God is our great bulwark against idolatry in its various forms.

B) The faithfulness of Samuel (vv.23-25)
"Moreover as for me, God forbid that I should sin against the Lord in ceasing to pray for you: but I will teach you the good and right way." This is an example to us all. Samuel did not "wash his hands" of Israel, even though they had effectively rejected him. He determined to be faithful to Israel in two ways: *(i)* in prayer and *(ii)* in teaching.

i) **His faithfulness in prayer.** Both Moses and Samuel were men who were outstanding in their intercession for Israel, so much so that God said, "Though Moses and Samuel stood before me, yet my mind could not be toward this people" (Jer 15.1). Samuel uses striking language: "God forbid that I should **sin against the Lord** in ceasing to pray for you." Israel had "sinned against the Lord" in demanding a king, and now we learn that it is possible to sin against the Lord by ceasing to pray for people! Rather searching, isn't it? Ceasing to pray for people could indicate several things. For example, it could mean that our interest in them has diminished: a case of "out of sight, out of mind." It could mean that we tend to "write off" people who don't agree with us, or people whose conduct and behaviour has caused us disappointment or annoyance. But, above everything else, ceasing to pray for people is a "sin against the Lord" because we fail to recognise **His** love and interest in them. We are to "continue in prayer" (Col 4. 2). Epaphras is a splendid example! See Colossians 4.12.

ii) **His faithfulness in teaching.** "I will teach you the good and right way." Samuel and Paul stand shoulder to shoulder here. See Acts 20.27: "I have not shunned to declare unto you all the counsel of God." The "good and right way" is not always acceptable, and like Samuel, the servant of God must be prepared to face opposition and rejection.

Samuel's faithfulness in this way teaches us another important lesson. Prayer and teaching went together. There is far more to Bible teaching than studying into the 'early hours' and then delivering an address. In any case, there is a vast difference between an address and a message! Prayer for those who listen to Bible teaching is an integral part of the ministry. We must pray for divine help and guidance in preparation and presentation, and we must pray for divine help and guidance for our hearers. This is a lesson for Sunday School teachers as well as "ministers of the word." (Do remember that the word "minister" often means "servant." It never refers to an official position).

Samuel concludes his address by repeating the alternatives. Their importance is stressed in this way. "Only fear the Lord (that's **reverence**), and serve him in truth with all your heart (that's **reality**): and consider how great things he hath done for you (that's **remembrance**). But if ye shall still do wickedly, ye shall be consumed, both ye and your king." Israel's future blessing did not depend on the existence of a king: it depended on their obedience and devotion to God. The Lord Jesus sad, "Ye are my friends, if ye do whatsoever I command you" (Jn 15.14).

CHAPTER 13

Saul's foolishness (1 Sam 13.1-23)

With this chapter Saul begins his campaign against the Philistines. He had been anointed for this purpose. "Thou shalt anoint him to be captain over my people Israel, that he may save my people out of the hand of the Philistines: for I have looked upon my people, because their cry is come unto me" (9.16). Victory over the Ammonites at Jabesh-Gilead had proved Saul's capability as a military leader, and this was a foretaste of victory over "all his enemies on every side." See 14.47-48. Sadly, Saul was eventually killed by the very people he had been anointed to defeat, and the seeds of his destruction are sown in this chapter. Like Uzziah centuries later, "he was marvellously helped, till he was strong. But when he was strong, his heart was lifted to his destruction: for he transgressed against the Lord his God" (2 Chron 26.15-16). The lesson is clear: "Let him that thinketh he standeth take heed lest he fall" (1 Cor 10.12).

Victory over the Philistines does not look at all likely in this chapter, so if you feel apprehensive, read the next chapter as well! The two chapters form one unit in the book. The chapter can be divided into three sections: *(1)* The distress of Israel (vv.1-7): "the people were distressed" (v.6); *(2)* The disobedience of Saul (vv.8-15): "thou hast not kept the commandment of the Lord thy God" (v.13); *(3)* The dominance of the Philistines (vv.16-23): they devastated and disarmed Israel.

1. The Distress of Israel (vv.1-7)

The chapter commences with a simple statement: "Saul reigned one year; and when he had reigned two years over Israel, Saul chose him three thousand men of Israel." Believe it or not, the underlying text has caused endless debate, and commentators spend considerable time weighing the *pros* and *cons* of various suggestions and counter-suggestions. J.N.Darby translates as follows: "Saul was...years old when he became king; and he reigned two years over Israel." The RSV has "Saul was...years old when he began to reign; and he reigned...and two years over Israel", with the footnote "the number is lacking in Hebrew." According to Ellicott's Commentary, "the only possible literal translation of the Hebrew of this verse is, "Saul was the son of one year" (i.e. one year old)." However, in spite of the technical difficulties, the Authorised Version appears to make good sense, and we will leave it there! It is more important to grasp the lessons of the passage, and we must therefore notice: **(A)** The assault at Gibeah (vv.2-4); **(B)** The anger of the Philistines (v.5); **(C)** The alarm in Israel (vv.6-7).

A) The assault at Gibeah (vv.2-4)

"Saul chose him three thousand men of Israel; whereof two thousand were with Saul in Michmash and in mount Bethel, and a thousand were with Jonathan in Gibeah of Benjamin: and the rest of the people he sent every man to his tent." This is the first mention of a standing army in Israel, and was the first step towards the development of Israel into a great military power. (Ellicott's Commentary). It seems reasonable to conclude, with Keil and Delitzsch that Israel was not sufficiently prepared at that time to wage war against the Philistines generally, and that Saul resolved to attack their outpost at Gibeah with a small number of picked soldiers. Jonathan (mentioned here for the first time) opened the campaign by smiting "the garrison of the Philistines that was in Geba." This was evidently the "garrison ('outpost' JND) of the Philistines" mentioned in 10.5. "Thou shalt come to the hill of God (literally 'Gibeah of God'), where is the garrison of the Philistines." There can be little doubt that Geba and Gibeah, both meaning "hill", are one and the same.

Jonathan's initiative reminds us that young people have an important role in the Lord's work. In this connection read Exodus 24. 5 (their role in worship) and 1 Kings 20.13-14 etc. (their role in warfare).

Gibeah, or Geba, was the home town of Saul, enabling us to say that Saul and Jonathan "nailed their colours to the mast" on their own doorstep! Gideon did exactly the same, only for him it probably was on his own literal doorstep! See Judges 6.25. In the spiritual battle, we must begin where we are, which is often the most difficult place to start. Saul and Jonathan tackled the enemy in their own town, and we must do the same. We shouldn't even think of crossing the seas to tell others about the Lord Jesus, if we are not prepared to cross our own street to tell someone about Him. The Lord Jesus told the ex-Gadarene demoniac, "Go home to thy **friends,** and tell them how great things the Lord hath done for thee" (Mk 5.19).

The attack on the Philistine outpost was well-publicised. In the first place, "the Philistines **heard** of it" (v.3), and in the second, "Saul blew the trumpet throughout all the land, saying, Let the Hebrews **hear.** (Note: this is the name usually employed by non-Israelites!). And all Israel (the name used by God for His people!) **heard** say that Saul had smitten a garrison of the Philistines" (v.4). So both Israel and the Philistines knew that Saul meant business. It is very important that leaders amongst God's people should display initiative, zeal and reality in leading the fight against spiritual enemies. However, like Queen Victoria, the Philistines were "not amused." Israel not only heard that "Saul had smitten a garrison of the Philistines"; they also heard that "Israel also was had in abomination with the Philistines" (v.4). This leads to

B) The anger of the Philistines (v.5)
"And the Philistines gathered themselves together to fight with Israel." Saul and Jonathan had "rocked the boat." It was a repetition of events in the days of Samson. See Judges 15. 11. It was also a repetition of events at Mizpeh in 1 Samuel 7. The Philistines made little or no effort to trouble Israel, as long as Israel behaved themselves, and kept quiet. Isn't it exactly the same in the spiritual realm? We can expect nice comfortable lives as long as we don't do anything silly, like witnessing for Christ and turning people "from darkness to light, and from the power of Satan unto God" (Acts 26.18). Christians who evangelise are a threat to Satan's interests, and must therefore be stopped in their tracks. Israel knew that the assault at Gibeah meant trouble, and they were right! It did not bode well for them: the Philistines arrived in Michmash with "thirty thousand chariots (that's a lot of chariots!), and six thousand horsemen, and people as the sand which is on the sea shore in multitude." We are not surprised to see:

C) The alarm in Israel (vv.6-7)
"When the men of Israel saw that they were in a strait, (for the people were distressed), then the people did hide themselves in caves, and in thickets, and in rocks, and in high places, and in pits. And some of the Hebrews went over Jordan to the land of Gad and Gilead. As for Saul, he was yet in Gilgal, and all the people followed him trembling." The word "distressed" means "pressed" or "harassed." (Gesenius). Compare Judges 6.2. See also Judges 5.6. In the days of Shamgar, it was the Philistines, again, who were responsible for depriving Israel of their liberty: see Judges 3.31.

It is a depressing picture, to put it mildly. God's people were obliged to hide from the enemy. Some decided to quit, and seek safety on the other side of Jordan, and Saul's army (the people that followed Saul) "shook in their shoes." This is just where Satan wants to get us too! He would be quite delighted if we were too scared to show our faces. He does not like people that "are not ashamed of the testimony of our Lord", and would very be pleased indeed if we opted out entirely, on the basis of "anything for a quiet life." He does not like people who "having done all...stand." People like Daniel and his three friends are not acceptable to him! See Dan. 3.16-18 etc. Satan would be quite delighted if we were reduced to nagging fears about the future. He does not like people who are "strong in faith, giving glory to God." From what follows, it is clear that Saul was also alarmed:

2. The Disobedience of Saul (vv.8-15)
It is imperative to read Samuel's original instructions to Saul before we explore these verses. "And thou shalt go down before me to Gilgal; and, behold, I will come down unto thee, to offer burnt-offerings, and to sacrifice sacrifices of peace-offerings: seven days shalt thou tarry, till I come to thee, and shew thee what thou shalt do" (10.8). Although some years had elapsed, those instructions were still in force. Samuel, a prophet, evidently foresaw conflict with the Philistines, and promised Saul guidance and help when the crisis came. We must now notice *(A)* Saul's impatience (vv.8-12) and *(B)* Saul's indictment (vv.13-14).

A) Saul's impatience (vv.8-12)
"And he tarried seven days, according to the set time that Samuel had appointed: but Samuel came not to Gilgal; and the people were scattered from him. And Saul said, Bring hither a burnt-offering to me, and peace-offerings. And he offered the burnt-offering. And it came to pass, that as soon as he had made an end of offering the burnt-offering, behold, Samuel came; and Saul went out to meet him, that he might salute him." Notice that Saul had not completed the sacrifices: he had only got as far as the burnt-offering. C.I.Scofield heads this paragraph, "Saul intrudes into the priest's office", but to be fair, the passage does not specifically state that Saul personally officiated at the altar. We know that Ahiah (also known as Ahimelech, 22.9,11,20), Eli's great-grandson, was priest at the time (see 14.3, 18-19). Perhaps we should be charitable, and say that it does not appear that Saul, unlike Uzziah, was actually guilty of usurping the priest's office.

But this did not mitigate Saul's guilt in disobeying the word of God. As we shall see, Samuel charged Saul with failing to keep "the commandment of the Lord thy God, which he commanded thee" (v.13). So the instructions given by Samuel to Saul perhaps two years before carried the weight of divine authority: "I will come down unto thee, to offer burnt-offerings, and to sacrifice sacrifices of peace-offerings: seven days shalt thou tarry, till I come to thee, and **shew thee what thou shalt do"** (10.8). The prophets were men who spake "from the mouth of the Lord" (2 Chron 36.12). Saul was certainly in dire straits, and we can understand his motives. The general panic had spread to his army, which was rapidly melting away (v.11), a Philistine attack seemed imminent (v.12), and Samuel had not come at the promised time. Under pressure, Saul's faith and obedience failed. (Rather like Peter in Matthew 14.28-31). It was not a case of ignorance. He knew exactly what he was doing: "I forced myself therefore, and offered a burnt-offering." He may have acted for the best of reasons, but what he did was wrong. Disobedience is foolishness; "thou hast done foolishly" (v.13). Saul thought that he could take the place of Samuel. He acted presumptuously.

There are solemn lessons for us all here. We can all be models of faith and obedience when everything is quiet and peaceful, but what happens when we are faced with adversity and difficulty? Centuries later, another Saul, who became Paul, could say, "we had the sentence of death in ourselves, that we should not trust in ourselves, but in God which raiseth the dead" (2 Cor 1.9).

All this reminds us of another King. He was in dire straits too, so much so that "his sweat was as it were great drops of blood falling down to the ground." But there was no lessening of His devotion and obedience. He was "obedient unto death, even the death of the cross."

B) Saul's indictment (vv.13-15)
"And Samuel said to Saul, Thou hast done foolishly: thou hast not kept the commandment of the Lord thy God, which he commanded thee: for now would the Lord have established thy kingdom for ever. But now thy kingdom shall not continue: the Lord hath sought him a man after his own heart, and the Lord hath commanded him to be captain over his people, because thou hast not kept that which the Lord commanded thee." The "man after his own heart" was, of course, David. As Keil and Delitzsch observe, this does not compel us "to assume an immediate rejection of Saul, even though Samuel said, "the Lord hath sought him a man after his own heart", for these words merely announce the purpose of God, without defining the

time of its actual realisation. Whether it would take place during Saul's reign, or after his death, was known only to God, and was made contingent upon Saul's further behaviour." As we shall see, Saul did not learn from events at Gilgal, and Samuel was later obliged to say, "The Lord hath rent the kingdom of Israel from thee this day, and hath given it to a neighbour of thine, that is better than thou" (15.28).

Once again, there are solemn lessons for us all here. Samuel himself emphasises them: "Hath the Lord as great delight in burnt offerings and sacrifices, as in **obeying** the voice of the Lord? Behold, to **obey** is better than sacrifice, and to hearken than the fat of rams. For rebellion is as the sin of witchcraft, and stubbornness is as iniquity and idolatry" (15. 22-23). We cannot emphasise too strongly the necessity to obey God's word. "Wherefore gird up the loins of your mind, be sober, and hope to the end for the grace that is to be brought to you at the revelation of Jesus Christ; as obedient children, not fashioning yourselves according to the former lusts in your ignorance" (1 Pet 1.13-14).

Having reprimanded Saul, Samuel leaves Gilgal en route for Gibeah (v.15). It does seem that friendly relations were maintained. It was not until Saul disobeyed God on the second occasion that the relationship was broken. See 15.35. It is interesting to note that Samuel went to Gibeah where, presumably, Jonathan was still located. It would be nice to think that Samuel counselled and encouraged Jonathan, but that is a little speculative! Saul does not seem to have had much success in reuniting his scattered army (see v.11): he is down to six hundred men! At least he didn't lose any more! See 14.2. This brings us to the final paragraph:

3. The Dominance of the Philistines (vv.16-23)
The narrative now moves on. Saul and Jonathan have linked up again at Gibeah. (We are told that this occurs as "Geba" in the original language, and Keil & Delitzsch suggest that it was a different place. But as the story unfolds in Chapter 14, Saul "tarried in the uttermost part of Gibeah under a pomegranate tree"). The Philistines were nearby, and it was not a pretty sight: **(A)** The Philistines devastated Israel (vv.17-18): "And the spoilers came out of the camp of the Philistines in three companies"; **(B)** The Philistines disarmed Israel (vv.19-22): "Now there was no smith found throughout all the land of Israel: for the Philistines said, Lest the Hebrews make them swords or spears." (vv.19-22) explain why Israel was unable to resist the Philistines. Israel had no weapons. The Philistines had evidently

made sure of this long before the current invasion. As a matter of policy, they closed every blacksmith's shop, so that Israel wouldn't even think about opposing them!

A) The Philistines devastated Israel (vv.17-18)
"And the spoilers came out of the camp of the Philistines in three companies: one company turned unto the way that leadeth to Ophrah, unto the land of Shual." This took them in a north-easterly direction. "And another company turned the way to Beth-horon" This was towards the west. "And another company turned to the way of the border that looketh to the valley of Zeboim toward the wilderness." This seems to have been in a south-easterly direction. So the "spoilers" went in all directions.

The very word "spoilers" suggests people who take "spoil." They loot, plunder and destroy. Just like the "thieves and robbers" described by the Lord Jesus: "the thief cometh not, but for to steal, and to kill, and to destroy." But He continued, *"I* am come that they might have life, and that they might have it more abundantly" (Jn 10.10). We all face "spoilers." The **world** will endeavour to "spoil" us with its allurements and enticements. Hence we read, "Love not the world, neither the things that are in the world." These are defined as "the lust of the flesh, and the lust of the eyes, and the pride of life" (1 Jn 2.15-16). The **religious world** will endeavour to spoil us too. Hence the injunction, "beware lest any man spoil you through philosophy and vain deceit" (Col 2.8). The **"flesh"**, the old nature within us, will endeavour to "spoil" us with its "affections and lusts" (Gal 5. 24). The **devil** will endeavour to "spoil" us by opposition and persecution. "Your adversary the devil, as a roaring lion", walketh about, seeking whom he may devour" (1 Pet 5. 8). The success of the "spoilers" was guaranteed by the fact that:

B) The Philistines disarmed Israel (vv.19-23)
As we have already noticed, the Philistines had taken steps beforehand to dissuade Israel from opposing them. "Now there was no smith found throughout all the land of Israel: for the Philistines said, Lest the Hebrews make them swords or spears: but all the Israelites went down to the Philistines, to sharpen every man his share (not easily identifiable: the word means "edge-tool": perhaps a kind of plough: some say that it was a sickle), and his coulter ("ploughshare" in Isaiah 2.4), and his axe, and his mattock (another "edge-tool": some say that it was a hoe)." J.N.Darby renders vv.19-20 as follows: "Now there was no smith found throughout all

the land of Israel: for the Philistines said, Lest the Hebrews make them swords or spears. And all Israel went down to the Philistines, every man to get his ploughshare, and his hoe, and his axe, and his sickle sharpened, when the edges of the sickles, and the hoes, and the forks, and the axes were blunted."

Whilst we may not be able to ascertain the precise nature of each tool, there is no doubt about the Philistines' intentions." After all, "plowshares" and "pruninghooks" could be turned into swords and spears (Joel 3.10), and that would never do! So the Philistines made sure that the agricultural implements stayed that way by servicing the Israelite's tools for them! With the result that "in the day of battle...there was neither sword nor spear found in the hand of any of the people that were with Saul and Jonathan: but with Saul and Jonathan his son was there found." Notice, incidentally, that swords and spears were not necessary for victory. See 17.47. Neither were superior numbers. See 14.6.

Do we need to say any more? Have we let the enemy deprive us of **our** spiritual weapons? "Take...the sword of the Spirit, which is the word of God...praying always with all prayer and supplication in the Spirit" (Eph 6.17-18). Nehemiah's men set us a splendid example here. See Nehemiah 4.16-18. If we have let the enemy take our weapons, the outlook is as grim for us as it seemed for Israel when "the garrison of the Philistines went out to the passage of Michmash".

CHAPTER 14A

Jonathan's initiative (14.1-23)

This is a long chapter, and will require "two bites of the cherry!" With this in mind, we will divide it as follows: **The deliverance from the Philistines** (vv.1-23): "So the Lord saved Israel that day" (v.23). **The deliverance of Jonathan** (vv.24-52), "So the people rescued Jonathan, that he died not" (v.45).

1. The Deliverance from the Philistines (vv.1-23)
There are two major parts to this section, and we will entitle these *(1)* The role of Jonathan (vv.1-15) and *(2)* The role of Saul (vv.16-23).

1. The Role of Jonathan (vv.1-15)
Like every other part of the Bible, these verses are full of interest and importance for us. No wonder Paul wrote, "whatsoever things were written aforetime were written for our learning!" (Rom 15.4). The three paragraphs which comprise this section are all introduced in the same way. *(A)* Jonathan's enterprise (vv.1-5): "Jonathan...said unto the young man that bare his armour"; *(B)* Jonathan's assurance (vv.6-12a): "Jonathan said unto the young man that bare his armour"; *(C)* Jonathan's assault (vv.12b-15): "Jonathan said to his armour-bearer."

A) Jonathan's enterprise (vv.1-5)
These verses paint three vivid pictures, and when we put two of them side by side, the contrast is inescapable. Here they are:

i) The initiative of Jonathan (v.1). "Now it came to pass upon a day, that Jonathan the son of Saul said unto the young man that bare his armour, Come, and let us go over to the Philistines" garrison that is on the other side. But he told not his father." So it was the young man who took the initiative in the conflict with the Philistines. God is still looking for young men and women with spiritual initiative. It was "the young men of the princes of the provinces" who led the attack on the Syrian army at Samaria. See 1 Kings 20.13-14,15,17,19. Jonathan looked for an opportunity to take the battle to the Philistines. This is stressed throughout the entire section: "Come, and let us **go over** to the Philistines" garrison that is on the other side...the passages, by which Jonathan sought to **go over** unto the Philistines" garrison...Come, and let us **go over** unto the garrison of these uncircumcised...Behold, we will **pass over** unto these men, and we will discover ourselves unto them" (vv.1,4,6,8). In two splendid articles on this chapter (published in *Counsel*), G.B.Fyfe writes as follows: "The moral in all this is clear. When things are at a low ebb spiritually, as they patently are in some places today, it needs young men to come forward with conviction and zeal to perform exploits for the honour of the Lord and for the deliverance of God's people. Some modern "Davids" and "Jonathans" are needed amongst us today!" Mr.Fyfe points out the parallel between David and Jonathan. In both cases, it was Philistine dominance that made their blood boil, in both cases, they faced the Philistines single-handedly (although Jonathan did have the help of his armour-bearer), and in both cases they were treated with contempt.

Notice that Jonathan did not share his intentions with his father. It does seem that Jonathan and Saul were frequently at cross-purposes. This chapter illustrates this clearly, as we will see. A word of warning is necessary here. Spiritual initiative should always be exercised in fellowship with fellow-believers, and in particular with assembly elders. This gives opportunity for prayer advice, encouragement and, if necessary caution. It is noteworthy that even Paul, who was led by God to visit Jerusalem when false teaching threatened the Gentile Christians (Gal 2.1-2), acted in full fellowship with the church at Antioch. See Acts 15.2-3. Now look at the next picture:

ii) The indolence of Saul (vv.2-3). "And Saul tarried in the uttermost part of Gibeah under the pomegranate tree which is in Migron: and the people that were with him were about six hundred men." Let's listen again to G.B.Fyfe: "Saul, instead of attempting to marshal Israel's sadly depleted forces, and seeking help from the Lord, is found lying under a pomegranate tree in the outskirts of Gibeah, far away from the probable battle zone. He remained completely inactive in the face of the threatening danger of an all-out attack by the strong Philistine forces. In other words, he had abandoned all confidence of defeating the foe." That says it all! It reminds us of the Reubenites, whose inactivity was highlighted by Deborah and Barak. See

Judges 5.15-16. Who are we like? Jonathan or Saul? The Christian life is a battle-ground, not a holiday camp. We are called to "fight the good fight of faith" (1 Tim 6.12).

Notice that in addition to the "six hundred men", Saul was accompanied by "Ahiah (elsewhere known as Ahimelech, 22.9,11,20), the son of Ahitub, I-chabod's brother, the son of Phinehas, the son of Eli, the Lord's priest in Shiloh, wearing an ephod." We shall meet him again shortly. Let's hope that he wasn't like his grandfather! Saul did not seek divine help through the priestly ministry of Ahiah (see v.18) until later, and we often fail in the same way. We are urged to "come boldly unto the throne of grace, that we may obtain mercy, and find grace to help in time of need" (Heb 4.16). How much do **we** use this wonderful facility?

iii) The immensity of the task (vv.4-5). Without even attempting to locate the exact spot, we cannot avoid the conclusion that Jonathan faced an uphill task in every sense! It involved rock-climbing, and when the time came, there wasn't a chair-lift in sight! Jonathan and his armour-bearer went up on hands and feet (v.13). It must have been particularly difficult for the armour-bearer! If you are going to do business for God, please don't expect an easy passage. Paul and Barnabas taught the early Christians that they "must through much tribulation (not the Great Tribulation) enter into the kingdom of God" (Acts 14.22). Serving God is not for the faint-hearted!

B) Jonathan's assurance (vv.6-12a)
This is a marvellous section! Jonathan isn't named in Hebrews 11, but he must be included with those who "through faith...waxed valiant in fight, turned to flight the armies of the aliens."

i) The confidence of Jonathan (v.6). "And Jonathan said to the young man that bare his armour, Come, and let us go over unto the garrison of these uncircumcised (think about that: two men versus a garrison!): it may be that the Lord will work for us: for there is no restraint to the Lord to save by many or by few." Jonathan had a right view of the enemy ("These uncircumcised": compare Judges 14.3), and a right view of the Lord (He could "save by many or by few"). He was not absolutely certain about the will of God at that time (this became clear later, see vv.8-12), but he was absolutely certain about the power of God! Jonathan had a strong and simple faith in God, and "God always honours faith like that!" (G.B.Fyfe).

1 Samuel

We have almost conditioned ourselves into thinking that since, we say, this is "the day of small things" (Zech 4.10), we can't expect too much. In reality, we have become "small people." As someone has said, "Blessed is he that expecteth nothing, for he shall receive the same!" But not Jonathan! What about us?

ii) The commitment of the armour-bearer (vv.7-10). "And his armour-bearer said unto him, Do all that is in thine heart: turn thee; behold, I am with thee according to thy heart." Let's turn the spotlight on this unnamed, but splendid, young man. Just look at his commitment: "Behold, **I am with thee** according to thy heart…And **both** of them discovered themselves unto the garrison of the Philistines…And the men of the garrison answered Jonathan and his **armour-bearer**…And Jonathan climbed up upon his hands and upon his feet, and his **armour-bearer** after him: and they fell before Jonathan; and his **armour-bearer** slew after him. And that first slaughter, which Jonathan and his **armour-bearer** made, was about twenty men" (vv.7,11,12,13,14). The "heart" of Jonathan reminds us of Hannah's "heart" (2.1), Eli's "heart" (4.13), and Saul's "heart" (10.9). That's just a start. Plenty of material for a good sermon here!

There was communication as well as commitment. The armour-bearer was thoroughly committed to Jonathan, and Jonathan took the armour-bearer completely into his confidence. See vv.8-10. This is a wonderful picture of standing "fast in one spirit, with one mind striving together for the faith of the gospel" (Phil 1.27). But we should carry on with the quotation: "and in nothing terrified by your adversaries." That was also true of Jonathan and his armour-bearer! But it is also a picture of the commitment we should have to our heavenly Captain, and He shares His purposes with us too. So;

> Only an armour-bearer, firmly I stand,
> Waiting to follow at the King's command;
> Marching if "onward" shall the order be;
> Standing by my Captain, serving faithfully.

iii) The contempt of the Philistines (vv.11-12). "And the Philistines said, Behold, the Hebrews come forth out of the holes where they had hid themselves (see 13.6). And the men of the garrison answered Jonathan and his armour-bearer, and said, Come up to us, and we will shew you a thing ("we will teach you a lesson")." The Philistines must have been the forerunners of Kaiser Wilhelm who described the British forces as "a contemptible little army!" Servants of God must be prepared to face mockery and ridicule. Paul was "mocked" by some at Athens, and Peter predicted that "there shall come in the last days scoffers ("mockers"), walking after their own lusts." Let's remember that the "preaching of the cross is to them that perish foolishness." We must not therefore be surprised if contempt is poured on the word of God, and on us personally as well.

C) Jonathan's assault (vv.12b-15)

"Assault" hardly seems the right word! Two people crawling up a precipice certainly doesn't look like an "assault!" But it was entirely successful.

i) The attack of Jonathan (vv.13b-14). He scaled the precipice with the assurance that "the Lord hath delivered them into the hand of Israel." Note this, not **"will** deliver them", but **"hath** delivered them." The outcome is a foregone conclusion! The Philistines were vastly superior in number, and had a vastly superior position. After all, they were just waiting for two men (although they may not have realised that it was only two men) to come puffing and blowing up the rock face. But Jonathan and his armour-bearer had received confirmation that God was on their side. See vv.8-10. It would have been pointless carrying the battle to the Philistines without the assurance of God's presence. After all, "If it had not been the Lord who was on our side, when men rose up against us: then they had swallowed us up quick" (Ps 124.1-3). Notice what happened when the Lord was **not** on the side of His people. See Numbers 14.40-45. It has been suggested that the words, "an half acre of land, which a yoke of oxen might plow", mean that a yoke of oxen could plough half an acre of land in a day. See JND footnote.

Bearing in mind that Jonathan was a Benjamite, he may have attacked the Philistines with bow and arrow, or sling and stone, or with his sword. See Judges 20.15-17; 1 Chronicles 12.2. The "first slaughter" reminds us of the power of **our** spiritual weaponry. We have "the sword of the Spirit, which is the word of God." While "the weapons of our warfare are not carnal", they are "mighty through God to the pulling down of strongholds" (2 Cor 10.4). Unlike Jonathan and his armour-bearer, we do not attack people, but we do attack the unseen powers of darkness that control people. They cannot be routed by any other means than "the sword of the Spirit." This is what the Lord Jesus used to defeat Satan. See Matthew 4.4,7,10. We dare not use any other method. It **must** be the word of God.

*ii) **The alarm of the Philistines.*** Jonathan's "first strike" resulted in mayhem amongst the Philistines. "And there was a trembling in the host, in the field, and among all the people: the garrison, and the spoilers, they also trembled, and the earth quaked: so it was a very great trembling." The AV margin and JND translate "a very great trembling" as "a trembling of God." Keil and Delitzsch describe it as "a supernatural terror miraculously infused by God into the Philistines." Jonathan and his armour-bearer certainly played their part, but even they could not cause an earthquake! No wonder we read, "So the **Lord** saved Israel that day" (v.23). Nothing causes the powers of darkness so much alarm as the power of God operating with and through His people. But Satan and his armies will be more than happy if, like Saul, we take it easy and just wait to see what will happen. This brings us to:

2) The Role of Saul (vv.16-23)
"And the watchmen of Saul in Gibeah of Benjamin looked; and, behold, the multitude melted away, and they went on beating down one another." This is exactly what happened to the Midianites in the dead of night after Gideon and his three hundred men blew their trumpets, broke their pitchers, and shouted "The sword of the Lord, and of Gideon." See Judges 7.20-22. Saul evidently realised that the panic amongst the Philistines had been caused by Israelites, and after a headcount, it became clear that Jonathan and his armour-bearer were somehow involved. We must now notice what followed:

*i) **Saul and the priest (vv.18-19).*** "And Saul said unto Ahiah (see v.3) bring hither the ark of God. For the ark of God was at that time with the children of Israel. And it came to pass, while Saul talked unto the priest, that the noise that was in the host of the Philistines went on and increased: and Saul said unto the priest, Withdraw thine hand." Commentators quibble with the reference to the ark, and prefer to follow the Septuagint version which reads, "And Saul said to Ahijah, Bring hither the ephod; for he bore the ephod in those days before the children of Israel." But one of these commentators (H.D.M.Spence in Ellicott's Commentary) goes on to say, "But the Hebrew and all the versions read as in our English version!" Without being uncharitable, some commentators will often look elsewhere if they don't think the Bible means what it says! We should be on our guard when writers talk about things which "have slipped out of the text", or "slipped into the text", or when they rearrange the text to suit their interpretation.

However, it is clear that Saul was unsure what to do, and sought divine guidance. The words "withdraw thine hand" evidently refer to the use of the

Urim and Thummim which were located in the fold of the breastplate worn by the high priest. See Exodus 28.30, Leviticus 8.8. It is generally presumed that the Urim and Thummim were two stones, but this is not actually stated in the Bible. They were certainly used, in some way not clearly expressed, to ascertain God's will in particular cases. See Numbers 27.21, 1 Samuel 28. 6, Ezra 2.63. It does seem that the high priest placed his hand on them: hence "withdraw thine hand." Israel was guided by God through the Urim and Thummim, but He guides *us* through the Holy Spirit.

The increasing noise from the Philistine camp made Saul feel that divine guidance was no longer necessary, and that events spoke for themselves. The ark gave place to arms! Saul's instinct as a general got the better of his desire for divine guidance! Some people start praying when they are unsure what to do, and then suddenly stop praying when everything seems clearer. Paul tells us to "pray without ceasing!"

ii) Saul and the Philistines (vv.20-23). "And Saul and all the people that were with him assembled themselves, and they came to the battle: and, behold, every man's sword was against his fellow, and there was a very great discomfiture." We have already noticed that Israel had been effectively disarmed by the Philistines (13.19-21), but now the Lord destroyed the enemy with their own weapons! They were destroyed by their own military advantage! It is most interesting to see who else arrived on the battlefield:

Firstly, there were the **defectors:** "Moreover the Hebrews (this is what foreigners called them) that were with the Philistines before that time, which went up with them into the camp from the country round about, even they also turned to be with the Israelites that were with Saul and Jonathan" (v.21). We can only presume that these people were serving in the Philistine army, on the basis "that if you can't beat them, join them." It wasn"t many years before that the men of Judah told Samson, "Knowest thou not that the Philistines are rulers over us? What is this that thou hast done unto us?" (Jud 15.11). It seems almost impossible that God's people should actually take the side of the enemy against their own fellow-countrymen. Jehu, the son of Hanani, reproved Jehoshaphat for the same thing: "Shouldest thou help the ungodly, and love them that hate the Lord?" (2 Chron 19.2). We must avoid the same pitfall. The Ecumenical Movement beckons, and it is not unknown for God's people to sacrifice truth in the interests of unity. (For "unity" read "uniformity"). Be warned, the pressure to conform will increase. In his book, *The Principality and Power of Europe*

1 Samuel

(Dorchester House Publications), Adrian Hilton demonstrates that the screw is already turning. Rome waits patiently, licking her lips.

But at least these defectors changed sides. Many true believers need to heed the clarion call from the throne of God, "Come out of her ("Babylon the great"), my people" (Rev 18.4)

Secondly, there were the **deserters.** "Likewise all the men of Israel which had hid themselves in mount Ephraim, when they heard that the Philistines fled, even they also followed hard after them in the battle" (v.22). These were the people of whom Saul said, "I saw that the people were scattered from me" (13.11), leaving him with "about six hundred men." These people did not defect to the other side when the going got tough, but they didn't stay with Saul either. They just opted out! That's another danger, isn't it? Faithfulness to God can bring terrible inconvenience and discomfort, so we just get out of the way. But at least they came back, even if they were "fair-weather" warriors! Paul was willing to stand alone, even when "all Asia" turned against him, and even when "all men" forsook him. See 1 Timothy 1.15 and 4.11.

It was a crushing defeat for the Philistines. But it was the Lord's victory. "So the **Lord** saved Israel that day: and the battle passed over unto Bethaven." We gladly say, "Not unto us, O Lord, not unto us, but unto thy name give glory" (Ps 115.1). Israel was victorious "that day", but that wasn't the end of the battle! "The battle passed over unto Bethaven." For us, the "battle" is ongoing. It will never cease until we reach heaven."

CHAPTER 14B

Jonathan's preservation (14.24-52)

In view of the length of this chapter, we have divided it into two parts as follows: **The deliverance from the Philistines** (vv.1-23); "So the Lord saved Israel that day" (v.23); **The deliverance of Jonathan** (vv.24-52); "So the people rescued Jonathan, that he died not" (v.45).

The Deliverance from the Philistines (vv.1-23)
The Philistines suffered a crushing defeat at the hands of Jonathan and Saul, although it would be more correct to say that they suffered a crushing defeat at the hand of God **through** Jonathan and Saul. "So the **Lord** saved Israel that day" (v.23). Jonathan took the initiative. Saul pitched in later. In our previous study, we noticed **(1)** The role of Jonathan (vv.1-15) and **(2)** the role of Saul (vv.16-23). We now come to the rather sad sequel to the story. Look at the contrast in (vv.23-24): "And the Lord saved Israel **that day**...and the men of Israel were distressed **that day**." The first was the result of confidence in God. The second was the result of selfish ambition. This brings us to:

1. The Deliverance of Jonathan (vv.24-52)
Bible history is never boring! The passage is full of wide-ranging lessons, and we will look at it like this: **(1)** The distress of Israel (vv.24-30); **(2)** The disobedience to the law (vv.31-35); **(3)** The deliverance of Jonathan (vv.36-46); **(4)** The defeat of the enemies (vv.47-48); **(5)** The details of Saul's family (vv.49-51); **(6)** The drafting for the army (v.52).

1) The Distress of Israel, (vv.24-30)
It is not surprising that they were "distressed that day", when we read "none of the people tasted any food" (v.24); "the people were faint" (v.28); "the people were very faint" (v.31). As we shall see, they were so famished that eventually they broke the law. We must now notice:

1 Samuel

A) Saul's prohibition (vv.24-26)
"And the men of Israel were distressed that day: for Saul had adjured the people (put them on oath), saying, Cursed be that man that eateth any food until evening, that I may be avenged of mine enemies." See also verse 28. G.B.Fyfe (writing in *Counsel)* calls this "sheer folly" and continues, "It sprang from the desire to save his face by avenging himself on his foes in the day of their confusion and weakness. This oath was the fulfilment of a fleshly desire for revenge, and not the honour of Israel and the glory of God...It nearly cost Jonathan his life. It drove the people into the sin of eating the flesh of animals with the blood. It prevented an all-out victory for Israel." This just proves the folly of imposing man-made rules and regulations, which have no sanction in the word of God, upon God's people, and only serve to bolster the ego of those who make them. The scribes and Pharisees were past-masters at it! The Lord Jesus roundly condemned their "legalism." See, for example, Matthew 23.1-36. A.McShane rightly observes that "a leader out of touch with the Lord never helps the saints to overcome their enemies, whether these be the world, the flesh, or the devil."

This incident also emphasises the need to carefully assess the possible consequences of our decisions, both for ourselves and for other people. What sometimes appears to be a short-term advantage can easily turn out to be a long-term disadvantage. Ahaz must have felt flushed with success when his alliance with the Assyrians resulted in the defeat of the Syrians, but it wasn't long before the Assyrians invaded Judah as well! Read 1 Kings 16 and Isaiah 7.

"An army marches on its stomach", and as "Christian soldiers" we need to maintain daily strength by reading and assimilating the word of God. Saul prohibited Israel from eating that day, but we must let nothing rob us of our spiritual food. As Jonathan pointed out, nourishment was essential for victory over the enemy. See verses 29-30.

B) Jonathan's protest (vv.27-30)
Jonathan knew nothing about his father's prohibition, and eagerly helped himself to some honey. He "put his hand to his mouth; and his eyes were enlightened." This has been rendered, "and his eyes became bright" (JND). In view of Proverbs 25.16, he probably didn't eat too much! The word of God is compared to honey in Psalm 19 and Psalm 119. Both passages refer to enlightenment. "The commandment of the Lord is pure, enlightening the eyes...sweeter also than honey and the honeycomb" (Ps 19.8-10). "How

sweet are thy words unto my taste! Yea, sweeter than honey to my mouth! Through thy precepts I get understanding" (Ps 119.103-104).

Jonathan rightly assessed the situation. "My father hath troubled the land: see, I pray you, how mine eyes have been enlightened, because I tasted a little of this honey. How much more, if haply the people had eaten freely today of the spoil of their enemies which they found? For had there not been now a much greater slaughter among the Philistines?" (vv.29-30). John makes it clear that the nourishment of the word of God enables us to wage successful spiritual warfare: "I have written unto you, young men, because ye are strong, and the word of God abideth in you, and ye have overcome the wicked one" (1 Jn 2.14). Don't expect to win spiritual victories if you are not feeding on the word of God.

2. The Disobedience to the Law (vv.31-35)
"And they smote the Philistines that day from Michmash to Aijalon: and the people were very faint. And the people flew upon the spoil, and took sheep, and oxen, and calves, and slew them on the ground: and the people did eat them with the blood." This contravened the covenant made with Noah and his descendants: "Every moving thing that liveth shall be meat for you; even as the green herb have I given you all things. But the flesh with the life thereof, which is the blood thereof, shall ye not eat" (Gen 9.3-4). It also contravened God's instructions to Israel. See Leviticus 17.10, Deuteronomy 12.23-25, etc. Leviticus 17 explains **why** "eating blood" was prohibited. **"For** the life of the flesh is in the blood: and I have given it to you upon the altar to make an atonement for your souls: for it is the blood that maketh an atonement for the soul. **Therefore** I said unto the children of Israel, No soul of you shall eat blood..." (vv.11-12). The lessons of the blood were so distinctive that it was **always** to be connected in their thoughts with **atonement.**

While Saul reprimanded the people for their transgression (v.33), he failed to recognise that he was responsible in the first place. It was his own harsh and unnecessary order that drove his men to desperation. There are certainly exceptions, but it is generally true to say that God's people appreciate good leadership. While leaders amongst God's people must be firm, they must also be gentle, considerate, and gracious. After all, they are shepherds, not butchers! Rehoboam made the mistake of following the counsel of the young men, who advocated rule by iron discipline, and lost most of his kingdom as a result. See 1 Kings 12.1-19. Bible teachers should also remember that their object is not to flatten God's people, but to warm their hearts and guide their feet with balanced teaching. Paul calls this, "speaking the truth in love" (Eph 4.15).

Prevention is better than cure, so while Saul made provision for his men to eat without contravening the law, it would have been far better if the problem had never arisen in the first place! To quote an old saying, "Better a fence at the top of the cliff, than an ambulance station at the bottom!" The "great stone" (v.33) was put in place, so that the animals could be slaughtered enabling "the blood to run off properly upon the ground, and the flesh be separated from the blood", Keil & Delitzsch. Compare verse 32: "The people...slew them on *the ground:* and the people did eat them with the blood."

We are not told why Saul built an altar (v.35), or why it is specifically described as "the first altar that he built unto the Lord." Perhaps Ellicott's Commentary is correct in saying: "the more obvious meaning...seems to be that this was the first public acknowledgement King Saul made to God for the mercy and goodness vouchsafed to him." On the other hand, Saul may have built the altar in view of Israel's sin in "eating blood", or, in view of his desire to pursue and destroy the Philistines. See verse 36.

3. The Deliverance of Jonathan (vv.36-46)
These verses can be conveniently considered as follows: **(A)** Saul's inquiry (vv.35-37); **(B)** Jonathan's identification (vv.38-44); **(C)** Israel's intervention, (vv.45-46).

A) *Saul's inquiry (vv.35-37)*
It is most interesting to notice what various people said here. "And Saul **said**...And they **said**...Then **said** the priest."

i) What Saul said. "And Saul said, **Let us** go down after the Philistines by night, and spoil them until morning light, and let us not leave a man of them." The words, "Let us", have an ominous ring about them. We have met them before in 1 Samuel: **"Let us** fetch the ark of the covenant of the Lord out of Shiloh unto us" (4.3). The words are first found on human lips in Genesis 11.3-4: "Go to, **Let us** make brick, and burn them throughly...Go to, **let us** build us a city and a tower...and **let us** make us a name." They made no reference whatsoever to God here, but He was watching. "And the Lord said...Go to, **let us** go down, and there confound their language" (vv.5-7).

Take time to be holy, let Him be thy Guide:
And run not before Him whatever betide:
In joy or in sorrow still follow thy Lord,
And, looking to Jesus, still trust in His word.

ii) What the people said. "And they said, Do whatsoever seemeth good unto thee." They said it again in verse 40. We get the impression that the people were rather disinterested. They certainly didn't seem to show great enthusiasm. It would have been nice to hear them say something like, "Go, and the Lord be with thee" (17.37). Perhaps they thought that it was all down to Saul anyway. After all, didn't they want a king to "go out before us, and fight our battles?" (8.20). One thing is clear; there is no mention of the Lord.

iii) What the priest said. At last, a spiritual voice! "Then said the priest, Let us draw near to God." Ahiah needed courage to say that! It was certainly a mild rebuke to Saul, who had earlier told the priest to "withdraw" his hand. See verse 19. Now we have the words, "Let us", in the very best context! But it was to no avail. "And Saul asked counsel of God, Shall I go down after the Philistines? Wilt thou deliver them into the hand of Israel? But he answered him not that day." In the words of Ellicott's Commentary, "the mysterious gems (referring to the Urim and Thummim) refused to shine, or in any way to signify divine approbation or disapproval." Saul concluded, rightly, that God had not answered because of sin in Israel, and we will have to decide who was actually guilty. But this does remind us that "if I regard iniquity in my heart, the Lord will not **hear** me" (Ps 66.18).

B) Jonathan's identification (vv.38-44)

"And Saul said, Draw ye near hither, all the chief of the people: and know and see wherein this sin hath been this day." Saul obviously suspected Jonathan: "For, as the Lord liveth, which saveth Israel, though it be in Jonathan my son, he shall surely die." Notice the silence of the people. "There was not a man among all the people that answered him." They all knew that Jonathan had unwittingly disobeyed his father, but "love covereth a multitude of sins" (1 Pet 4.8 RV). Their response, "Do what seemeth good unto thee", also seems to convey their reluctance to betray him.

The "perfect lot" (v.41) pointed to Jonathan, and Saul pronounced the death sentence. "Thou shalt surely die, Jonathan." Jonathan found this quite incredible: "With the end of my staff which is in my hand I tasted a little honey, and behold, I must die!" (v.43 JND). He could scarcely believe his ears! It would have been another matter entirely if he had deliberately transgressed a divine commandment. But he had unwittingly transgressed a commandment issued by his father without divine authority. It was Saul who was blameworthy, rather than Jonathan and, like Herod, he was prepared for his "oath's sake" (Mt 14.9) to see Jonathan die. At least Herod was "sorry", but there is no hint of sorrow here. The "perfect lot" did not point an accusing finger at Jonathan. It pointed to his innocence, and this follows:

C) Israel's intervention (vv.45-46)
"And the people said unto Saul, Shall Jonathan die, who hath wrought this great salvation in Israel? God forbid: as the Lord liveth, there shall not one hair of his head fall to the ground; for he hath **wrought with God this day.** So the people rescued Jonathan, that he died not." The people recognised that Jonathan's victory was nothing else than a divine verdict on the case. Notice that it does not say that God "wrought with Jonathan", but that Jonathan "wrought with God." It is very important for us to remember that we are involved in "the Lord's work." We are at His disposal. Notice too that while God "answered Saul not **that day**" (v.37), Jonathan had "wrought with God **this day** (v.45)." The people were more spiritually minded than their king. Saul was obsessed with self-vindication, when he should have been rejoicing in victory.

It all resulted in failure to completely destroy the Philistine army, and this reminds us that we can be so obsessed with our own interests, that we forget the work in hand. Sadly, it is not unknown for Christians to defend their particular ideas, or their party position, to the bitter end, with devastating results for God's work and God's people. It was happening at Corinth. See 1 Corinthians 1.10-17. In the case before us, Saul went off in a huff, and the Philistines got back home without further loss. "Then Saul went up from following the Philistines: and the Philistines went to their own place" (v.46). There was no doubt that the Philistines had been routed, but it could have been an even greater victory if Saul had acted more reasonably.

4. The Defeat of the Enemies (vv.47-48)
In spite of all this, the defeat of the Philistines served to give Saul "regal authority over the Israelites." (Keil & Delitzsch). "So Saul took the kingdom over Israel." He was certainly successful in battle. It was a far cry from the days when "all the Israelites went down to the Philistines, to sharpen every man his share, and his coulter, and his axe, and his mattock…so it came to

pass in the day of battle, that there was neither sword nor spear found in the hand of any of the people that were with Saul and Jonathan" (13.20-22). Now, under Saul, Israel was becoming a formidable force in the Middle East.

However, Saul was never completely victorious. He "vexed" the Philistines, but he never destroyed them. See verse 52. If Saul had pursued and completely destroyed the Philistines, Goliath would never have challenged and derided Israel. Ultimately, they defeated and destroyed Saul. It is significant that David's first victory was over the Philistines, and ultimately the Lord gave him "rest round about from all his enemies" (2 Sam 7.1). Are **we** winning victories in "the good fight of faith?"

5. The Details of Saul's Family (vv.49-51)
Only three of Saul's sons are mentioned. Jonathan, Ishui and Mechishua all fell with their father on Mount Gilboa. See 31.2. Ishui and Abinadab are one and the same. There was a fourth son, Esh-baal or Ish-bosheth: see 1 Chronicles 8.33 and 2 Samuel 2.8. We will meet Saul's daughters, Merab and Michal, again in 1 Samuel 18. Michal did not have a very happy life. See 2 Samuel 3.13-16: 6.20-23. Saul's cousin, Abner, was the captain of his army. A.McShane has the following to say about him: "Whatever ability he may have manifested on the battlefield, he certainly never showed any trace of godliness. He possibly was put into his position because of his relationship to the king. True leaders must ever get beyond natural relationships when seeking men to share with them in responsibility."

6. The Drafting for the Army (v.52)
"And there was sore war against the Philistines all the days of Saul: and when Saul saw any strong man, or any valiant man, he took him unto him." Samuel was right (of course): "This will be the manner of the king that shall reign over you: He will take your sons, and appoint them for himself, for his chariots, and to be his horsemen; and some shall run before his chariots" (8.12). But let's end on a practical note. This is how Keil & Deltizsch see it: "The meaning might be expressed in this manner: And as Saul had to carry on a severe war against the Philistines his whole life long, he drew to himself every powerful man and every brave man that he met with."

We too are involved in a life-long battle. It is not a case of "too old at forty." There is no retirement age. There is "no discharge" in this war, Ecclesiastes 8.8. We must marshal all our spiritual resources for the conflict. Let's remember that "his divine power hath given unto us all things that pertain unto life and godliness" (2 Pet 1.3). Or, looking at it from a different point of view, we are required to serve in the army of a heavenly King. Saul's men did not have an "opt out" clause in their contract. As their king, he had sovereign rights over them. The Lord Jesus has every right to our allegiance. Army service is mandatory. We must be "willing in the day of his power" (Ps 110.3).

CHAPTER 15

To obey is better than sacrifice (1 Sam 15.1-35)

We have read and studied some exciting chapters in 1 Samuel, but there are important lessons for us in the solemn passages as well, and this is one of them. The chapter spells out the sobering consequences of disobedience. It ends with the words, "and the Lord repented that he had made Saul king over Israel." We disregard the lessons of this chapter at our peril.

The chapter can be divided as follows: **(1)** The command to Saul (vv.1-9); **(2)** The confrontation of Saul (vv.10-23); **(3)** The confession by Saul (vv.24-31); **(4)** The consequences for Saul (vv.32-35).

1. The Command to Saul (vv.1-9)
This paragraph covers **(A)** The destruction of the Amalekites (vv.1-3); **(B)** The deliverance of the Kenites (vv.4-6); **(C)** The disobedience of Saul (vv.7-9).

A) The destruction of the Amalekites (vv.1-3)
Before giving Saul instructions to destroy Amalek, Samuel reminds him of his responsibility. "The Lord sent me to anoint thee to be king over **his** people, over Israel: now **therefore** hearken thou unto the voice of the words of the Lord." The king was not a free agent: he ruled over **God's** people, and must therefore obey **God's** will. Spiritual leadership does not lie in a strong personality and a fund of new ideas, but in ascertaining and implementing the word of God. "He that ruleth over men must be just, ruling in the fear of God" (2 Sam 23.3). The scriptures frequently emphasise that privilege determines responsibility. See, for example James 3 chapter 1, "My brethren, be not many masters (teachers), knowing that we shall receive the greater condemnation ("greater judgment", JND)."

The Amalekites were evidently descended from Esau (Gen 36.12), although people of the same name are mentioned in Genesis 14.7. They attacked Israel shortly after they had crossed the Red Sea (Ex 17.8-16), and were located in the south of Canaan. See Numbers 13.9. Balaam called them "the first of the nations" (Num 24.20). The Scofield Bible has a note against this: "Or, the first of the nations that warred against Israel." We learn a little more about their attack from Deuteronomy 25 verses17-19. Amalek showed no mercy to an estimated 2.5 million asylum-seekers. Notice that they "smote the hindmost of thee, even all that were feeble behind thee, when thou wast faint and weary; and he feared not God." The enemy hasn't changed. He still picks off weak, vulnerable Christians. But, given the opportunity, he will pick off **any** Christian! We must **all** therefore ensure that we are "nourished up in the words of faith and of good doctrine" (1 Tim 4.6), and "strong in the Lord, and in the power of his might" (Eph 6.10). God's people were not to be like the Amalekites: they were to show a completely different attitude to sojourners. See, for example Leviticus 19.33-34.

The time had come to fulfil the instructions of Moses: "Thou shalt blot out the remembrance of Amalek from under heaven; thou shalt not forget" (Deut 25.19). Should anybody object to this on the ground that it all happened four hundred years before, just read 1 Samuel 15 again. The current generation of Amalekites are called "the sinners the Amalekites" (v.18), and their king, Agag, had "made women childless" (v.32). Amalek had not changed. In any case, "God requireth that which is past" (Eccl 3.15), and wicked men will be "judged out of those things...written in the books", however many years have elapsed since the entries were made. God was prepared to spare Sodom if there were as few as ten righteous people in the city. The complete destruction of the Amalekites must therefore imply that there were no righteous people among them at all. It was an act of mercy towards the whole human race that such wicked people should be destroyed. Compare Genesis 15.16.

B) The deliverance of the Kenites (vv.4-6)
The Amalekites **"laid wait"** for Israel "when he came up from Egypt", but the Kenites **"shewed kindness** to all the children of Israel, when they came up out of Egypt." (Numbers 24 verse 21 suggests that the Kenites were not always kind to Israel). Since Jethro, or Raguel, Moses's father in law, is called a Kenite (Jud 1.16) as well as a Midianite (Num 10.29), it seems that the Kenites were probably a branch of the Midianites. Midian was the son of Abraham and Keturah (Gen 25.1-2). We do not have details of the kindness shown by the Kenites, unless this refers to Num 10.29-32, but

C) The disobedience of Saul (vv. 7-9)

Saul was under instructions to "smite Amalek, and utterly destroy all that they have, and spare them not." Sadly, he had a better idea: "But **Saul** and the people (keep these words in mind) spared Agag, and the **best** of the sheep...oxen...fatlings...lambs, and all that was good, and would not utterly destroy them: but every thing that was vile and refuse, **that** they destroyed utterly." (Compare 22.17-19, where Saul spared nothing in his rage against David). We can understand, humanly speaking, why they wanted to keep the best animals, but it is not quite so easy to ascertain why Agag was spared. Possibly, Saul wished to display him as a trophy of war. Call it "incomplete obedience", or "selective obedience", if you like, but it was nothing less than rank disobedience, and this is stressed throughout the chapter. See vv.11,19,23. It was also a challenge to Samuel's authority.

Are **we** selective in our obedience to God's word? Do **we** just practice what happens to be convenient, or what suits **our** own interests? Notice that Israel was warned against "picking and choosing" when it came to idolatry. See Deuteronomy 7.25-26. "The graven images of their gods shall ye burn with fire: thou shalt not desire the silver or gold that is on them, nor take it unto thee, **lest** thou be snared therein." It is all too easy to give up some things which are wrong, but not others, especially if we can see some advantage in retaining them. God expects us to make "a clean break" with the evil things which once commanded our attention.

2. The Confrontation of Saul (vv.10-23)

This section can be divided into two parts: **(A)** Samuel's grief (vv.10-11) and **(B)** Saul's guile (vv.12-23).

A) Samuel's grief (vv.10-11)

"Then came the word of the Lord unto Samuel, saying, It repenteth me that I have set up Saul to be king: for he is gone back from following me, and hath not performed my commandment. And it grieved Samuel; and he cried unto the Lord all night." Notice three things here:

i) God's repentance. "It repenteth me that I have set up Saul to be king." Repentance is essentially a change of mind. But unlike us, God does not feel "the pain of remorse" (Ellicott's Commentary) because He has erred in the past. Note that He never could or did err. Changed circumstances mean that God must act differently. Repentance is a change of attitude. The repentance of Nineveh (they "turned from their evil way") enabled God to "repent of the evil, that he said he would do unto them" (Jon 3.10). He was able to look favourably upon them. We have the reverse in Genesis 6 verse 6, where God's "repentance" is connected with sorrow over sin. We must notice that God's purposes and promises are unalterable. See v.29. Compare Psalm 110 verse 4. There is no "repentance" here!

ii) Saul's sin. "He is gone back from following me, and hath not performed my commandment." Saul had turned round from following God, in order to go his own way. Compare Isaiah 53 verse 6. Quite obviously, we cannot follow the Lord and, at the same time, disobey Him.

iii) Samuel's anger. "It grieved Samuel; and he cried unto the Lord all night." The word "grieved" *(charah)* means "to burn", and is expressive of anger, rather than sorrow. Although Samuel was justly angry at the way in which God had been dishonoured by Saul's disobedience, he still interceded for him, but to no avail.

B) Saul's guile (vv.12-23)
Saul made three attempts to extricate himself (vv.13,15,20-21), and in each case Samuel silenced his arguments. Notice the recurring pattern in these verses: "Saul said" (vv.13, 15,20); "Samuel said" (vv.14,16,22). Saul was evidently very pleased with himself: "Saul came to Carmel, and behold, he set him up a place (literally "a hand", *yad,* meaning "a monument", JND)." Compare Absalom's pillar, which was called "Absalom's place" *(yad)* (2 Sam 18. 8). Samuel finally met him in Gilgal. Sadly, Saul was "uncircumcised in heart and ears." Remember what happened at Gilgal (Josh 5.2-9).

i) He attempted to deceive Samuel (vv.12-14). Notice the confidence with which Saul opens the conversation: "Blessed be thou of the Lord: I have performed the commandment of the Lord." Very impressive! But Saul must have been fully conscious that he had failed to carry out the commandment of God. He could hear the "bleating of the sheep" and the "lowing of the oxen" as easily as Samuel! This reminds us of the attempted deceit of

Ananias and Sapphira. Like Saul, they "kept back part of the price", (Acts 5.2). In both cases, the deceit was soon exposed, but do remember that while you may succeed, at least for a time, to create a false impression in other people's minds, you cannot deceive God.

ii) He attempted to defend his sin (vv.15-19). Saul now changes his tactics. "They have brought them from the Amalekites: for the people spared the best of the sheep, and the oxen, to sacrifice unto the Lord thy God; and the rest we have utterly destroyed." Notice that he implies that the people were responsible: **"They** have brought them from the Amalekites: for the **people** spared the best of the sheep, and the oxen." This was blatantly false: as we have noticed, both **"Saul** and the people spared...the best of the sheep" etc., (v.9). Saul returns to this argument later, but notice how he endeavoured to side-step the issue on religious grounds. The best animals had been spared for sacrifice! So that made everything right! It's a familiar argument isn't it? "Never mind about sticking strictly to the Bible, it's your motives which are important .God doesn't worry too much about fine details, as long as your heart's right!" Do you think that Saul's conscience was troubling him as he was speaking? He refers to the Lord as "the Lord **thy** God." See also v.21 and v.30.

Samuel cuts the argument short. Both Gesenius and Keil & Delitzsch state that the word "Stay" means "Leave off!" Saul's early humility had given place to arrogance. "When thou wast little in thine own sight (referring to Saul's own words in 9.21), wast thou not made head of the tribes of Israel, and the Lord anointed thee king over Israel?" This reminds us that God "resisteth the proud, and giveth grace to the humble" (1 Pet 5.5-6). The Lord Jesus taught that "he that humbleth himself shall be exalted" (Mt 23.12). He was a wonderful example of His own ministry! See Philippians 2.8-9. But like Uzziah (2 Chron 26.16), Saul's exaltation had gone to his head, and he interpreted the commandment of God (v.18) to suit himself. Pride is self-assertion. Saul's argument that he acted with God's best interests in view (that is, if we take his words at face value) is dismissed as "evil in the sight of the Lord" (v.19). Saul had disobeyed God, and no argument could alter that. "Wherefore then didst thou not obey the voice of the Lord?" But Saul hasn't finished.

iii) He attempted to deny responsibility (vv.20-23). "Yea, I have obeyed the voice of the Lord, and have gone the way which the Lord sent me, and have brought Agag the king of Amalek, and have utterly destroyed the

Amalekites. But the people took of the spoil, sheep, and oxen, the chief of the things which should have been utterly destroyed, to sacrifice unto the Lord thy God in Gilgal." Saul now admits that the animals should have been destroyed, but puts the blame fairly and squarely upon the people. **"I have obeyed the voice of the Lord...But the people took of the spoil!"** It has a familiar ring about it! "And the man said, The woman whom thou gavest to be with me, she gave me of the tree, and I did eat. And the Lord God said unto the woman, What is this that thou hast done? And the woman said, The serpent beguiled me, and I did eat" (Gen 3.12-13). There is an interesting parallel between Adam and Saul. Both were given dominion, both were given commandments, both disobeyed God, both assigned blame to someone else, and both lost the blessings of fellowship with God.

The fact remains that Saul was more culpable than the people. He was the king. He was responsible. There is no evidence that the people defied Saul. He was equally enthusiastic about "the spoil." He wasn't under pressure from his men. His argument was spurious. Saul's bad leadership reminds us that while overseers are not responsible to the flock, they are responsible **for** the flock. They are "stewards of God" (Tit 1. 7). An overseer must hold fast "the faithful word, as he hath been taught, that he may be able by sound doctrine both to exhort and to convince the gainsayers" (Tit 1.9). It is an abdication of responsibility to blame others in the assembly, when things get out of control. Potential problems need to be 'nipped in the bud.'

Samuel answers Saul's attempt to shift the blame, by emphasising God's delight in **obedience,** and His abhorrence of **disobedience.** "Hath the Lord as great delight in burnt-offerings and sacrifices, as in obeying the voice of the Lord? Behold, to obey is better than sacrifice, and to hearken than the fat of rams. For rebellion is as the sin of witchcraft, and stubbornness is as iniquity and idolatry." Samuel is not, for one moment, devaluing the importance of sacrifice. But sacrifice without obedience is no better than idol worship. Compare Isaiah 1.11-17, Malachi 1.10. The reason for God's delight in obedience is clear: when a man offered a sacrifice, he offered an animal; but when he obeyed God, he offered himself. See Mark 12.32-33. The Lord Jesus delighted to do God's will. His perfect obedience flowed from His complete devotion to God-Psalm 40.6-8. He said to His disciples, "If ye love me, keep my commandments."

> When we walk with the Lord,
> In the light of His word,
> What a glory He sheds on our way!
> While we do His good will
> He abides with us still,
> And with all who will trust and obey!

There are other things that God prefers to sacrifice. "I delight in lovingkindness, and not sacrifice; and the knowledge of God more than burnt-offerings" (Hos 6.6 JND). See also Matthew 9.13, "But go ye and learn what that meaneth, I will have mercy, and not sacrifice." The terrible results of Saul's disobedience are spelt out with chilling clarity: "Because thou hast rejected the word of the Lord, he hath also rejected thee from being king."

3. The Confession by Saul (vv.24-31)
While Saul responds to Samuels' solemn indictment by twice confessing his sin, he pleads mitigating circumstances in the first case (v.24) and his own prestige in the second (v.30).

A) "I have sinned" (vv.24-29)
i) Saul's request (vv.24-25). "I have sinned: for I have transgressed the commandment of the Lord, and thy words: because I feared the people, and obeyed their voice. Now therefore, I pray thee, pardon my sin, and turn again with me, that I may worship the Lord." Before we condemn Saul out of hand, let's remember that **we** often blame our circumstances for failure! Saul's attempt to make his sin appear as small as possible shows that his sense of guilt was superficial. C. V. Lapide (quoted by Keil & Delitzsch) rightly observes that "it was not true and serious repentance or the result of genuine sorrow of heart because he had offended God, but was merely repentance of the lips arising from fear of losing the kingdom, and of incurring public disgrace. This is apparent even from verse 25, but still more from verse 30."

ii) Samuel's response (vv.26-29). The divine sentence would not be rescinded: "I will not return with thee: for thou hast rejected the word of the Lord, and the Lord hath rejected thee from being king over Israel." This repeats the sentence in verse 23, and reminds us of 2 Chronicles 15.2, "The Lord is with you, while ye be with him; and if ye seek him, he will be found of you; but if ye forsake him, he will forsake you." Saul's attempt to restrain Samuel from leaving resulted in accidental damage to the prophet's mantle, and this served to illustrate the end of Saul's sovereignty. "The Lord hath rent the kingdom from thee this day, and hath given it to a neighbour of thine, that is better than thou." We first heard about Saul's "neighbour" in 13.14, and we will meet him in the next chapter. It was God's settled intention to give him the crown. "And also the Strength of Israel (God is the guarantor of His own purposes) will not lie nor repent: for he is not a man, that he should repent." The word "Strength" can be rendered "Trust." It "signifies constancy, endurance, then confidence, trust, because a man can trust in what is constant." (Keil & Delitzsch).

B) "I have sinned" (vv.30-31)
i) Saul's request (v.30). "I have sinned: yet honour me now, I pray thee, before the elders of my people, and before Israel, and turn again with me, that I may worship the Lord thy God." As we have already noticed, Saul was more concerned about his prestige, than his guilt. He was desperate to maintain the *status quo* before others, rather than "hiding in shame, and mourning in secret before the Lord", A.McShane. It was "a strange penitence" (Ellicott's Commentary).

ii) Samuel's response (v.31). Rather surprisingly, Samuel acceded to his request, and this has been variously explained. There could be some mileage in the suggestion given in Ellicott's Commentary: it was "a desire to prevent any disaffection towards the monarchy. Samuel's known disapproval of Saul's conduct and his declining the king's earnest prayer to stay, would probably have been the signal to the discontented spirits to revolt, under the pretext that such a result would be pleasing to the great seer." This may or may not have been the case.

4. The Consequences for Saul (vv.32-35)
The rejection of Saul had three immediate effects. *(A)* He lost the final honour (vv.32-33); *(B)* He lost the fellowship of Samuel (vv.34-35); *(C)* He lost the favour of God (v.35).

A) He lost the final honour (vv.32-33)
Agag obviously thought that since he had not been put to death earlier, his life was to be spared. "Surely the bitterness of death is past." He had a rude awakening. "Samuel hewed Agag in pieces before the Lord in Gilgal." It was a case of "whatsoever a man soweth, that shall he also reap." Agag had obviously conducted his wars with great cruelty. Through disobedience,

Saul lost the honour of completing the destruction of the Amalekites, and therefore the honour of fulfilling God's promise (Ex 17.14), and vindicating His name. Will the Lord say to **us,** "Well done, good and faithful servant?"

B) He lost the fellowship of Samuel (vv.34-35)
"Then Samuel went to Ramah; and Saul went up to his house to Gibeah of Saul. And Samuel came no more to see Saul until the day of his death: nevertheless Samuel mourned for Saul." Disobedience interrupts our fellowship with the Lord's people and, of course, with the Lord Himself. "If we **walk in the light,** as he is in the light, we have fellowship one with another" (1 Jn 5.7). Samuel and Saul did meet again, but Samuel did not come from Ramah. He came from beyond the grave. See 28.4-25. Notice too that "Samuel mourned for Saul." His disobedience caused Samuel sorrow. Paul wrote 1 Corinthians "out of much affliction and anguish...with many tears" (2 Cor 2.4). We are quick to condemn and criticise others, but how many tears do we shed over their waywardness?

C) He lost the favour of God (v.35)
"And the Lord repented that he had made Saul king over Israel." This does not contradict the earlier statement that "the Strength of Israel will not lie nor repent: for he is not a man, that he should repent" (v.29). Saul's disobedience brought about a change in God's attitude towards him, but nothing would change God's intention to give the kingdom to another man. Although Saul lost divine favour, he clung to power until his death on Mount Gilboa. As A.McShane observes, "Only by divine help can any man bear the burdens of leadership in the assembly, and all who attempt this task without it are sure to fail just as miserably as Saul did."

CHAPTER 16

"This is he" (1 Samuel 16.1-23)

We now reach the third major division of 1 Samuel. As we have already noticed, in chapters 1-7, **Samuel** is prominent; in chapters 8-15, **Saul** is prominent; in chapters 16-31, **David** is prominent. Saul's disobedience lost him the kingdom. His disobedience at Gilgal obliged Samuel to say "But now thy kingdom shall not continue: the Lord hath sought him a man after his own heart, and the Lord hath commanded him to be captain over his people, because thou hast not kept that which the Lord commanded thee" (13.14). That was bad enough, but worse was to follow. Saul's failure to completely destroy the Amalekites brought even stronger censure from Samuel: "the Lord hath rent the kingdom of Israel from thee this day, and hath given it to a neighbour of thine, that is better than thou" (15.28).

The "man after God's own heart", and the "neighbour that is better than thou", was David, and we meet him for the first time in this chapter.

The chapter can be divided into two sections: **(1) The anointing of David (vv.1-13).** "Thou shalt anoint unto me him whom I name unto thee (v.3)…Surely the Lord's anointed is before him (v.6)…Then Samuel took a horn of oil, and anointed him (v.13)." **(2) The attributes of David (vv.14-23).** Notice particularly verse 18: "cunning in playing, and a mighty valiant man, and a man of war, and prudent in matters, and a comely person, and the Lord is with him." The chapter proves, yet again, that "whatsoever things were written aforetime were written for our learning" (Rom 15.4). There are practical lessons here. But there are also beautiful pictures of the Lord Jesus, who is in every way "the man after God's own heart." He is David's Lord and David's Son (Mt 22.42-45). He is "the root and offspring of David" (Rev 22. 16).

1) The Anointing of David (vv.1-13)
We will divide this section of the chapter as follows: **(A)** Samuel's command

from God (vv.1-5); **(B)** Samuel's conclusion about Eliab (vv.6-10); **(C)** God's choice of David (vv.11-13).

A) Samuel's command from God (vv.1-5)
Notice the expressions, "I will send thee" (v.1), and "I will shew thee" (v.3). Samuel enjoyed divinely-given directions and divinely-given discernment. While, in his youth, "Samuel did not yet know the Lord" (3.7), he certainly knew Him now! "And the Lord said unto Samuel...and Samuel said...and the Lord said..." (vv.1-2). See also verses 7 & 12. The Lord and Samuel communicated with each other with ease.

i) Samuel's orders (v.1).
"How long wilt thou mourn for Saul, seeing I have rejected him from reigning over Israel? Fill thine horn with oil, and go; I will send thee to Jesse the Beth-lehemite: for I have provided me a king among his sons."

We can understand Samuel's grief. Saul's failure, and rejection by God, must have been a bitter blow to him, which reminds us that life can hand out some hard knocks. Our cherished dreams and bright ambitions for ourselves, and for others, can suddenly crash. Disappointment and discouragement can be intense, so that "even the strongest men are loath to try again" (A.McShane). It is therefore encouraging to learn that Saul's failure did not leave God unprepared. He had anticipated the situation, and made provision. His gentle rebuke for Samuel reminds us that circumstances can overwhelm us to the extent that we become spiritually inactive and lose our spiritual vision. Even in the midst of disappointment, we should be "always abounding in the work of the Lord."

Unlike Saul, David was not anointed at the request of the people. God had given them the king **they** wanted: now He is going to give them the king **He** wanted. It would be long years before David ascended the throne. In the intervening period, he defeated an immensely powerful enemy, only to be rejected and persecuted. But the crowning day came, and "all the elders of Israel...anointed David king over Israel" (2 Sam 5.1-3). In the same way, Israel's final King, still "despised and rejected of men", will ultimately reign from the "holy hill of Zion" (Ps 2.6). Samuel's visit to Bethlehem therefore reminds us that God has provided another King from the same family. "There shall come forth a rod out of the stem of Jesse, and a Branch shall grow out of his roots", (Is 11.1). Bethlehem was the birth-place of David, and the birth-place of "great David's greater Son." (See Mic 5.2), "But thou,

Beth-lehem Ephratah, though thou be little among the thousands of Judah, yet out of thee shall he come forth unto me that is to be ruler in Israel; whose goings forth have been from of old, from everlasting."

ii) Samuel's objection (vv.2-3). "How can I go? If Saul hear it, he will kill me." (Compare Acts 9.10-16, where another Saul was involved!). It has been suggested that "headstrong as Saul was, he owed too much to the prophet to put him to death"." (The Pulpit Commentary). On the other hand, Samuel's worst fears were certainly justified later. Just think about Saul's attempts to kill David! Perhaps Samuel accurately read Saul's character at this early stage and knew that he would not tolerate a rival. Quite clearly, Samuel's statement that God had given "the kingdom of Israel...to a neighbour of thine, that is better than thou", was never far from Saul's mind. See 18.8 & 20.30-31.

There is no duplicity in the Lord's answer: "Take an heifer (a female animal: this emphasises the submission and feelings of Christ) with thee, and say, I am come to sacrifice to the Lord." This was perfectly true. Samuel did offer a sacrifice. It served, however, to conceal the principle object of his visit. Quite clearly, there was no treason involved, and it would be many years before David commenced to reign. He was anointed in view of an event that lay years ahead. It has been nicely said that "all charitable, well-disposed persons suppress much, and keep a guard over their lips, lest they should stir up strife and hatred." (The Pulpit Commentary). We need to be "as wise as serpents, and harmless as doves" (Mt 10.16).

iii) Samuel's obedience (vv.4-5). "And Samuel did that which the Lord spake, and came to Bethlehem." He did exactly as commanded. The lesson is obvious. Just remember 15.22. Samuel exemplified his own ministry! Notice that we have here another local sacrifice. Compare 9.12-13. Whilst this may seem to contradict the clear teaching in Deuteronomy 12, we must remember that Shiloh had been abandoned (Ps 78.60), and Jerusalem, which became the "place which the Lord your God shall choose", was not yet occupied by Israel. See 2 Samuel 5.6-9. It seems that Samuel himself instituted the practice of "occasionally holding sacrifices, now at one place and now at another, to keep alive a sense of religion in the hearts of the people." (The Pulpit Commentary).

B) Samuel's conclusion about Eliab (vv.6-10)
Appearances can be deceptive! "He looked on Eliab, and said, Surely the

Lord's anointed is before him. But the Lord said unto Samuel, Look not on his countenance, or on the height of his stature; because the Lord hath refused him: For the Lord seeth not as man seeth; for man looketh on the outward appearance, but the Lord looketh on the heart."

It isn't long before we have the opportunity to see the heart of David and the heart of Eliab. David was quite appalled when Goliath challenged Israel. "Who is this uncircumcised Philistine that he should defy the armies of the living God." But Eliab didn't even pay lip service to David's deep concern for God's glory: "And Eliab's anger was kindled against David, and he said, Why camest thou down hither? And with whom hast thou left those few sheep in the wilderness? I know the naughtiness of thine heart; for thou art come down that thou mightest see the battle" (17.26-29). Time certainly proved that God was right in rejecting Eliab! Paul warned Timothy about hasty decisions: "Lay hands on no man suddenly...Some men's sins are open beforehand (so it is quite obvious that they are ineligible for service)...and some men they follow after (it takes time for their deficiencies to show). Likewise also the good works of some are manifest beforehand (so it is quite obvious that they are eligible for service); and they that are otherwise cannot be hid (those who do not show their eligibility at first will make it clear later)."

We must never forget the omniscience of God. The Lord Jesus censured the religious leaders for their pretence: "Ye hypocrites, well did Esaias prophesy of you, saying, This people draweth nigh unto me with their mouth, and honoureth me with their lips, but their heart is far from me" (Mt 15.7-8). Let's remember that "neither is there any creature that is not manifest in his sight: but all things are naked and opened unto the eyes of him with whom we have to do" (Heb 4.13). His knowledge is global: "For the eyes of the Lord run to and fro throughout the whole earth" (2 Chron 16.9). This is why the wheels of His chariot throne are "full of eyes round about them four" (Ezek 1.18). Compare Revelation 4. 6.

Eliab was followed by Abinadab, Shammah, and four other brothers, with the conclusion, "The Lord hath not chosen these" (v.10). On a technical note, 1 Chronicles 2.13-15 gives us a total of only seven sons, including David, which strongly suggests that one of those seen by Samuel died later. In all this, we should not overlook the role of Jesse. His simple obedience to Samuel's request is delightful. He is honoured in Scripture. See Isaiah 11.1 & 10. David never forgot him. See Psalm 72. 20.

C) God's choice of David (vv.11-13)

"And Samuel said unto Jesse, Are here all thy children? And he said, There remaineth yet the youngest, and, behold, he keepeth the sheep. And Samuel said unto Jesse, Send and fetch him: for we will not sit down (literally "surround": i.e. to surround the meal table) until he come hither. And he sent, and brought him in. Now he was ruddy, and withal of a beautiful countenance, and goodly to look to. And the Lord said, Arise, anoint him: for this is he." We should notice at least three things here:

i) David's activity (v.11). "He keepeth the sheep." God chose a shepherd. See Psalm 78.70-72, "He chose David also his servant, and took him from the sheepfolds: from following the ewes great with young he brought him to feed Jacob his people, and Israel his inheritance. So he fed them according to the integrity of his heart; and guided them by the skilfulness of his hands."

It is most significant that the "man after God's own heart" was completely overlooked at first, and this reminds us that "the stone that the builders rejected, the same is become the head of the corner" (Mt 21.42). The Lord Jesus was unrecognised. In fact, He came unto his own, and his own received him not." But although overlooked, David was busy with the sheep, reminding us that although unrecognised, the Lord Jesus worked tirelessly in the interests of men and women. He saw them as "sheep not having a shepherd" (Mk 6.34).

God loves shepherd work. It was David, the shepherd-king who wrote, "The Lord is my shepherd." This isn't the only place in the Old Testament where the Lord is described as a shepherd. See, for example (Is 40.10-11). The Lord Jesus is "the good shepherd...the great shepherd...the chief shepherd." Abel was a shepherd. He "brought of the firstlings of his flock and of the fat thereof", Genesis 4. 4. Moses was a shepherd, both literally (Ex 3.1) and metaphorically: "Thou leddest thy people like a flock by the hand of Moses and Aaron," (Ps 77.20). Assembly elders are described in shepherd language. The word "feed" (Acts 20. 28, 1 Pet 5. 2) means "tend" or "act as a shepherd." Compare John 21.15-17 where *bosko* ("feed") is used in vv.15 & 17, and *poimaino* ("tend") in v.16.

ii) David's appearance (v.12). "Now he was ruddy, and withal of a beautiful countenance, and goodly to look to." The word "ruddy" denotes "the reddish colour of the hair, which was regarded as a mark of beauty in southern lands, where the hair is generally black", Keil & Delitzsch. These commentators translate "withal of a beautiful countenance, and goodly to look to", as "also of beautiful eyes and good looks." Compare JND margin: "beautiful-eyed." Moses was "exceeding fair" (literally, "fair to God", JND margin), Acts 7. 20.

For obvious reasons, the New Testament does not describe the physical appearance of the Lord Jesus. It emphasises the beauty of His character, and we sing

> What grace, O Lord, and beauty shone
> Around Thy steps below!
> What patient love was seen in all
> Thy life and death of woe!

"Thou art fairer than the children of men; grace is poured into thy lips: therefore God hath blessed thee for ever" (Ps 45.2). Men saw "no beauty" in Him, but to us He is "altogether lovely" (Song 5.16).

iii) David's anointing (v.13). "Then Samuel took a horn of oil, and anointed him in the midst of his brethren: and the Spirit of the Lord came upon David from that day forward. So Samuel rose up and went to Ramah." This reminds us that the Lord Jesus, "made of the seed of David according to the flesh" (Rom1.3), was "anointed...with the Holy Ghost and with power: who went about doing good, and healing all that were oppressed of the devil; for God was with him" (Acts 10. 38).

David means "beloved", and when the Lord Jesus was "anointed...with the Holy Ghost, God said "This is my **beloved** Son, in whom I am well pleased" (Mt 3.16-17). It is wonderful to remember that He loves to be "in the midst of his brethren."

> With Jesus in our midst,
> We gather round the board,
> Though many, we are one in Christ,
> One body in the Lord.

2. The Attributes of David (vv.14-23)

We can divide this section of the chapter into three parts as follows: *(A)* Saul's agitation (vv.14-17); *(B)* David's attractiveness (v.18); *(C)* David's acceptance (vv.19-23).

1 Samuel

A) Saul's agitation (vv.14-17)

"And the Spirit of the Lord came upon David from that day forward...But the Spirit of the Lord departed from Saul, and an evil spirit from the Lord troubled him. And Saul's servants said unto him, Behold now, an evil spirit from God troubleth thee." This is an extremely solemn passage. As Keil & Delitzsch point out, this was not "merely an inward feeling of depression at the rejection announced to him, which grew into melancholy, and occasionally broke out in passing fits of insanity, but a higher evil power, which took possession of him." This emphasises the fearful dangers of disobedience. Saul was subject to demon power because he had rejected the word of God. See 15. 23 & 26. It was a divine punishment. Compare 2 Thessalonians 2.11-12. "For this cause God shall send them strong delusion, that they should believe a (the) lie: that they might all be damned who believed not the truth, but had pleasure in unrighteousness." Believers enjoy the "peace of God, which passeth all understanding", but "the wicked are like the troubled sea, when it cannot rest, whose waters cast up mire and dirt. There is no peace, saith my God, to the wicked" (Is 57.20-21). We should add that whilst believers now are permanently indwelt by the Holy Spirit (Jn 14.16-17), and therefore do not pray "take not thy Holy Spirit from me" (Ps 51.11), disobedience still brings disquiet and agitation.

The servants of Saul recognised that music would give some relief, and one of the young men (the word "servants" in v.18 is different) knew just the man for the job:

B) David's attractiveness (v.18)

"I have seen a son of Jesse the Beth-lehemite, that is cunning in playing, and a mighty valiant man, and a man of war, and prudent in matters, and a comely person, and the Lord is with him." All these features had been developed in David's **early life,** long before he hit the headlines. How well are **we** preparing ourselves for future responsibility? See 1 Timothy 4.12, 2 Timothy 2.15 etc. Notice David's attributes:

i) "Cunning in playing." David is described as "the man who was raised upon high, the anointed of the God of Jacob, and the sweet psalmist of Israel" (2 Sam 23.1).

He employed his musical ability in praising God, and helping others. Through his playing, "Saul was refreshed, and was well, and the evil spirit departed from him" (v.23). Through David, there was some relief for the man who, because of disobedience, was deprived of divine blessing.

While, apart from Hebrews 2.12, there is no reference to musical ability in connection with the Lord Jesus. He exceeds David in bringing peace to men and women troubled by sin. We "have peace with God through our Lord Jesus Christ" (Rom 5.1). David only brought Saul temporary peace of mind. Rather like modern tranquillisers. The Lord Jesus can bring permanent peace to minds troubled because of sin. He deals with the problem at source.

We have a ministry of restoration. See Galatians 6.1, "Brethren, if a man be overtaken in a fault, ye which are spiritual, restore such an one in the spirit of meekness; considering thyself, lest ye also be tempted." Note Colossians 4.11, where "comfort" means "to sooth". We too have a ministry of praise. See Ephesians 5.19.

ii) "A mighty valiant man, and a man of war." As Keil & Delitzsch observe, "the description of David as "a mighty man' and "a man of war", does not presuppose that he had already fought bravely in war, but may be perfectly explained, as he himself later affirmed, by his conflicts with lions and bears." See 17.34-35. David proved himself locally, before he proved himself nationally. He was victorious in the obscurity of the hillside before he was victorious in the glare of publicity in the valley. As we shall see, David did not avoid confrontation with the enemy. He was willing to take responsibility and to expose himself to risk. Compare Romans 16.4.

The Lord Jesus was "a mighty valiant man." Although fully aware of His future sufferings, which were known to Him from "before the foundation of the world", let alone in time, He nevertheless "stedfastly set his face to go to Jerusalem" (Lk 9.51). He was, equally, "a man of war." See, for example (Lk 11.21-22). His greatest victory was at Calvary. See Hebrews 2.14-15. It will not be long before the world sees Him as "a man of war." See Psalm 45.3-5: "Gird thy sword upon thy thigh, O most might...thy right hand shall teach thee terrible things...Thine arrows are sharp in the heart of the king's enemies." See Revelation 19.11-16.

We should be "valiant for the truth" (Jer 9.3). We should "earnestly contend for the faith" (Jude 3). Compare 1 Corinthians 2.2, 15.58 etc. David was "a mighty valiant man" in protecting the flock, that is, in his shepherd-character. We should be "men of war." See Ephesians 6.

iii) "Prudent in matters." David was "skilled in speech" (JND). He learnt to control mind and mouth. This became even more evident as time passed. See 18.5 etc.

The Lord Jesus was "skilled in speech." They said, "Never man spake like this man" (Jn 7.46), and "all bare him witness, and wondered at the gracious words which proceeded out of his mouth (Lk 4.22)." See Psalm 45.2.

We too should be "skilled in speech." "Let no corrupt communication proceed out of your mouth, but that which is good to the use of edifying, that it may minister grace to the hearers" (Eph 4.29). "Let your speech be always with grace, seasoned with salt (not pepper!), that ye may know how ye ought to answer every man" (Col 4.6). Read James 3.

iv) "A comely person." "And of good presence." (v.18 JND). It was a pleasure to be with David. His anointing by Samuel did not go to his head. Having served Saul, he went back to the sheep! (17.15). After defeating Goliath, he "behaved himself wisely in all his ways; and the Lord was with him…all Israel and Judah loved David, because he went out and came in before them." (1 Sam 18.14-16). (This is explained in 2 Samuel 5.2). The people who resorted to David in the cave of Adullam (1 Sam 22.1-2, obviously regard him as "a man…of good presence!" What do people think of **our** company?

The Lord Jesus is "a man…of good presence." The two disciples en route to Emmaus proved this. "Did not our heart burn within us, while he talked with us by the way, and while he opened to us the scriptures?" (Lk 24.32).

We must emulate Tychicus. He was obviously "a man of good presence!" "All my state shall Tychicus declare unto you, who is a beloved brother, and a faithful minister and fellowservant in the Lord" (Col 4.7).

v) "The Lord is with him." See also 18.12 & 14. That was an enviable testimony! Do **we** convey the impression that God is with us? It ought to be true of our assembly life as well as our personal life. People should "report that God is in you of a truth" (1 Cor 14.25).

C) David's acceptance (vv.19-23)
David received a warm welcome at court. "And David came to Saul, and stood before him: and he loved him greatly; and he became his armourbearer.

Chapter 16

And Saul sent to Jesse, saying, Let David, I pray thee, stand before me; for he hath found favour in my sight. At this point, obviously, Saul had no suspicion that David was his anointed successor, and although David was well aware of his destiny, he never claimed it. He waited God's time. There can be no doubt that David's presence at Saul's court was part of his training for future responsibility. But before he reigns, "his faith must be put to the test by all manner of sufferings. He must be the dependent man, the humbled man, despised, hated, persecuted; in the midst of this life of renouncements and strife, he will experience that His God is sufficient for everything" (H.L.Rossier).

CHAPTER 17A

"Have ye seen this man that is come up?" (17.1-30)

The confrontation between David and Goliath must be one of the best-known stories in the Bible. While it is "stock in trade" for every Sunday School teacher, it is brimful of important lessons for **every** age group! Since the narrative occupies a long chapter, we will have to divide the passage into two sections: **(1)** The defiance of Goliath (vv.1-30). Just listen to him: "I defy the armies of Israel this day" (v.10). **(2)** The death of Goliath (vv.31-58). "So David...smote the Philistine, and slew him" (v.50).

1. The Defiance of Goliath (vv.1-30)
The section can be divided into four paragraphs as follows: **(A)** The champion from Gath (vv.1-7). "And there went out a champion out of the camp of the Philistines" (v.4). **(B)** The challenge to Israel (vv.8-11). "Give me a man, that we may fight together" (v.10). **(C)** The carriage of supplies (vv.12-24). "Take now for thy brethren an ephah of this parched corn, and these ten loaves...and carry these ten cheeses" (vv.17-18) **(D)** The concern of David (vv.25-30). "Who is this uncircumcised Philistine, that he should defy the armies of the living God?" (v.26).

A) The champion from Gath (vv.1-7)
The Philistines are back! We last saw them retreating to "their own place", after Jonathan and Saul had smitten them "from Michmash to Aijalon" (14.31 & 46). (Aijalon, also spelt Ajalon, was the site of another great victory: see Joshua 10.12). However, 1 Samuel 14 ends with the statement: "And there was sore war against the Philistines all the days of Saul." According to the dates given in the Scofield Bible, twenty-four years had passed since the last battle, but the "auld enemy" had not abandoned their desire to dominate Israel. This reminds us of another enemy who will never admit defeat! He even persisted with the Lord Jesus: "And when the devil had ended all the temptation, he departed from him **for a season**" (Lk

4.13). He evidently persisted with the apostle Paul: "Wherefore we would have come unto you, even I Paul, **once and again;** but Satan hindered us" (1 Thess 2.18). We can be sure, therefore, that he will persist with us! Notice:

i) The confrontation (vv.1-3)
"And the Philistines stood on a mountain on the one side, and Israel stood on a mountain on the other side: and there was a valley between them." It is interesting to notice that the Philistines "were gathered together at Shochoh, which belongeth to **Judah.**" It is worth remembering that, strictly speaking, the Philistines actually lived in territory belonging to Judah. In Joshua's day, it was part of the "land to be possessed." See Joshua 1.1-3. But the Philistines did not remain in their coastal strip, and took every opportunity to press inland. Failure to deal with the enemy all those years before had far-reaching results. However, at least the battle lines were clear. The two sides were clearly divided. "There was a valley between them." Compromise and infiltration are infinitely more dangerous. Just think of the havoc caused by Israel's liaisons with the Canaanite nations. We must remember "whose I am, and whom I serve." (Acts 27.23).

Notice that unlike Jonathan, who took the battle to the Philistines (see 14.1,8 etc.), Saul had evidently allowed the Philistines to take the initiative. The Lord Jesus said, "Go ye into all the world, and preach the gospel to every creature." The best means of defence is attack! Notice too that the Philistine challenge was vested in one man, which reminds us that the guiding and controlling genius of all opposition to God's word and God's people is vested in Satan.

ii) The champion (vv.4-7)
He looked invincible! The description of Goliath begins with his **size.** That was daunting enough! His height was "six cubits and a span." He was at least nine feet tall. His impressive height was matched by impressive **armour.** **(a)** "An helmet of brass." **(b)** "A coat of mail" or, "a corselet of scales" (JND). The word "mail" is translated "scales" in Leviticus 11.9-10 and Deuteronomy 14.9-10. So it was "a coat made of plates of brass lying one upon another like scales" (Keil & Delitzsch). Its weight in modern terms is not easily calculated, but it is thought by some that "five thousand shekels" is approximately 150 pounds. **(c)** "Greaves of brass upon his legs." His impressive height and impressive armour were matched by impressive **weapons. (a)** "A target of brass between his shoulders." The word "target"

refers to a lance or small spear: some say a javelin. It was evidently slung over his shoulders. **(b)** "And the staff of his spear was like a weaver's beam (see also 2 Sam 21.19); and his spear's head weighed six hundred shekels of iron." That is, about seventeen pounds. **(c)** We also know that Goliath carried a sword (see v.51). He was preceded by a shield-bearer. Compare, item by item, the armour listed here with the armour described in Ephesians 6.

All this reminds us of the way in which the Lord Jesus describes Satan: "When a strong man armed keepeth his palace, his goods are in peace: but when a stronger than he shall come upon him, and overcome him, he taketh from him all his armour wherein he trusted, and divideth his spoils" (Lk 11.22). Goliath is certainly a picture of Satan! Like Goliath, he cannot be overthrown by human strength. Like Goliath he has immensely powerful weapons. Like Goliath, he has plenty of help in deflecting opposition. His shield-bearers include humanists, who have no room for supernatural powers, and satirists, comedians and cartoonists, who poke fun at him, and therefore imply that he doesn't exist at all.

We cannot leave these verses without reminding ourselves that God wears armour! See Isaiah 59.17, "He put on righteousness as a breastplate, and an helmet of salvation upon his head; and he put on the garments of vengeance, and was clad with zeal as a cloke." God's people must wear armour too: see Ephesians 6.13-17, 2 Corinthians 6. 7, 1 Thessalonians 5.8. Like Goliath, Satan is well-prepared for battle. It is therefore imperative that we should be well-prepared too.

B) The challenge to Israel (vv.8-11)
We should notice *(i)* the demand by Goliath (vv.8-9); *(ii)* the defiance of Goliath (v.10); *(iii)* the dismay of Israel (v.11).

(i) The demand by Goliath (vv.8-9)
"And he stood and cried unto the armies of Israel, and said unto them, Why are ye then come out to set your battle in array? Am I not a Philistine, and ye servants to Saul? Choose you a man for you, and let him come down to me. If he be able to fight with me, and to kill me, then we will be your servants: if I prevail against him, and kill him, then shall ye be our servants, and serve us." Like Goliath, Satan will do all in his power to gain the upper hand in the affairs of God's people. Notice the derogatory way in which he described Israel: "Am I not a Philistine, and ye servants to Saul?" Compare

JND here: "Am I not **the** Philistine, and ye servants of Saul?" Goliath represented and embodied the power of Philistia. But they were just the "servants of Saul." He doesn't even call them Israelites! Such was his disdain for God's people. It still happens! Gospel preachers are increasingly called "fundamentalists", and reduced to cult status.

Goliath demanded settlement of the conflict by single combat. There was no need for a fully-fledged battle ("why are ye come out to set your battle in array?"): the matter could be decided between two people. Hence his cry, "choose you a man...give me a man." This reminds us that we enjoy deliverance from bondage to sin, because the Lord Jesus defeated Satan in single combat at Calvary. He was not chosen by men. Like David, he undertook to engage the enemy voluntarily. "Forasmuch then as the children are partakers of flesh and blood, he also himself likewise took part of the same; that through death he might destroy him that had the power of death, that is, the devil; and deliver them who through fear of death were all their lifetime subject to bondage" (Heb 2.14-15). Goliath thundered, "Give me a man." We point to the Lord Jesus, and say, "Behold the man!" Compare 1 Corinthians 15.47.

(ii) The defiance of Goliath (v.10)
"And the Philistine said, I defy the armies of Israel this day; give me a man, that we may fight together." The word "defy" means "to reproach." Keil & Delitzsch translate as follows: "I have mocked the ranks of Israel this day." So far as Goliath was concerned, he defied "the armies of **Israel.**" David saw it quite differently: "Who is this uncircumcised Philistine, that he should defy the armies of **the living God?**" (v.26). This emphasises the difference between the "natural man" and the "spiritual man." See 1 Corinthians 2.14-15. It also emphasises that people who oppose God's people, oppose God Himself.

(iii) The dismay at Goliath (v.11)
"When Saul and all Israel heard those words of the Philistine, they were dismayed, and greatly afraid." The giant seemed unassailable. There was no man qualified to engage him in hand to hand combat. The future looked decidedly bleak. What Saul did not know was that God had the right man ready. He seemed totally unqualified, and arrived in a most undistinguished way, but he defeated the giant! All of which reminds us that when salvation seemed impossible, God made provision. "And he saw that there was **no man,** and wondered that there was no intercessor: therefore **his arm** brought

1 Samuel

salvation unto him; and his righteousness, it sustained him" (Is 59.16). We are now introduced to "the man" who would enter the valley of Elah, and destroy the enemy. He certainly did not arrive in a blaze of glory! So:

C) The carriage of supplies (vv.12-24)
That's how he arrived! "Take now for thy brethren an ephah of this parched corn, and these ten loaves; And carry these ten cheeses" (vv.17-18). Not very impressive is it?! But the lessons are most impressive! Our attention is drawn to *(i)* David's family (vv.12-14); *(ii)* David's humility (vv.15-20); *iii)* David's arrival (vv.20-24). In this connection, notice the perfect timing!

i) *David's family (vv.12-14)*
Reference is made *(a)* to his father (v.12) *(b)* to his brothers (v.13), and *(c)* to his age (v.14). At first glance, it is difficult to understand why this information is given at this point in the story. After all, we met the family in Chapter 16. On reflection, however, these verses form an introduction to what follows by summarising the role of the family in "the remarkable chain of circumstances by which David was led to undertake the conflict with Goliath." (Keil & Delitzsch).

a) His father (v.12). "Now David was the son of that Ephrathite of Bethlehem-Judah, whose name was Jesse; and he had eight sons: and the man went among men for an old man in the days of Saul." The names are most interesting. David means "beloved", and Jesse possibly means "wealthy" (Gesenius). Bethlehem-Judah means "the house of bread and praise." Centuries later, the "bread of life" (Jn 6.48), God's beloved Son, came to Bethlehem, "the house of bread", and "suddenly there was with the angel a multitude of the heavenly host, praising God" (Lk 2.13). It has been suggested that the reference to Jesse's age explains why he had not been drafted into the army.

b) His brothers (v.13). "And the three eldest sons of Jesse went and followed Saul to the battle: and the names of his three sons that went to the battle were Eliab the firstborn, and next unto him Abinadab, and the third Shammah". Quite obviously, this was no "quirk of fate." It was the providence of God. Their army service was part of His plan.

c) His age (v.14). "And David was the youngest: and the three eldest followed Saul." This emphasises that David was the most unlikely person in the family to engage Goliath. He wasn't even a soldier! See v.33: "Thou art not able to go against this Philistine to fight with him: for thou art but a youth." But "God hath chosen the weak things of the world to confound the mighty" (1 Cor 1.27). Compare Gideon: Judges 6.15.

ii) David's humility (vv.15-19)
These verses emphasise that although David had been anointed king, he was willing to undertake the most humble tasks. Notice his humility as **(a)** a shepherd, and **(b)** as a servant.

a) As a shepherd. "The three eldest followed Saul. But David went and returned from Saul to feed his father's sheep at Beth-lehem." David was not therefore in the permanent service of Saul. He went backwards and forwards from Saul to feed his father's sheep in Bethlehem. Compare 16.11 & 19. Shepherding sheep could be dangerous work. See (vv.34-35). The "youth" who delivered the lamb out of the lion's mouth was destined to deliver Israel from the Philistine champion. His diligence and care as a shepherd is emphasised in (v.20). He "left the sheep with a keeper." This was the man whom God took "from the sheepfold...to feed Jacob his people, and Israel his inheritance" (Ps 78.70-72). This illustrates Proverbs 15.33: "Before honour is humility." The future king was not afraid to get his hands dirty!

David was not the only king to be born in Bethlehem, and he was not the only king who was accustomed to shepherd work. The "King of kings", who is "made of the seed of David according to the flesh", is none other than "the good shepherd." He gave "his life for the sheep." Think about **His** humility!

Notice, too, the way in which verses 15-16 paint two pictures side by side. On the one hand we have David keeping the sheep: on the other we have Goliath challenging Israel. God was preparing His man in verse 15 to meet the crisis in verse 16.(Notice that Goliath confronted Israel for forty days. In Scripture, forty is the number of testing. Israel was tested for forty days, and found wanting. The Lord Jesus was triumphant after forty days and forty nights. This is repeated in verses 17-19, where we move quickly from pastoral Bethlehem to the battle-front. This brings us to the second aspect of David's humility:

b) As a servant. "Take now for thy brethren an ephah of this parched corn, and these ten loaves, and run to the camp of thy brethren; and carry these

1 Samuel

ten cheeses unto the captain of their thousand, and look how thy brethren fare, and take their pledge." According to Keil & Delitzsch, this means "a pledge that they are alive and well." David might have protested that this was beneath him. After all, he was the coming king. He had been anointed by no less a person than Samuel! But not a word of it!

Similarly, there was not a word of complaint, or the slightest hint of resentment, on the part of the Lord Jesus, God's anointed King, when He came "not to be ministered unto, but to minister, and to give his life a ransom for many." He was also sent by His Father, and like David (v.28), He was ill-received by His brethren. See John 1.11.

iii) David's arrival (vv.20-24)

David "rose up early." So did Joshua (Josh 3.1), and Gideon (Judg 7.1). So did the Lord Jesus (Mk 1.35). Perhaps the Lord Jesus is saying to us, "Take up thy bed and walk!" We cannot fail to notice that David arrived at exactly the right moment. Speaking generally, he arrived after Israel had been tested for forty days, and their weakness had been exposed. Speaking specifically, "he came to the trench (the wagon-rampart, or wagon-defence), *as* the host was going forth to the fight, and shouted for the battle" (v.20). "**As** he talked with them (his brethren), behold, there came up the champion, the Philistine of Gath, Goliath by name, out of the armies of the Philistines, and spake according to the same words: and David heard them." (v.23). Here is another example of the providence of God. There is nothing coincidental about this! We noticed another example of God's perfect timing in 9.14.

God's timing is always perfect. See Galatians 4.4-5, "When **the *fulness of the time was come,*** God sent forth his Son, made of a woman, made under the law, to redeem them that were under the law, that we might receive the adoption of sons." The Lord Jesus came after men and women had been tested by the law, and left "in bondage under the elements of the world" (vv.1-3).

David not only saw and heard Goliath. He witnessed the fear of Israel. "And all the men of Israel, when they saw the man, fled from him, and were sore afraid." Saul's army quickly retreated when he appeared. Compare verses 19 and 24. Compare Philippians 1.28. H.D.M. Spence (Ellicott's Commentary) makes the following observation: "A dull, cowardly torpor had come over Saul, the punishment for his self-will and disobedience, and the king's helpless lethargy had settled now on the hearts of the soldiers he had trained so well in his earlier and nobler days."

D) The concern of David (vv.25-30)
We can consider this paragraph as follows: **(i)** Saul's reward (v.25); **(ii)** David's reaction (vv.26-27); **(iii)** Eliab's rebuke (vv.28-30).

i) Saul's reward (v.25)
"And the men of Israel said (evidently amongst themselves), Have ye seen this man that is come up? Surely to defy Israel is he come up: and it shall be, that the man who killeth him, the king will enrich him with great riches, and will give him his daughter, and make his father's house free in Israel." (Compare Esther 6.6-9). There was a bright future for the man who could despatch the giant, and without pressing the details too far, this reminds us that following His great victory over Satan and his forces at Calvary, the Lord Jesus has been "highly exalted." God "raised him up from the dead, and gave him glory" (1 Pet 1.21). He, too, has received a bride and, changing the metaphor, his victory has brought liberty to all belonging to "his father's house." While the liberty promised by Saul probably meant freedom from taxation and public responsibilities, every Christian enjoys liberty from sin. "If the Son...shall make you free, ye shall be free indeed" (Jn 8.34-36).

ii) David's reaction (vv.26-27)
"And David spake to the men that stood by him, saying, What shall be done to the man that killeth this Philistine, and taketh away the reproach from Israel? (compare 11.2 etc). For who is this uncircumcised Philistine, that he should defy the armies of the living God?" The "men of Israel" saw Goliath as a major military obstacle (after all, he looked like a walking tank!), but David saw him through different eyes. He felt very deeply about the situation. How concerned do **we** feel about the general weakness of God's people? How concerned do we feel about our **own** weakness?

a) It was unthinkable that **God's people** should be so completely intimidated and cowed by Goliath. After all, Israel means "soldier of God", and how could an "uncircumcised Philistine", having no relationship with God at all, inflict such fear on them. It was certainly a reproach. No such reproach could be laid at the door of the apostles. The Jewish leaders saw "the boldness of Peter and John" (Acts 4.13). They were "in nothing terrified" by their adversaries, Philippians 1.28. What about **us?**

> Ashamed to be a Christian!
> Ashamed the world should know
> I'm on my way to Zion
> Where joys eternal flow!

b) It was unthinkable that **God's name** should be brought into such disrepute. Goliath had defied not just Israel, but "the armies of the living God." How do people perceive God through **us?** After all, we "turned to God from idols, to serve the living and true God" (1 Thess 1.9).

This reminds us that the Lord Jesus came to make us "more than conquerors" (Rom 8.37), and to bring endless glory to God.

iii) Eliab's rebuke (vv.28-30)
Had Eliab forgotten that David had been anointed by Samuel? We are told that "Samuel took the horn of oil, and anointed him in the **midst of his brethren"** (16.13). Perhaps, like the Lord's brethren, he just didn't believe that his youngest brother was the future king of Israel. Compare John 7.5. It is comforting to remember that the Lord Jesus "was in all points tempted like as we are, yet without sin" (Heb 4.15), and this includes misunderstanding and misrepresentation in the family circle. He perfectly understands the difficulties experienced by Christians who have no like-minded relatives.

As Keil & Delitzsch point out, "Eliab sought for a splinter in his brother's eye, and was not aware of the beam in his own (Mt 7.3-5). The very things with which he charged his brother – presumption and wickedness of heart – were most apparent in his scornful reproof." It is to David's credit that he gave a "soft answer." See Proverbs 15.1. "What have I now done? Is there not a cause?" This is generally understood to mean, "What have I now done? It was only a word." However, J.N.Darby renders the verse as follows: "What have I now done, Was it not laid upon me?" This may simply mean, "You seem bitterly displeased with my zeal in this matter, but surely, is there not such a good cause for my passionate emotion here – such an insult to our God" (Ellicott's Commentary). It does seem, however, that David was expressing more than concern. It does not seem unreasonable to suggest that David was beginning to feel that he was the "man" demanded by Goliath, and that his convictions about this were very clear by the time he was summoned by Saul.

Chapter 17A

The first publicly-recorded words of the Lord Jesus reveal **His** convictions. "Wist ye not that I must be about my Father's business?" (Lk 2.49). David's convictions took him into the valley of Elah, and the divine convictions of the Lord Jesus took Him to Calvary.

CHAPTER 17B

"I come to thee in the name of the Lord of hosts" (17.31-58)

In view of the length of this chapter, we have divided it into two parts as follows: **(1)** The defiance of Goliath (vv.1-30); **(2)** The death of Goliath (vv.31-58).

1. The Defiance of Goliath (vv.1-30)
"And the Philistine said, I defy the armies of Israel this day; give me a man, that we may fight together. When Saul and all Israel heard those words of the Philistine, they were dismayed, and greatly afraid." It isn't surprising that there were no volunteers for the job! Not even Jonathan! The sheer size of the man made him a daunting proposition, let alone his impregnable armour and massive spear.

But whilst Israel trembled with fear, a young shepherd-boy trembled with indignation. How dare this Philistine "defy the armies of the living God?" David found it unthinkable that God's name should be brought into such disrepute. But he was prepared to go further. His reply to Eliab, "What have I now done, Was it not laid upon me" (v.29 JND) strongly suggests that he was prepared to be the "man" to face Goliath. This explains why Saul sent for him, which brings us to:

2. The Death of Goliath (vv.31-58)
These famous verses can be divided as follows: **(A)** David's willingness to fight (vv.31-32); **(B)** David's trust in God (vv.33-37); **(C)** David's equipment for battle (vv.38-40); **(D)** David's response to Goliath (vv.41-47); **(E)** David's victory over Goliath (vv.48-53); **(F)** David's return to Saul (vv.54-58).

A) David's willingness to fight (vv.31-32)
"And David said to Saul, Let no man's heart fail because of him; thy servant will go and fight with this Philistine." David began by encouraging faint

hearts. We need people like that! He was not deterred by the overwhelming odds that faced him. He was not deterred by the awesome responsibility involved. After all, Israel's future was at stake. Goliath made this clear: "If he be able to fight with me, and to kill me, then will we be your servants: but if I prevail against him, and kill him, then shall ye be our servants, and serve us" (v.9). But David was resolute: "thy servant will go." There was nothing half-hearted about his decision. Notice what the Scriptures say about wholeheartedness. See Deuteronomy 11.13; 13.3, 1 Kings 2.4; 14.8.

Centuries later, Isaiah "heard the voice of the Lord, saying, Whom shall I send, and who will go for us?" The prophet responded by saying, "Here am I; send me." Are **we** willing to say with David, "thy servant will go", or with Isaiah, "here am I; send me?" But don't expect anything sensational. In most cases, God's service involves the "home front", and you will be expected to "stay the course" through "thick and thin." Do expect, however, to face giants! See Ephesians 6.12.

The willingness of David reminds us that the Lord Jesus was willing to "go and fight." He said, "Lo, I come: in the volume of the book it is written of me, I delight to do thy will, O my God: yea, thy law is within my heart" (Ps 40.7-8), quoted (with interesting omissions) in Hebrews 10.7-9. He came to "**give** his life a ransom for many." Why not make a list of the New Testament passages which emphasise the willingness of the Lord Jesus to engage the enemy on our behalf? See, for example, Galatians 1.4, Titus 2.14. He "gave himself." David's victory over Goliath delivered Israel from the prospect of bondage to the Philistines, and the victory of the Lord Jesus over Satan (Heb 2.14-15) has delivered us from bondage to sin. The alternative is unthinkable.

B) David's trust in God (vv.33-37)
This section begins with Saul saying, "Thou art **not able to go",** and ends with Saul saying, **"Go,** and the Lord be with thee." We must notice the striking difference between the way in which the two men assessed the situation. Saul's assessment was based on human reasoning, but David's assessment was based on faith in God. Saul compared David with Goliath, but David compared Goliath with God!

i) Saul's assessment (v.33)
"Thou art not able to go against this Philistine to fight with him: thou art but a youth, and he a man of war from his youth." That wasn't a very encouraging

1 Samuel

start for David! Let's be careful that **we** don't deter others with spiritual ambition. In Saul's opinion, the young shepherd-boy from Bethlehem didn't stand a chance against the seasoned warrior from across the valley. It was a foolhardy proposition! People once said the same about Saul himself. See 10.27. In fact, we can almost hear Saul saying, "How shall this man save us?" He didn't know that God "hath chosen the foolish things of the world to confound the wise; and God hath chosen the weak things of the world to confound the things which are mighty" (1 Cor 1.27-28).

History repeated itself when the Lord Jesus came. "We preach Christ crucified, unto the Jews a stumblingblock, and unto the Greeks **foolishness**." To preach salvation through a man on a cross was ridiculous! "But unto them which are called", He is "Christ the power of God, and the wisdom of God." Saul soon discovered that what seemed to be human foolishness was actually divine wisdom, and what seemed to be human weakness was actually divine strength.

ii) David's assessment (vv.34-37)
This was based on his experience of God's power (vv.34-35), and on his expectation of God's power, (vv.36-37).

a) His experience (vv.34-35). Unknown to Saul, David had already triumphed over brute strength. "Thy servant kept his father's sheep, and there came a lion and a bear, and took a lamb out of the flock: and I went out after him, and delivered it out of his mouth: and when he arose against me, I caught him by his beard, and smote him, and slew him." David is certainly not 'blowing his own trumpet here!' He acknowledged that "the **Lord**...delivered me out of the paw of the lion, and the paw of the bear" (v.37). David knew from experience that he could rely on God to help him. He was the "living God" (both plural words): see 1 Kings 17.1, 1 Thessalonians 1: 9 etc. (In the millennium, lions and bears will no longer pose a threat! See Isaiah 11.7).

Let's remember that God "chose David also his servant, and took him from the sheepfolds: from following the ewes great with young he brought him to feed Jacob his people, and Israel his inheritance" (Ps 78.70-72). The shepherd who "kept his father's sheep" and delivered the lamb from the predator's mouth, did exactly the same in later years. See, for example (1 Sam I 30), where David delivered the women and children from the Amalekites, whom he then "smote...from the twilight even unto the evening of the next day." David was a good shepherd in both ways! It reminds us that there are still predators who will attack "the flock." See Acts 20.28-31. Remember, too, that the "good shepherd" gave "his life for the sheep" at Calvary.

We cannot leave this without noting that if David was already skilled in warfare, then the Lord Jesus was skilled in recovering sheep from the greatest predator of all, before He destroyed him at Calvary. See, for example, Acts 10.38, and Luke 13.10-19.

B) His expectation (vv.36-37). Past help from God gave David confidence for the future. "Thy servant slew both the lion and the bear: and this uncircumcised Philistine shall be as one of them, seeing he hath defied the armies of the living God…The Lord that delivered me out of the paw of the lion, and out of the paw of the bear, he will deliver me out of the hand of this Philistine." We sing

> His love in times past forbids me to think
> He'll leave me at last in ruin to sink.
> Each sweet Ebenezer I hold in review
> Confirms His good pleasure to see me right through.

If David was confident of victory over the Philistine, then the Lord Jesus was confident of victory over Satan. He put it like this: "When a strong man armed keepeth his palace, his goods are in peace: but when a stronger than he shall come upon him, and overcome him, he taketh from him his armour wherein he trusted, and divideth his spoils" (Lk 11.21-22).

Saul was impressed! "And Saul said unto David, Go, and the Lord be with thee." But he must have wondered about the outcome when David refused to wear any armour. This brings us to:

C) David's equipment for battle (vv.38-40)
His refusal to wear Saul's armour and carry Saul's sword reminds us of some important lessons:

i) We should not imitate the methods of the world. It was worldy-wise to equip David with armour resembling that of Goliath. David was given a "helmet of brass" and "a coat of mail." Compare (v.5) although different words are used to describe the "coat of mail." Sadly, many Christians have resorted to worldly methods in their service for God. Prayer, Bible study, and Gospel preaching have been set aside in favour of entertainment and social activities.

ii) We should not try to wear somebody else's armour. It is important to keep company with other Christians, but they cannot give us their faith and confidence in God. We have a great deal to learn from each other, but we cannot carry somebody else's "shield of faith" or wear somebody else's "breastplate of righteousness." We have got to wear our own armour!

iii) We cannot effectively use weapons with which we are unfamiliar. It has been rightly said that we should not "traffic in unfelt truth." We must feel the weight of God's word in our own lives before we share it with others. This is why the message of the prophets is often called a "burden." David said, "I cannot go with these; for I have not proved them."

Having "put them off him", David "took his staff in his hand, and chose him five smooth stones out of the brook, and put them in a shepherd's bag which he had, even in a scrip ('into a pocket', JND); and his sling was in his hand: and he drew near to the Philistine." We get the distinct impression that whilst David had not "proved" Saul's armour, he was thoroughly versed in the art of hurling stones! But it didn't look very promising. It looked about as hopeful as a peashooter against a Churchill tank! But, as we shall see, "David prevailed over the Philistine with a sling and a stone" (v.50). There was not even "a sword in the hand of David." His foolish weapons were wonderfully effective. It reminds us that "though we walk in the flesh, we do not war after the flesh: for the weapons of our warfare are not carnal, but mighty through God to the pulling down of strongholds" (2 Cor 10.3-4). It reminds us, again, that "the preaching of the cross is to them that perish foolishness; but unto us which are saved it is the power of God" (1 Cor 1.18). Let's continue to use our "foolish" weapons!

It is usually said that David selected five stones in case Goliath's four brothers appeared! See 2 Samuel 21.15-22. David certainly got them all in the end!

D) David's response to Goliath (vv.41-47)
Notice ***(i)*** Goliath's contempt, (vv.41-44): "he disdained him: for he was but a youth." ***(ii)*** David's confidence, (vv.45-47): "this day will the Lord deliver thee into mine hand."

i) Goliath's contempt (vv.41-44). "And when the Philistine looked about, and saw David, he disdained him: for he was but a youth, and ruddy, and of a fair countenance" The repetition of David's description here, "ruddy, and of a fair countenance" (see 16.12), emphasises that there was nothing rugged or threatening about David. He looked too nice for the job! Goliath felt quite insulted. Israel obviously thought that he could be defeated by a boy! (very well, he would make short work of their representative. Listen to ***(a)*** his indignation: "Am I a dog that thou comest to me with staves" (v.43); ***(b)*** his imprecation: "And the Philistine cursed David by his gods" (v.43); ***(c)*** his intention: "Come thou to me, and I will give thy flesh unto the fowls of the air, and to the beasts of the field" (v.44).

ii) David's confidence (vv.45-47). We should carefully notice that whilst David was confident, he was not self-confident. "Thou comest to me with a sword, and with a spear, and with a shield: but I come unto thee in the name of **the Lord of hosts**, the **God of the armies of Israel**, whom thou hast defied. This day will **the Lord** deliver thee into mine hand; and I will smite thee...that all the earth may know that there is a **God** in Israel. And all this assembly shall know that **the Lord** saveth not with sword and spear: for the battle is **the Lord's**, and he will give you (plural: the entire Philistine army) into our hands." David recognised that it was "not by might, nor by power, but by my Spirit, saith the Lord of hosts" (Zech 4.6). Notice too that he gave glory to God ***before*** slaying Goliath. There was no doubt about his faith in God!

This illustrates 1 John 5.4, "Greater is he that is in you, than he that is in the world." The title, **"Lord of hosts"** *(Jehovah Tsebahoth)*, emphasises the immense resources of God. He "governs all the powers of heaven, both visible and invisible, as He rules in heaven and on earth." (Keil and Delitzsch). See Daniel 4.35, "He doeth according to his will in the army of heaven, and among the inhabitants of earth." David uses the divine title **"God"** twice here: **"God** *(Elohim)* of the armies of Israel", and "a **God** *(Elohim)* in Israel." *Elohim* is a plural word, and first occurs in Genesis 1.1. Its root *(ahlah)* means "to worship, to adore, and presents God as the one supreme object of worship, the Adorable One", Thomas Newberry. The title, **"the Lord"** *(Jehovah)*, is "a combination in marvellous perfection of the three periods of existence in one word, the future, the present, and the past", Thomas Newberry. Goliath "cursed David by ***his*** gods", but there was no comparison! No wonder David was so confident!

1 Samuel

David's reply to Goliath emphasises his deep concern for God's glory. He was not just concerned about national interests, or even about his own interests. Notice his words, "that **all the earth** may know that there is a God in Israel. And **all this assembly** shall know that the Lord saveth not with sword and spear." Not just "all this assembly", but "all the earth!" This should be our priority too. Notice the order in Matthew 6.9-13. The prayer commences with God's interests: "**thy** name...**thy** kingdom...**thy** will." It then continues with our interests: "give **us**...forgive **us**...lead **us**." We should be able to sing with deep feeling:

> Oh, the joy to see Thee reigning,
> Thee, my own beloved Lord!
> Every tongue Thy Name confessing,
> Worship, honour, glory, blessing,
> Brought to Thee with one accord;
> Thee, my Master and my Friend,
> Vindicated and enthroned,
> Unto earth's remotest end
> Glorified, adored, and owned!

E) David's victory over Goliath (vv.48-53)

In this section, we must notice **(i)** the defeat of the Philistine champion (vv.48-51a) and **(ii)** the defeat of the Philistine army (vv.51b-53). Notice that it was the Lord's victory (v.47), David's victory (vv.50-51), and Israel's victory (v.52). David certainly illustrated 1 Samuel 14.6, "for there is no restraint to the Lord to save by many or by few."

i) The defeat of the Philistine champion, (vv.48-51a).

Notice that David "hastened, and ran toward the army to meet the Philistine." Compare (v.40), "he drew near to the Philistine". He certainly couldn't have "hastened" if he had been wearing Saul's armour! David was on the attack! This reminds us that the Lord Jesus made no attempt to avoid Satan. He was "led by the Spirit into the wilderness, being forty days tempted of the devil" (Lk 4.1). When the party came to arrest Him, He said to His disciples, "Rise up, let us be going: behold, he is at hand that doth betray me" (Mt 26.46). On the cross, He destroyed "him that had the power of death, that is, the devil." The Lord Jesus took the battle to him.

The passage emphasises the unusual way in which David slew Goliath. "And David put his hand in his bag, and took thence a stone, and slang it, and smote the Philistine in his forehead, that the stone sunk into his forehead (pin-point accuracy: the only exposed part of his body); and he fell on his face to the earth (just like his god, Dagon: see 4.3-4). So David prevailed over the Philistine **with a sling and with a stone,** and smote the Philistine; but there was no sword in the hand of David." David's artillery looked totally ineffective against such a formidable foe. But it was completely successful! He returned alive from the battle! The victory of the Lord Jesus was even more amazing. He triumphed through death! See, for example, Colossians 2.14-15, "Blotting out the handwriting of ordinances that was against us, which was contrary to us, and took it of the way, nailing it to his cross; and having spoiled principalities and powers, he made a shew of them openly, triumphing over them in it (that is, in the cross, or better, by His work on the cross)." He too returned alive from the battle!

> Through weakness, like defeat,
> He won the mead and crown;
> Trod all our foes beneath His feet,
> By being trodden down.
>
> He hell in hell laid low;
> Made sin, He sin o'erthrew;
> Bowed to the grave, destroyed it so,
> And death, by dying, slew.

It is also significant that David slew Goliath **twice!** "So David prevailed over the Philistine with a sling and with a stone, and smote the Philistine, and **slew him**...David ran, and stood upon the Philistine, and took his sword, and drew it out, and **slew him**, and cut off his head therewith." The Lord Jesus destroyed (the word "destroy", Hebrews 2.14, means to annul) Satan at Calvary, and He will finally destroy him at the end of the Millennium. See Revelation 20.10.

ii) The defeat of the Philistine army (vv. 51b-53). "And when the Philistines saw that their champion was dead, they fled." These verses are quite self-explanatory, and remind us of the ultimate defeat, not only of Satan, but of his entire unseen army.

F) David's return to Saul (vv. 54-58)
"And David took the head of the Philistine, and brought it to Jerusalem; but he put his armour in his tent." We also know that Goliath's sword was

placed with the priestly garments in the tabernacle. See 1 Samuel 21.9. We can summarise this by saying that the evidence of David's victory was displayed **manward:** Goliath's head was taken to Jerusalem; **selfward**: his armour was placed in David's tent; **Godward,** his sword was placed in the tabernacle. This reminds us that the results of our Lord's victory should be seen in our public life, in our personal life, and in our priestly life. However, we also look at this in the following way:

i) The head of Goliath in Jerusalem was evidence of David's victory. The city could see that the enemy was defeated. It was proclaimed publicly. Centuries later, the same city rang with the message, "This same Jesus hath God raised up whereof we all are witnesses" (Acts 2.32). "And with great power gave the apostles witness of the resurrection of the Lord Jesus" (Acts 4.33). We have no reason to be ashamed of the gospel of Christ.

There is no anachronism in the reference to Jerusalem here. "The assertion made by some that Jerusalem was not yet in possession of the Israelites, rests upon a confusion between the citadel of Jebus upon Zion, which was still in the hands of the Jebusites, and the city of Jerusalem, in which Israelites had dwelt for a long time (see at Joshua 15.63, and Judges 1.8)." (Keil & Delitzsch).

ii) The armour of Goliath in David's tent was evidence of David's victory. Every visitor to the tent would see that armour! Every Christian home should display evidence that "Jesus Christ is Lord." Hezekiah was asked, "What have they seen in thine house?" Christian homes should be places which reflect the supremacy of Christ. Just think about it: the very same tent could have been the home of nothing more than a Philistine slave!

iii) The sword of Goliath in the Lord's presence was evidence of David's victory. This reminds us that heaven witnesses the triumph of the Lord Jesus. "This Jesus hath God raised up, whereof we all are witnesses…for David is not ascended into the heavens: but he saith himself, The Lord said unto my Lord, Sit thou on my right hand, until I make thy foes thy footstool" (Acts 2.32-36)

The chapter closes with a conversation between Saul and Abner about David before his victory; "and when Saul saw David **go forth** against the Philistine" (vv.55-57); and a conversation between Saul and David after his victory "and as David **returned** from the slaughter of the Philistine, Abner took him and brought him before Saul" (vv.57-58). In both cases, the question was the same: "whose son is this youth?" (v.55); "whose son art thou, young man?" (v.58). The ignorance of Abner and Saul reminds us of John 7.27. A.McShane suggests that since "the victor was to have the king's daughter to wife, we need not be surprised if Saul is interested in the pedigree of his future son-in-law." That sounds like a sensible suggestion! In reply, David certainly didn't make any grandiose claims for himself. He was happy to acknowledge that he was "the son of thy servant Jesse the Beth-lehemite." This is typical of David's attitude throughout the whole chapter.

There was no doubt about David's victory: "Abner brought him before Saul **with the head of the Philistine in his hand!**" The Lord Jesus has "led captivity captive."

CHAPTER 18

"Then Jonathan and David made a covenant" (18.1-30)

The life of David could be broadly summarised as follows: *(i)* The saviour of Israel, 1 Samuel 16-17; *(ii)* The servant at court, 1 Samuel 18-19; *(iii)* The sufferer in exile, 1 Samuel 20-31; *(iv)* The sovereign on the throne, 2 Samuel 1-24 & 1 Kings 1-2. David's training at court (16.14-23) now gives place to his testing at court (18.1-19: 17), but "David behaved himself wisely in all his ways" under the most intense provocation.

This chapter can be divided into five paragraphs as follows: *(1)* The covenant with Jonathan (vv.1-4; *(2)* The popularity of David (vv.5-7); *(3)* The animosity of Saul (vv.8-16); *(4)* The offer of Merab (vv.17-19); *(5)* The marriage to Michal (vv.20-30).

1. The Covenant with Jonathan (vv.1-4)
The friendship between David and Jonathan makes an excellent study in brotherly relations. Notice *(i)* Jonathan's devotion to David (18.4), *(ii)* Jonathan's delight in David (19.2); *(iii)* Jonathan's defence of David (19.4); *(iv)* Jonathan's desire to please David (20.4;1-42); *(v)* Jonathan's danger because of David (20.33); *(vi)* Jonathan's distress over David (20.34). That will do for a start!

This is the first recorded encounter between David and Jonathan. Notice *(A)* Jonathan's devotion to David, (vv.1-3), and *(B)* Jonathan's deference to David, (v.4).

A) Jonathan's devotion to David (vv. 1-3)
"And it came to pass, when he had made an end of speaking unto Saul, that the soul of Jonathan was knit with the soul of David, and Jonathan loved him as his own soul" (v.1). (In this chapter, David is loved by Jonathan (v.1); by "all Israel and Judah" (v.16); and by Michal (v.20). See also (v.22).

Chapter 18

The word translated "knit" occurs elsewhere in the Old Testament. Its meaning is beautifully illustrated in Genesis 44. 30. "his life (Jacob's life) is **bound up** with the lad's life (Benjamin's life)." That gives us a good idea of the depth of Jonathan's love for David, and we hear the Saviour's voice, "Lovest **thou** me?" Paul puts it like this: "For to me to live is Christ." In the case of Jonathan, it was "love...strong as death." In the case of Saul, it was "jealousy...cruel as the grave" (Song 8. 6). After the death of Saul and Jonathan on mount Gilboa at the hands of the Philistines, David uttered his celebrated words, "I am distressed for thee, my brother Jonathan: very pleasant hast thou been unto me: thy love to me was wonderful, passing the love of women" (2 Sam 1.26).

Jonathan loved David **(i)** because of his victory and **(ii)** because of his virtues. After all, Jonathan owed his own liberty to David. See 17. 9. He reminded his father that he too was indebted to David: "His works have been to thee-ward very good: for he did put his life in his hand, and slew the Philistine, and the Lord wrought a great salvation for all Israel: thou sawest it, and didst rejoice" (19.4-5). But Jonathan was also impressed with David's character. It was after David "had made an end of speaking unto Saul" that "the soul of Jonathan was knit with the soul of David." David won hearts as well as battles! His humility evidently impressed Jonathan. David identified himself simply as "the son of thy servant Jesse the Beth-lehemite." The chapter stresses the winsomeness of David's character. See (vv.5.14,16,30). We love the Lord Jesus for the same reasons:

> We love Thee for the glorious worth
> Which in Thyself we see;
> We love Thee for the shameful cross
> Endured so patiently.

The covenant (v.3) between David and Jonathan was mutual. They pledged loyalty and fidelity to each other. This is very clear in Chapter 20. Note (vv.8,12-17). See, particularly (v.42): "And Jonathan said to David, Go in peace, forasmuch as we have sworn **both of us** in the name of the Lord, saying, The Lord be between thee and me, and between my seed and thy seed forever." See also 23.18. If Jonathan's loyalty to David reminds us that we must be loyal to Christ, then David's loyalty to Jonathan reminds us that He will not fail us. See, for example (Jn 10.28), "I give unto them eternal life; and they shall never perish", and John 17.19. "And for their sakes I sanctify myself, that they also might be sanctified through the truth" (Jn 17.19).

We have noticed *(i) the intimacy* of Jonathan's love for David ("knit") and *(ii) the intensity* of his love for David ("as his own soul"). Now we must notice *(iii) the integrity* of his love for David. He displayed the reality of his love for him: so

B) Jonathan's deference to David (v.4)
Jonathan expressed his love for David in three ways: "And Jonathan stripped himself of *(i)* the robe that was upon him, and gave it to David, and his garment, even *(ii)* to his sword, and to his bow, and *(iii)* to his girdle", (v.4). He did this voluntarily. David did not put pressure on him. It was an act of love. The fearless fighter became a faithful friend. But it was costly for Jonathan. It cost him everything, in the same way that allegiance to Christ cost Paul everything. See Philippians 3.7-8. "But what things were gain to me, those I counted loss for Christ."

i) He surrendered "the robe" and "his garment." These were the garments of a prince! But it was more than the surrender of princely garments: Jonathan was surrendering his future prospects. Saul knew this only too well: "Thou son of the perverse rebellious woman, do not I know that thou hast chosen the son of Jesse to thine own confusion...For as long as the son of Jesse liveth upon the ground, thou shalt not be established, nor thy kingdom" (1 Sam 20.30-31). But Jonathan thought only of the exaltation and honour of David. "Thou shalt be king over Israel" (23.17). Are we prepared to give the Lord Jesus first place in our lives, and arrange our affairs "that in all things he might have the pre-eminence?"

ii) He surrendered "his sword" and "his bow." Jonathan was no mean warrior. He "smote the garrison of the Philistines that was in Geba" (1 Sam 13. 2-3), and climbed up the rock "upon his hands and his feet" to the Philistine garrison near Gibeah" (14.13). He was not lacking in initiative! But he now surrenders his initiative and military genius to David. Henceforward, David would command the armies of Israel. Only as we place ourselves under the command of the "captain of the host of the Lord" (Josh 5.14), will we be "strong in the Lord, and in the power of his might" (Eph 6.10).

iii) He surrendered "his girdle." The girdle was the emblem of service." Men "girded their loins" in order to engage in unobstructed and unimpeded service. The Lord Jesus did this: see John 13.4. Jonathan therefore gave to David the right to direct his future service. It was far more than a gesture.

"Whatsoever thy soul desireth, I will even do for thee" (1 Sam. 20.4). Are we prepared to say "Lord, what wilt thou have me to do?" (Acts 9.6), and then become "doers of the word, and not hearers only?" (Jas 1.2).

It is all summed up in Romans 12. 1-2, "I beseech you therefore, brethren, by the mercies of God, that ye present **your bodies** a living sacrifice, holy, acceptable unto God, which is your reasonable service. And be not conformed to this world: but be ye transformed by the renewing of **your mind**, that ye may prove what is that good, and acceptable, and perfect, will of God."

2. The Popularity of David (vv. 5-7)
David was popular for the best of reasons, and this reminds us that the Lord Jesus "increased in wisdom and stature, and in favour with God and man" (Lk 2.52). But, like David, it wasn't long before He incurred the wrath of the leadership. Pilate knew that "for envy they had delivered him" (Mt 27.18). We must notice **(A)** The conduct of David (v.5), and **(B)** The celebration of David (vv.6-7).

A) David's conduct (v. 5)
"And David went out (JND 'went forth' i.e. 'for warlike raids') whithersoever Saul sent him, and behaved himself wisely." We must remember that David had been anointed king, but this did not go to his head. He was willing to serve Saul. The future king of Israel evidently believed that "before honour is humility" (Prov 15.33), and waited God's time. Whilst the three references to David's wisdom in this chapter (vv.5, 14-15, 30) seem to refer particularly to his military expertise (note the context in each case), his qualities were certainly recognised in all directions: he was "over the men of war, and he was accepted in the sight of all the people, and also in the sight of Saul's servants." We can all behave wisely in favourable circumstances as (v.5), but David behaved himself wisely in unfavourable circumstances as well! See (vv.14-15, 30). When the Lord Jesus came, "the common people heard him gladly" (Mt 12.37). They said "a great prophet is risen up among us" (Lk 7.16). The "officers" sent by the chief priests and Pharisees said, "Never man spake like this man" (Jn 7.46).

B) David's celebration (vv. 6-7)
Some people see difficulties in the chronological order of these verses, but Ellicott's Commentary is probably right in saying, "The triumphant return of the young soldier does not refer to the home-coming after the death of the giant, but to the close of the campaign that followed that event." The women

sang "in alternate choruses" (Keil & Delitzsch): they "answered one another as they played." We can understand the joyful reception given to David and Saul, but it might have been better if they had chosen another song! It wasn't very diplomatic to sing, "Saul hath slain his thousands, and David his tens of thousands!" (See also 21.11). Perhaps the chorus was factual, and David **had** slain more Philistines than Saul, but it isn't always wise to make comparisons in public! Hero-worship can be dangerous in other ways. In this case, the Lord was completely excluded. He isn't even mentioned by the singers! Compare the song of the women in Exodus 15.20-21. Popularity can be dangerous, but David remained unaffected. Notice how the Lord Jesus handled popularity. See Mark 1.37-38 and John 6.15.

3. The Animosity of Saul (vv.8-16)
"And Saul was very wroth, and the saying displeased him; and he said, They have ascribed unto David ten thousands, and to me they have ascribed but thousands: and what can he have more but the kingdom? And Saul eyed David from that day and forward." Saul certainly hadn't learnt the New Testament lessons: "in lowliness of mind let each esteem other better than themselves" (Phil 2.3); "in honour preferring one another" (Rom 12.10). There can be little doubt that Saul realised that David was the "neighbour of thine, that is better than thou" (15.28). Solomon put it like this. "Jealousy is cruel as the grave: the coals thereof are coals of fire, which hath a most vehement flame" (Song 8.6).

Saul's anger was vented in two murderous attempts on David's life. Once again, there is a striking parallel between David's experience, and the experience of the Lord Jesus. Both were subject to bitter hatred.

i) Saul "eyed David from that day forward", and "the scribes and Pharisees watched" the Lord Jesus (Lk 6.7). "They watched him" (Lk 14.1). "They watched him, and sent forth spies" (Lk 20.20).

ii) Saul was under the control of the "evil spirit from God" (see our comments on 16.14-15) when he attempted to kill David. The men who plotted the death of the Lord Jesus were also under Satan's power: see John 8. 40-44, "But now ye seek to kill me…Ye are of your father the devil, and the lusts of your father ye will do. He was a murderer from the beginning."

Notice the reference to Saul "prophesying." Scholars have noted that the conjugation employed in the original Hebrew (the *Hithpael*) is never used by an Old Testament writer of true prophecy, which is always expressed by the *Niphal* conjugation. The pronouncements of Saul were not engendered by the Holy Spirit, but by the evil spirit.

iii) Saul said, "I will smite David even to the wall with it (his javelin)", and the "Pharisees went out, and held a council against him, how they might destroy him", (Mt 12.14). See also Luke 19.47 etc.

It has been said that "a man with envy in his heart will soon have a javelin in his hand." The javelin may take the form of a poisoned word, a slanderous remark, or a defamatory report. No wonder Paul writes, "Let no corrupt communication proceed out of your mouth, but that which is good to the use of edifying, that it may minister grace unto the hearers" (Eph 4. 29).

iv) Saul failed on two occasions to kill David. David "avoided out of his presence twice", and the Lord Jesus "passing through the midst of them went his way" (Lk 4.29-30). See also John 8.59; 10.39.

v) Saul "was afraid of David because the Lord was with him" (see also v.14 and v.28), and, centuries later, we catch the desperation in the voices of the Jewish counsel, "What do we? For this man doeth many miracles. If we let him alone, all men will believe on him: and the Romans will come and take away both our place and nation", (Jn 11. 47-48). See also 12.19. The Lord Jesus was "Approved of God...by miracles and wonders and signs which God did by him in the midst of you, as ye yourselves also know" (Acts 2.22). As A.McShane observes, "it is strange that, in such circumstances, it was Saul, not David who was afraid."

In all this, plus his removal from court (v.13: Saul deprived himself of the only man able to soothe and help him), David "behaved himself wisely in all his ways; and the Lord was with him." It reminds us of Joseph (see Genesis 39. 2, 21): both men were in adverse circumstances, but both enjoyed the Lord's presence, and both acted wisely. It's worth noticing that David did not retaliate, and he didn't quit his post. This only intensified Saul's fear (see also (v.29), but "all Israel and Judah loved David, because he went out and came in before them." The expression "went out and came in before them" is explained in 2 Samuel 5.2, "when Saul was king over us, thou wast he that leddest out and broughtest in Israel." This combines the pictures of shepherd and military commander, and the tribesmen therefore continued:

1 Samuel

"And the Lord said unto thee, Thou shalt feed my people Israel, and thou shalt be a captain over Israel."

The Lord Jesus "behaved himself wisely" in the face of the severest provocation. "Who, when he was reviled, reviled not again; when he suffered he threatened not; but committed himself to him that judgeth righteously" (1 Pet 2.23).

Having failed to kill David with his javelin, Saul then turned to other means. Keil & Delitzsch sum it up by entitling (v.17-30), "The craftiness of Saul in the betrothal of his daughters to David." This brings us to:

4. The Offer of Merab (vv.17-19)
"And Saul said to David, Behold my elder daughter Merab, her will I give thee to wife: only be thou valiant for me, and fight the Lord's battles. For Saul said, Let not mine hand be upon him, but let the hand of the Philistines be upon him." It has been pointed out that whilst Saul had been under the influence of "the evil spirit from God" when he threw the javelin at David, now he is plotting in cold blood. There was nothing genuine in Saul's offer to David. But we must notice David's genuine humility, "Who am I? And what is my life, or my father's family in Israel, that I should be son in law to the king?" As A.McShane observes, David "could have justly claimed the offered bride as his right (see 17.25), and have bluntly told Saul that apart from him he would have had no daughters to offer to anyone. But no man who is always fighting for his rights is fit for leadership."

We are not told how David reacted when Merab was "given unto Adriel the Meholathite to wife." (We know from 2 Samuel 21.8-9 that Merab and Adriel had five sons, and that all five were hanged by the Gibeonites "in the hill before the Lord"). We are not told, either, what made Saul change his mind. We can conjecture! It has been suggested that this happened, at least in part, because Merab had no love for David. This could be inferred from a comparison of (vv.17-18 with v.20). We do know, however, that Saul was not a man of his word. We should be people who mean what we say, and say what we mean. Read 2 Corinthians 1:13-20.

5. The Marriage to Michal (vv.20-30)
"And Michal Saul's daughter loved David: and they told Saul, and the thing pleased him." But it was not a case of a proud father giving away his daughter! Read on: "And Saul said, I will give him her, that she may be a

snare to him, and that the hand of the Philistines may be against him. Wherefore Saul said to David, Thou shalt this day be my son in law in the one of the twain (JND 'a second time')." Sadly, David himself did exactly the same to Uriah the Hittite. See 2 Samuel 11.

Negotiations were conducted through Saul's servants. If Saul maintained his subtlety "Behold, the king hath delight in thee, and all his servants love thee", then David maintained his humility: "Seemeth it to you a light thing to be a king's son in law, seeing that I am a poor man, and lightly esteemed?" The words "lightly esteemed" mean "humble." If Saul thought that he could make "David fall by the hand of the Philistines" (v.25), he was mistaken. David delivered twice the price demanded (vv.25 & 27) by the appointed time (v.26), and Saul was obliged to give David "his daughter to wife" (v.27). David's continuing success only served to increase Saul's conviction that "the Lord was with him", and now his own daughter loved David. It all served to increase his fear, and "Saul became David's enemy continually" (vv.28-29).

Neither David or Michal knew that their domestic life held many sorrows in store for them. In the place of "first love" (v.28), Michal ultimately "despised him in her heart" and publicly rebuked him (2 Sam 6.16 & 20). It is a sad story. Read, in addition to the above, 1 Samuel 19. 8-17, 25. 44, 2 Samuel 3.14-16. She ended up caring for her sister's children (2 Sam 21. 8-9), and saw them all hanged. Dreadful!

We must notice David's progress in the chapter. He "behaved himself wisely" (v.5), he "behaved himself wisely in all his ways" (v.14), he "behaved himself very wisely" (v.15), and he "behaved himself more wisely" (v.30). This reminds us of Samuel's steady progress in Chapters 2 & 3. It also reminds us of the need to "grow in grace, and in the knowledge of our Lord and Saviour Jesus Christ (2 Pet 3.18). We must notice, however, that Saul's opposition increased as well. See (vv.8-9,17, 21 and .29, where he "became David's enemy continually." We have already noticed that the references to David's wise conduct are related to his military expertise. So: "And the princes of the Philistines went forth (i.e. to battle, as in (v.5), and it came to pass, whenever they went forth, that David succeeded better than all the servants of Saul; and his name was much esteemed" v.30 ("set by", AV, JND). David excelled in warfare. How are we progressing in "the good fight of faith?" (1 Tim 6.12).

1 Samuel

The words "set by" mean "precious" and the Hebrew word *(yaqar)* is usually translated in that way. So David's name was precious! Just like the name of the Lord Jesus. See 1 Peter 2.4-7. Is **He** really precious to us?

CHAPTER 19

"So David fled" (19.1-24)

In Genesis 49, Jacob summoned his sons for the last time. "Gather yourselves together, that I may tell you that which shall befall you in the last days." We could call his last words "the prophecy of Jacob", and it is most interesting to read what he said about Benjamin. "Benjamin shall ravin as a wolf: in the morning he shall devour the prey, and at night he shall devour the spoil" (v.27). Saul the son of Kish was a true Benjamite. David certainly proved this: notice what he said in 1 Samuel 26.20. Saul of Tarsus was a true Benjamite as well. See Acts 26.9-11. He persecuted Christians "even unto strange cities." Both "ravined as a wolf."

In this chapter, Saul begins his relentless persecution of David. It lasted for something like seven years. (BC 1063-1056 according to C.I.Scofield). "David fled" (v.10); "And he went, and fled" (v.12); "So David fled" (v.18); "And David fled" (20.1); "And David arose, and fled" (21.10). But he ultimately ascended the throne. One day God's King, at present "despised and rejected of men", will sit "upon the throne of his father David, to order it, and to establish it with judgment and with justice, from henceforth even for ever" (Is 9.7).

There are five paragraphs in this chapter. *(1)* Saul's antagonism (vv.1-3); *(2)* Jonathan's advocacy (vv.4-7); *(3)* David's alertness (vv.8-10); *(4)* Michal's advice (vv.11-17); *(5)* God's aegis (protection) (vv.18-24).

1. Saul's Antagonism (vv.1-3)
"And Saul spake to Jonathan his son, and to all his servants, that they should **kill David.**" Saul's hatred punctuates the chapter. See vv.1, 10-11, 16, 20 etc. We must notice **(A)** Saul's designs on David (v.1), and **(B)** Jonathan's delight in David (vv.2-3).

A) Saul's designs on David (v.1)

Notice the connection between 18.30 and 19.1. "David behaved himself more wisely than all the servants of Saul; so that his name was much set by. And Saul spake to Jonathan his son, and to all his servants that they should kill David." Compare Mark 15.10, "For he (Pilate) knew that the chief priests had delivered him for envy." It all goes back to 1 Samuel 18.6-9.

Saul's attempt to eliminate David is a picture of a future worldwide attempt, spearheaded by its rulers, to eliminate "great David's greater Son." For two thousand years the world has cried, "We will not have this man to reign over us" (Lk 19.14), and its hostility will increase until, at the end-time, the world will unite against Him. See Psalm 2.2, "The kings of the earth set themselves, and the rulers take counsel together, against the Lord, and against his anointed." Saul hated David "without a cause" (v.5) and the world hates Christ "without a cause" as well. See John 15.25. We must not therefore be surprised if **we** experience the hatred of the world. See John 15.18-21.

Although rejected by the world, the Lord Jesus found great joy in His disciples. "They...have known surely that I came out from thee, and they have believed that thou didst send me" (Jn 17.8). David must have found great joy in the devotion of Jonathan, who recognised that he was God's anointed king. So:

B) Jonathan's delight in David (vv.2-3)

"But Jonathan Saul's son delighted much in David." In fact, "Jonathan loved him as his own soul"; see 18.1 and 20.17. The strength of Jonathan's feelings for David is stressed by the words "delighted **much** in David." One man rejected David, but the other man delighted in him! Sadly, Saul did not mean what he said when he "commanded his servants, saying, Commune with David secretly, and say, Behold the king hath delight in thee" (18.22). The unreality of Saul contrasts vividly with the reality of Jonathan!

It was David who wrote, "Delight thyself also in the Lord; and he shall give thee the desires of thine heart" (Ps 37.4). Do **we** "delight" ourselves "in the Lord?" God delights in Him. See Isaiah 42.1. Can **we** say, "I sat down under his shadow with **great delight,** and his fruit was sweet to my taste?" (Song 2.3). We can either take "delight" in ourselves and in our own interests, or in Him and in His interests. This is spelt out in Isaiah 58.13-14, "If thou turn away thy foot from the sabbath, from doing **thy** pleasure on my holy day...not doing **thine** own ways, nor finding **thine** own pleasure, nor speaking

***thine* own words: then shalt thou delight thyself *in the Lord.*"** It's worth noticing that Jonathan delighted in David personally. He loved David for what he was, as well as for what he had done. His advice to David should stand us all in good stead when we are under pressure: "Take heed to thyself until the morning, and abide in a secret place, and hide thyself" (v.2). See Matthew 6.6.

Jonathan proved his delight in David, by representing him before Saul, and this follows:

2. Jonathan's Advocacy (vv.4-7)
In verses 1-3, Jonathan spoke *to* David. That was communion. In verses 4-5, Jonathan spoke *of* David. That was communication. The man who "delighted much in David" was not ashamed to speak about him! Quite obviously, Jonathan would have found it very irksome to represent David if he didn't love him. But his "delight" in David enabled him to overcome reticence and fear in view of Saul's hostility. The Lord's work has never been easy, but our love for Christ is a compelling motive for faithful service. Simon Peter was told, "Feed my lambs…Feed my sheep"…Feed my sheep", but each command was preceded by the question, "Simon, son of Jonas, lovest thou me?" (Jn 21.15-17). It was not a question of "loving the work", or "loving the sheep", but love for Christ. Jonathan's witness before Saul is an excellent model for us.

i) **He emphasised the purity of David.** "Let not the king sin against his servant, against David; because he hath not sinned against thee, and because his works have been to thee-ward very good." When the mob demanded the death of the Lord Jesus, Pilate cried, "Why, what evil hath he done?" The Saviour "went about doing good, and healing all that were oppressed of the devil" (Acts 10.38). He was, indeed, the "lamb without blemish and without spot." Everything about Him is "very good!"

ii) **He emphasised the victory of David.** "He did put his life in his hand, and slew the Philistine, and the Lord wrought great salvation for all Israel: thou sawest it, and didst rejoice." Jonathan stressed the willingness of David to engage Goliath. He did this voluntarily. "He did put his life in his hand." David put his life at risk. Through him, "the Lord wrought great salvation." All Israel benefited from his victory. His triumph could not be denied: "thou sawest it, and didst rejoice." This reminds us of the victory of the Lord Jesus. He "gave himself" willingly. He accomplished "so great salvation"

(Heb 2.3). Through His death, salvation is available to all men. The facts of His death and resurrection are well-attested. In the words of Paul before Agrippa, "This thing was not done in a corner" (Acts 26.26).

iii) He emphasised the sin of rejecting David. "Wherefore then wilt thou sin against innocent blood, to slay David without a cause? Notice the striking parallel in Matthew 27.4, "I have sinned in that I have betrayed the innocent blood." Jonathan challenged Saul, in the same way that the early gospel preachers challenged their hearers. See, for example, Acts 3.14-19, "But ye denied the Holy One and the Just, and desired a murderer to be granted unto you; and killed the Prince of life...Repent ye therefore, and be converted, that your sins may be blotted out..."

Jonathan's advocacy gained temporary respite for David: "And Saul hearkened unto the voice of Jonathan: and Saul sware, As the Lord liveth, he shall not be slain. And Jonathan called David, and Jonathan shewed him all those things. And Jonathan brought David to Saul, and he was in his presence, as in times past." It all looked promising, but, sadly, it didn't last. How often this happens!

3. David's Alertness (vv.8-10)
It is rather significant that David's further victory over the Philistines (v.8) was immediately followed by a further attempt on his life (vv.9-10). No doubt Saul was filled with insane jealousy at David's triumph. Compare 18.6-8. The fact that the "evil spirit from the Lord *(Ruach Jehovah;* it is *Ruach Elohim* in 18.10; see also 16.14-15) was upon Saul" at the time, does not mean that the Lord initiated the murderous intentions of Saul! He had rejected "the word of the Lord", and the Lord had rejected him. (See 15.26). In consequence, the man who once enjoyed divine power, was now deliberately exposed to Satan's power. While God was therefore in complete control of the situation, it does illustrate Satan's avowed intention to oppose His will. If you are winning spiritual victories, don't be surprised if you find yourself under attack. Paul wrote, "I will tarry at Ephesus until Pentecost. For a great door and effectual is opened unto me, and there are many adversaries" (1 Cor 16.8-9). David was certainly at risk as he endeavoured to bring peace of mind to Saul, and we are equally at risk as we preach "peace by Jesus Christ" (Acts 10.36).

David was saved from death three times in this chapter. He was saved from death at court (v.10), at home (v.12), and at school (vv.20-24). Here, he was saved because he was alert. David knew by experience that he was in danger. See 18.10-11. Whilst David played the harp with "his hand", Saul played with the javelin in "his hand" (v.9). But David was not "ignorant of his devices!" He wasn't so absorbed in his music that he forgot to keep one eye on Saul! His alertness enabled him to "slip away out of Saul's presence, and he smote the javelin into the wall." Notice how Phinehas used his javelin-Numbers 25.7-8.

We too need to be watchful and vigilant. See, for example (1 Pet 5.8), "Be sober, be vigilant; because your adversary the devil, as a roaring lion, walketh about, seeking whom he may devour." Watchfulness is the order of the day. See Acts 20.31, "Therefore **watch** and remember." The elders from Ephesus were to "watch" in view of the "grievous wolves" and "men...speaking perverse things." See 1 Thessalonians 5.6, "Let us **watch** and be sober", in view of the Lord's coming. See Revelation 3.2, "Be **watchful,** and strengthen the things that remain." The Lord Jesus urged His disciples to "watch and pray" (Mt 26.41). Whilst David evidently anticipated Saul's attempt to murder him, trouble sometimes comes from the most unexpected places and unexpected people. David's own wife let him down. See verse 17.

So "David fled, and escaped that night" (v.10). This is the first of four references to David escaping. See also (vv.12,17,18). This attack took place at night, and the next night wasn't any better! This brings us to

4. Michal's Advice (vv.11-17)
Notice three things here: *(A)* She advised David to escape (v.11); *(B)* She helped him to escape (vv.12-16); *(C)* She misrepresented him after his escape (v.17).

A) She advised him to escape (v.11)
"Saul also sent messengers unto David's house, to watch him, and to slay him in the morning: and Michal David's wife told him, saying, If thou save not thy life tonight, tomorrow thou shalt be slain." It was certainly a case of, "Boast not thyself of tomorrow; for thou knowest not what a day may bring forth." Centuries before, Lot was told, "Escape thou for thy life; look not behind thee, neither stay thou in all the plain; escape to the mountain, lest thou be consumed" (Gen 19.17). David describes his danger at this time in Psalm 59. Just read the title!

On this occasion, David was saved because he took advice, reminding us of the oft-quoted text, "How shall we escape if we neglect so great salvation?" We must warn people to "flee from the wrath to come." But the Scriptures advise **us** to flee from certain things. We are to "flee fornication" (1 Cor 6.18); "flee from idolatry" (1 Cor 10.14); "flee also youthful lusts" (2 Tim 2.22).

B) She helped him to escape (vv.12-16)
"So Michal let David down through a window: and he went, and fled, and escaped." Michal provided the means of escape, and we must do the same. We assist unsaved people to escape from death by telling them about the gospel, and we assist God's people to escape spiritual and moral danger by Bible teaching and exhortation. It was a rather humiliating exit for David. After all, he was the king's son-in-law, but more than that, he was the coming king! But then, we do have to humble ourselves to be saved, don't we? David wasn't the first man to escape through a window. See Joshua 2.15. He wasn't the last man either! See 2 Corinthians 11.32-33.

Michal put the image *(teraphim)* in the bed to make sure that David was well on his way before his escape was detected. The ruse certainly worked, but as As A.McShane observes, we might well ask, "Why was an image in the home of David?" Keil & Delizsch suggest that the figure in the bed was "in all probability an image of the household gods of the size of life, and, judging from what follows, in human form." They continue, "Michal probably kept *teraphim* in secret, like Rachel, because of her barrenness." (Gen 31.19). Perhaps we had better leave it there! Just look at Saul's bitter hatred. "Bring him up to me in the bed, that I may slay him."

C) She misrepresented him after his escape (v.17)
"And Saul said unto Michal, Why hast thou deceived me so, and sent away mine enemy, that he is escaped? And Michal answered Saul, He said unto me, Let me go; why should I kill thee?" It is regrettable that Michal should misrepresent David in this way. Let's be careful that **we** don't create a false impression about other people. We can contrast Michal with Jonathan. "How different her heart is from Jonathan's who openly, at his own risk and peril, took up the defence of the one whom he tenderly loved" (H.L.Rossier).

5. God's Aegis (vv.18-24)
Notice here **(A)** David's presence with Samuel (vv.18-19); **(B)** David's pursuit by Saul (vv.20-24); **(C)** David's protection by God, (also vv.20-24) i.e. the same verses as the preceding section!.

A) David's presence with Samuel (vv.18-19)

"So David fled, and escaped, and came to Samuel to Ramah, and told him all that Saul had done to him. And he and Samuel went and dwelt in Naioth." There are important lessons for us here. In his perplexity and distress:

i) David went to Samuel. He went to the right man! Samuel was a man in touch with God. He was a priestly man. He was a spiritual man. When you are in difficulty and under pressure, don't seek the company, sympathy and help of worldly people. After their grilling by the Jewish leaders, the apostles "went to **their own company**, and reported all that the chief priests and elders had said unto them" (Acts 4.23).

This reminds us that in our problems and difficulties, we can come to another Priest. The Lord Jesus is "touched with the feeling of our infirmities." (Heb 4.5). The disciples of John the Baptist buried him, and "went and told Jesus" (Mt 14.12).

ii) David spoke to Samuel. He "told him all that Saul had done to him." It is always helpful to share our concerns with other believers. This secures prayerful support. Whilst it is neither wise nor necessary to reveal all our secrets, some Christians do seem to rob themselves of prayerful fellowship by being deliberately secretive about everything!

We must, of course, lift this to a higher level, and remind ourselves that we can always speak freely to God. "Let us therefore come boldly unto the throne of grace, that we may obtain mercy, and find grace to help in time of need" (Heb 4.16). The word "boldly" denotes "primarily, freedom of speech, unreservedness of utterance", (W.E.Vine). We can tell Him everything!

iii) David dwelt with Samuel. "And he and Samuel went and dwelt in Naioth." So it was not a brief visit. There was ongoing fellowship with Samuel. Some Christians appear to specialise in brief visits! It's a far cry from the time when "all that believed were together!" (Acts 2.44). Notice where David and Samuel lived. They "went and dwelt in Naioth." It was here that Samuel presided over a school! See verse 20. So David lived in a place where the word of God was heard. Let's therefore remember that Christian fellowship does not consist of cups of tea and a good chinwag, but in spiritual activities! The word of God will strengthen us when we are under pressure.

The so-called "the schools of the prophets" are mentioned again in the days of Elijah and Elisha. The "scholars" are called "the sons of the prophets." See 1 Kings 20.35. They lived in considerable numbers at Gilgal, Bethel and Jericho. See 2 Kings 2.3, 5, 7, 15; 4.3. They evidently lived together. According to Keil & Delizsch, Naioth comes from a word signifying "dwellings." The "sons of the prophets" evidently lived with Elisha in 2 Kings 6.1. They certainly ate with him in 2 Kings 4.38. Bearing in mind the low spiritual state of the entire nation in the days of Samuel, and of the northern kingdom in the days of Elijah and Elisha it does seem that these three prophets established "schools" to ensure the propagation of the word of God.

B) David's pursuit by Saul (vv.20-24)
"And it was told Saul, saying, Behold, David is at Naioth in Ramah. And Saul sent messengers to take David...he sent other messengers...Saul sent messengers again the third time...then went he also to Ramah...and he went thither to Naioth in Ramah."

Saul was determined to get David. "Jealousy is cruel as the grave: the coals thereof are coals of fire, which hath a most vehement flame" (Song 8.6). It all reminds us of another bitter enemy who never gives up. His avowed intention is to "take us out of the equation.'" This can involve relentless persecution, but it can also involve subtlety. "The roaring lion" can just as easily become "an angel of light." We should expect Satan to act like that, but sometimes, alas, Christians can persist in their antagonism towards fellow-believers. David was more at risk from Saul than he was from Goliath! Beware of a carnal Christian! But God was on David's side! So...

C) David's protection by God (vv.20-24)
The "evil spirit from the Lord was upon Saul" in verse 9, and "the Spirit of God was upon him" in verse 23. That seems strange! We must remember, of course, that the Spirit of God did not rest on either Saul or his servants in blessing, but to restrain them by controlling their minds. Compare Balaam. In the words of John Calvin, God "holds the hearts of men in His hand and power, and turns and moves them according to His will." Scholars tell us that the Hebrew and Greek words rendered "naked" do not always signify complete nudity, but also apply to a person "with his upper garment off" (Keil & Delizsch, and W.E.Vine).

We should notice that Saul did not learn from the experience of his messengers. He refused to accept that God was protecting David, and persisted in his bitter campaign against him. It is tragic if we do not learn from our own experiences, and from the experiences of others. The proverb, "Is Saul also among the prophets?" (see also 10.12), is an expression of astonishment.

Let's remember that the Holy Spirit **indwells** every Christian. The Lord Jesus said, "He dwelleth with you, and shall be in you" (Jn 14.17).

CHAPTER 20

"Jonathan...loved him as he loved his own soul" (Ch 20.1-42)

This chapter marks the parting of the ways for David and Jonathan. It ends as follows: "And Jonathan said to David, Go in peace, forasmuch as we have sworn both of us in the name of the Lord, saying, The Lord be between me and thee, and between my seed and thy seed for ever. And he arose and departed: and Jonathan went into the city" (v.42). They did meet once more. See 23.16-18. But David was now an exile. He was no longer welcome at court under any circumstances.

This is a long chapter, but as it contains a large amount of narrative, we will attempt to cover it at one sitting! It can be analysed as follows: **(1)** David's perplexity before Jonathan (vv.1-3); **(2)** David's proposal to Jonathan (vv.4-10); **(3)** David's promise to Jonathan (vv.11-13); **(4)** David's promotion by Jonathan (vv.24-34); **(5)** David's parting from Jonathan (vv.35-42).

1. David's Perplexity before Jonathan (vv.1-3)
We should notice **(A)** David's resentment (v.1); **(B)** Jonathan's reassurance (v.2) **(C)** David's reservation (v.3).

A) *David's resentment, (v.1)*
David is on the run again. Although he had enjoyed divine protection at Naioth, the presence of Saul obviously made it unsafe for him to stay there. "And David fled from Naioth in Ramah, and came and said before Jonathan, What have I done? What is mine iniquity? And what is my sin before thy father, that he seeketh my life?" David protested his innocence. It has been pointed out that his words here "are found in substance in not a few of his Psalms, where, in touching language, he maintains how bitterly the world had wronged and persecuted a righteous, innocent man." (Ellicott's Commentary). See, for example, Psalms 7 & 17. Jeremiah protested in the same way. See 15.10.

David's experience reminds us that although the Lord Jesus was "a man approved of God", He was "taken, and by wicked hands...crucified and slain" (Acts 2.22-23). When the crowd demanded the crucifixion of the Lord Jesus, Pilate said "Why, what evil hath he done?" (Lk 23.22). They "hated Him without a cause" (Jn 15.25). Centuries before, Cain slew his brother, simply because "his own works were evil, and his brother's righteous" (1 Jn 3.12).

The message is clear: "All that will live godly in Christ Jesus shall suffer persecution" (2 Tim 3.12). Now read 1 Peter 3.13-17. Godly people suffer because they are godly people, leading John to say, "Marvel not, my brethren, if the world hate you." We must ensure, of course, that we "give none occasion to the adversary to speak reproachfully" (1 Tim 5.14).

David's reaction to Saul's hostility also reminds us of the need for self-restraint when we are provoked. In the circumstances, David was very restrained! He can be forgiven for asking, "Why?" But pressure can bring loss of self-control, and push us into saying and doing things which we later regret. The Lord Jesus "answered never a word" (Mt 27.14). "When he was reviled, reviled not again; when he suffered, he threatened not; but committed himself to him that judgeth righteously" (1 Pet 2.23).

(B) Jonathan's reassurance (v.2)
Bearing in mind that Jonathan was well aware of his father's desire to kill David (see, for example, 19.2-5: note the words "Saul my father seeketh to kill thee"), his reply can hardly mean that Saul "had not uttered a single word to him about his deadly hatred, or his intention of killing David." (Keil & Delitzsch). Jonathan's reply assured David that he had a friend at court who would ensure his safety! "God forbid: thou shalt not die: behold my father will do nothing, either great or small, but that he will shew it me: and why should my father hide this thing from me? It is not so." However, David was not convinced that Saul would reveal his intentions to Jonathan.

C) David's reservation (v.3)
"Thy father certainly knoweth that I have found grace in thine eyes; and he saith, Let not Jonathan know this, lest he be grieved; but truly, as the Lord liveth, and as thy soul liveth, there is but a step between me and death." The words, "there is but a step between me and death", emphasise the brevity and uncertainty of life. What a solemn warning to unsaved men and women! What a solemn challenge to **us!**

1 Samuel

> Only one life, 'twill soon be past,
> Only what's done for Christ will last.

In view of his precarious position, David decides to put Saul's intentions towards him beyond any further doubt.

2. David's Proposal to Jonathan (vv.4-10)

Jonathan's desire to help David is beautifully expressed: "Whatsoever thy soul desireth, I will even do it for thee." There were no reservations! The man who had symbolically surrendered his right to the throne in 18.4, now proves the reality of his devotion to David. This reminds us that the Lord Jesus prayed, "O my Father, if it be possible, let this cup pass from me! Nevertheless, not as I will, but as thou wilt" (Mt 26.39).

Can **we** say this to the Lord Jesus, "Whatsoever thy soul desireth, I will even do it for thee?" The words, "Not so, Lord" (Acts 10.14) are a contradiction in terms. However, we ought to add a rider here. Jonathan's unqualified promise landed him in a web of deceit. See (vv.5-6 & 28-29). Unqualified devotion to Christ will never lead **us** into wrong paths!

Notice here **(A)** David's proposition (vv.5-7); **(B)** Jonathan's probity (vv.8-9); **(C)** David's problem (v.10).

A) David's proposition (vv.5-7)

The details are self-explanatory (vv.5-6), and the purpose is clear: "If he say thus, It is well; thy servant shall have peace: but if he be very wroth, then be sure that evil is determined by him (v.7)". We know that the "new moons", or "beginnings of your months", were to be marked by sacrifice (see Numbers 28.11-15), but it was evidently the practice to hold some kind of civil festival as well. It was also evidently the practice for families to hold an annual sacrifice. Compare 1 Samuel 1.3. Strictly speaking, these should be held at the tabernacle (see Deuteronomy 12), but "at this time, when the central sanctuary had fallen into disuse, they were held in different places, wherever there were altars to Jehovah as, for example, at Bethlehem. See 16.2." (Keil & Delitzsch). The same commentators add, "We see from these words that David did not look upon prevarication as sin." In the words of a British politician, he was "economical with the truth." We should **not** follow David's example. "Wherefore putting away lying, let every man speak truth with his neighbour" (Eph 4.25).

B) Jonathan's probity (vv.8-9)
David appeals to Jonathan on the basis of their covenant (18.3). He expects Jonathan to be "straight up and down." If he was guilty and had rightly incurred Saul's wrath, then let Jonathan slay him, but no trickery! David did not want Jonathan to get him back to court by creating the false impression that all was well. There is a note of indignation in Jonathan's reply: "Far be it from thee: for if I knew certainly that evil were determined by my father to come upon thee, then would I not tell thee?"

This serves to remind us of our obligations to each other as Christians. See, for example (Col 3.9-14). "Lie not one to another, seeing that ye have put off the old man with his deeds; and have put on the new man which is renewed in knowledge after the image of him that created him...Put on therefore, as the elect of God, holy and beloved, bowels of mercies, kindness, humbleness of mind, meekness, longsuffering; forbearing one another, and forgiving one another, if any man have a quarrel against any: even as Christ forgave you, so also do ye."

C) David's problem (v.10)
A practical problem! How was he going to find out about Saul's reaction? "Who shall tell me? Or what if thy father shall answer thee roughly?" Jonathan has the answer (vv.18-23), but before he gives the details, he solemnly promises to act with complete integrity. Perhaps this reflects his indignation in (v.10). In turn, he seeks the assurance of David that he will deal kindly with him. This brings us to:

3. David's Promise to Jonathan (vv.11-23)
We can summarise this section as follows: **(A)** The promise made by Jonathan (vv.12-13); **(B)** The promise made by David (vv.14-17); **(C)** The problem solved by Jonathan (vv.18-23).

It is worth noticing that whilst the conversation between David and Jonathan was in private, Jonathan was aware that God was listening! See v.12. While not all conversations are suitable for public consumption, we must never forget that the ear of God is not "heavy, that it cannot hear" (Is 59.1).

A) The promise made by Jonathan (vv.12-13)
We can take the text exactly as it stands. "O Lord God of Israel, when I have sounded my father about tomorrow any time, or the third day, and, behold, if there be good toward David, and I then send not unto thee, and shew it

thee; the Lord do so, and much more to Jonathan: but if it please my father to do thee evil, then will I shew it thee, and send thee away, that thou mayest go in peace: and the Lord be with thee, as he hath been with my father." The opening words, "O Lord God of Israel", do not need amendment, as some suggest! ("The Lord of Israel *is my witness*"). Jonathan appeals **directly** to God as he makes his promise to David. Is there a touch of sadness in his voice as he says, "and the Lord be with thee, as he **hath been** with my father?" See 16.14. Compare Joshua 1.5, "As I was with Moses, so I **will be** with thee." It would be a terrible tragedy if all **we** can do is to look back to past experiences of the presence of God. This haunted Saul to the day of his death. At the end of his life he lamented, "God is departed from me" (1 Sam 28.15). It is more likely, however, that Jonathan is expressing here his expectation that David would one day replace Saul on the throne.

B) The promise made by David (vv.14-17)
The terms of David's oath to Jonathan are set out in (vv.14-15). "And thou shalt not only while I yet live, shew me the kindness of the Lord, that I die not; but also thou shalt not cut off thy kindness from my house for ever; no, not when the Lord hath cut off the enemies of David every one from the face of the earth." So the covenant required kindness on the part of David towards Jonathan personally, and to Jonathan's family. When David's enemies were "cut off", he was not to "cut off" his kindness to Jonathan's family. Once again, Jonathan anticipated that David would triumph over all his enemies. The Lord would "cut off the enemies of David every one from the face of the earth."

Do notice Jonathan's concern, not only for himself, but for future generations. J.Hay (writing in the Believer's Magazine) comments: "Never be like Hezekiah. When warned of danger for a coming generation, he seemed complacent, content that he would never see it himself!" "Is it not good, if peace and truth be in my days?" (2 Kings 20.19). Remember, we do have an obligation to the next generation.

The words at the end of v.16, "Let the Lord require it at the hand of David's enemies", are usually regarded as the comment of the man who wrote 1 Samuel. Hence the rendering, "And Jehovah required it (what Jonathan had predicted) at the hand of David's enemies." Notice that the word "saying" is italicised. However, it makes good sense to attribute the words to Jonathan himself.

But why was Jonathan so willing to acknowledge David in this way? After all, he was the crown prince! Why surrender his right to David? Saul was bitterly angry about this: "Thou son of the perverse rebellious woman, do not I know that thou hast chosen the son of Jesse to thine own confusion" (v.30). The answer is clear: Jonathan loved David! He "loved him as he loved his own soul." See 18.1,3. Jonathan wanted the reassurance of the man whom he loved. "And Jonathan caused David to swear again, because he loved him." Why do we forego our own interests and rights in favour of Christ? For the same reason. We love Him!

We are happy to report that David was a man of his word. His enemies were "cut off...from the face of the earth" in 2 Samuel 8 (read it), and in 2 Samuel 9, David said, "Is there yet any that is left of the house of Saul, that I may shew him kindness for Jonathan's sake?...And Ziba said unto the king, Jonathan hath yet a son, which is lame on his feet." It is worth pointing out that David went further than just preserving Jonathan's son. He decreed that Mephibosheh should eat at his table "as one of the king's sons." David's grace and generosity exceeded the bounds of duty!

Once again, this reminds us of the Lord Jesus. The dying thief cried, "Lord, remember me when thou comest into (in) thy kingdom", but the answer far exceeded his request, **"Today** shalt thou be with me in paradise."

C) The problem solved by Jonathan (vv.18-23)
David had said, "Who shall tell me? Or what if thy father answer thee roughly?" (v.10). Here is Jonathan's answer! The narrative here is perfectly clear. No comment needed! J.Hay notes that "the contrast has often been drawn between what Jonathan called an empty seat (v.18) and an empty *place.*" He continues, "At the end of life will we leave only an empty seat, or a real gap in the ranks?" Challenging, isn't it? Notice too that David's empty seat meant loss of fellowship for Jonathan. Need we say more?!

4) David's Promotion by Jonathan (vv.24-34)
In this paragraph, we should notice **(A)** Saul's anxiety and David's absence (vv.25-29), and **(B)** Saul's anger and Jonathan's answer (vv.30-34).

A) Saul's anxiety and David's absence (vv.25-29)
Once again, the narrative is perfectly clear. Saul was deeply concerned that "David's place was empty" (vv.25 & 27), not because he missed his

music, but because he wanted to kill him. This is clear from v.31. The javelin was ready! See v.33.

Jonathan offered the rehearsed excuse, with additions! Compare vv.28-29 with v.6. Lies take on a life of their own! The web of deceit gets increasingly complicated. As J.Hay points out, Jonathan "stressed the insistence of David's brother (v.29), thus implicating an innocent party." He continues: "he appealed to sentiment by quoting David as saying, "Let me…see my brethren." But none of this carried weight with Saul." Which brings us to

B) Saul's anger and Jonathan's answer (vv.30-34)
i) Saul's anger. "Thou son of the perverse rebellious woman (what a way to describe your wife!), do not I know that thou has chosen the son of Jesse (it seems as if Saul can hardly bear to mention David's name) to thine own confusion, and to the confusion of their mother's nakedness? For as long as the son of Jesse liveth upon the ground, thou shalt not be established, nor thine kingdom. Wherefore now send and fetch him unto me, for he shall surely die."

So Saul was well aware of Jonathan's loyalty to David. He had "chosen the son of Jesse." Are people aware of our allegiance to Christ? Have we "nailed our colours to the mast?" Or have we "nailed them to the fence!" Timothy was told, "Be not ashamed of the testimony of our Lord", and Paul was an example of his own ministry: "For the which cause I also suffer these things: nevertheless I am not ashamed." Neither was Onesiphorus: "he oft refreshed me, and was not ashamed of my chain" (2 Tim 1.8,12,16).

Saul also knew that Jonathan's loyalty to David involved the ascendancy of David, and he therefore appeals to Jonathan to look after his own interests. But while Saul was jealous for his son's future, Jonathan was **not** concerned for his own interests! His attitude was akin to the attitude of John the Baptist: "he must increase, but I must decrease" (Jn 3.30). But if you intend to give Christ first place in your life, expect trouble.

ii) Jonathan's answer. "Wherefore shall he be slain? What hath he done?" Notice Jonathan's concern for David as opposed to himself: "Wherefore shall **he** be slain? What hath **he** done?" His loyalty to David earned him a brush with death. "And Saul cast a javelin at him to smite him: whereby Jonathan knew that it was determined of his father to slay David." So Jonathan's loyalty to David earned him his father's hostility, to put it mildly.

This reminds us of the Lord's teaching: "Remember the word that I said unto you, The servant is not greater than his lord. If they have persecuted me, they will also persecute you" (Jn 15.20). The Lord Jesus knew the cost of allegiance only too well. See Romans 15.3, "For even Christ pleased not himself; but, as it is written, The reproaches of them that reproached thee fell on me."

We must notice that Jonathan was grieved, not over the insult to himself, and to his mother, but over the insult to David, "So Jonathan arose from the table in fierce anger, and did eat no meat the second day of the month: for he was grieved for David, because his father had done him shame." How much do we feel the insults levelled at the Lord Jesus? People use His name in blasphemy. Religious leaders deny His deity and reduce Him to the level of a mere religious leader. National leaders, even royalty, bent on "political correctness", just give Him a place with others in our so-called "multi-faith" society. Shame on us if we are not "grieved."

5. David's Parting from Jonathan (vv.35-42)
Following the prearranged signal (vv.19-22), David emerged from hiding. We come now to the parting of the ways. Notice the following: **(A)** They parted under pressure (vv.39-40); **(B)** They parted with tears (v.41); **(C)** They parted in peace (v.42).

A) They parted under pressure (vv.39-40)
Jonathan "stands as an illustration of one, who, having put his hand to the plough, looked back (Lk 9.62). Was it loyalty to his father that hindered him? Was it the stigma of being associated with an outlaw that kept him back? Did the love of material and physical comforts stifle ambitions for wholehearted commitment?" (J.Hay). He seems to be serving notice of his intentions by returning his weapons to the city. He obviously wasn't going to use them in the cause of David! Whatever the reason, he went back to the city. It reminds us of Demas. See 2 Timothy 4.10: "Do thy diligence to come shortly unto me: for Demas hath forsaken me, having loved this present world." The stigma of association with a man in chains was too much for him.

J.Hay continues: "David's course led him to the throne. Jonathan was left impaled to the wall of Beth-shan. Had he stuck by David he would have been "in safeguard" (22.23). How vital to make the right choices at the crossroads of life!"

These are weighty words. We must notice that while David did not ask Jonathan to accompany him into exile, the Lord Jesus made self-sacrifice a pre-requisite: "If any man will come after me, let him deny himself, and take up his cross, and follow me" (Mt 16.24). We should add that some feel that Jonathan was not in a position to forsake Saul and follow David. His place was with his father, to whom he owed allegiance, and that, in any case, he could best serve David by remaining at court. Even David would do nothing to harm Saul. He continued to regard him as "the Lord's anointed." See, for example 24.6. David waited God's time. See 26.8-11.

B) They parted with tears (v.41)
"And as soon as the lad was gone, David arose out of a place toward the south, and fell on his face to the ground, and bowed himself three times: and they kissed one another, and wept one with another, until David exceeded." Whilst Jonathan's loveable and sympathetic character endears him to us, he shared David's rejection in heart alone. "He did not have enough faith to **follow** the rejected king" (H.L.Rossier). The words, "until David exceeded", remind us that the love of Christ for us exceeds our love for Him! Notice too, that this took place without human observers. "The lad was gone." Don't we all have times like that-alone with Christ?

C) They parted in peace (v.42)
"And Jonathan said to David, Go in peace, forasmuch as we have both sworn in the name of the Lord, saying, The Lord be between my seed and thy seed for ever." There wasn't going to be much peace for David over the next seven years or so, but at least they parted in peace! That's an important lesson for us all! The contention between Paul and Barnabas was "so sharp between them, that they departed asunder one from the other" (Acts 15.39). We must endeavour to avoid that!

CHAPTER 21

"Give me five loaves of bread" (ch 21.1-15)

This chapter continues the story of David's exile. He is "on the run" from Saul. Events in his life at this time remind us that whilst there are striking similarities between his experiences and those of the Lord Jesus, there are also striking dissimilarities. In Chapter 20 we noticed that he was "economical with the truth" in connection with his absence from the feast (see vv.5-6), and in this chapter he resorts to deception on two occasions. In the first case, it had a disastrous result for the priesthood. Eighty-five priests lost their lives, plus "woman, children, and sucklings" (22.18-19).

David's faith lapsed under pressure, and people died as a result, The Lord Jesus never wavered under pressure, and countless multitudes have eternal life! "For the joy that was set before him", He "endured the cross, despising the shame, and is set down at the right hand of the throne of God." He "endured such contradiction of sinners against himself" (Heb 12.2-4).

We can easily divide the chapter as follows: *(1)* David at Nob (vv.1-9). Sadly, we notice his false explanation to Ahimelech. *(2)* David at Gath (vv.10-15). Sadly, we notice his feigned insanity before Achish. The Psalmist said, "The Lord is on my side; I will not fear: what can man do unto me?" (Ps 118.6). This chapter shows us what can happen when we forget this.

1. David at Nob (vv.1-9)

We learn from Isaiah 10.32, that Nob lay between Anathoth and Jerusalem. It is called "the city of the priests" (22.19), and this title is explained by the presence of the tabernacle there. We know that the ark of the covenant was in the house of Abinadab at Kirjath-jearim (1 Sam7.12), where it remained (but see 1 Sam 14.18) until its removal to Jerusalem after David's coronation. See 2 Samuel 6. However, the tabernacle, minus the ark, was at Nob. This is clear from the references to the showbread ("hallowed bread"

203

(vv.4-6), and to the ephod (v.9). Ahimelech and Ahiah are one and the same. Compare 14.3,18 with 22.9,11-12, 20.

We must notice *(A)* The fear of Ahimelech, (v.1); *(B)* The explanation of David (v.2); *(C)* The offer of showbread (vv.3-6); *(D)* The presence of Doeg (v.7); *(E)* The sword of Goliath (vv.8-9).

A) The fear of Ahimelech (v.1)
"Then came David to Nob, to Ahimelech the priest; and Ahimelech was afraid at the meeting of David, and said unto him, Why art thou alone, and no man with thee?"

i) The reason for David's visit
It has been suggested that David went to Nob solely to relieve his hunger and retrieve the sword of Goliath, but perhaps the main reason for his visit was to seek divine guidance through Ahimelech, the high priest. Saul later accused him of aiding David in all three ways. See 22.13-15. Ahimelech made it perfectly clear to Saul that he was unaware that David was a fugitive, and therefore had no intention of assisting him against Saul. Quite possibly then, David's primary reason for visiting Nob was to seek help from God, and he took the opportunity to ask for food and weapons. If this was David's motive in fleeing to Nob, it is a great pity that he went about it in the wrong way, and ended up telling lies However, we must not let the opportunity pass without reminding ourselves of the necessity to "come boldly to the throne of grace, that we may obtain mercy, and find grace to help in time of need" (Heb 4.16).

ii) The reaction to David's visit
"Ahimelech was afraid." Whilst he was evidently unaware that David was fleeing from Saul (see 22.14-15), he must have known about the strained relations between them, and this undoubtedly made him uneasy at the sudden and lone appearance of the king's son-in-law.

B) The explanation of David (v.2)
"The king hath commanded me a business, and hath said unto me, Let no man know anything of the business whereabout I send thee, and what I have commanded thee; and have appointed ("directed", JND) my servants to such and such a place." David was evidently afraid that if he told the truth, Ahimelech would refuse to assist him for fear of reprisals from Saul. Sadly, David's deception resulted in the massacre of the priests at Nob,

and David had to confess to Abiathar, "I have occasioned the death of all the persons of thy father's house" (22.22).

David's conduct reflected his lack of faith in God, and this is all the more surprising when we remember how God had preserved him in the past. He had evidently forgotten events at Naioth in Ramah. See 19.18-24. But none of us have the right to criticise David! It is all too easy to lie our way out of trouble. Let's remember that a "half-truth" is as bad as a downright lie. We know, of course that David told lies to secure his own well-being, rather than to cover his wrong-doing and we can do the same. For example, loyalty to Christ can land us in trouble, and we can be tempted to make life as comfortable as we can for ourselves by avoiding the reproach of Christ. Remember that "the fear of man bringeth a snare: but whoso putteth his trust in the Lord shall be safe" (Prov 29.25).

C) The offer of showbread (vv.3-6)
David's request for "five loaves...or what may be found" (JND), could only be met from the showbread. It is called "hallowed bread" to distinguish it from "common bread." (It seems strange that there was no ordinary bread available. Perhaps this indicates that the priests were not supported by the people as required by Numbers 18 etc. New loaves of "shewbread" (Ex 25.30) were placed upon the "table of shewbread" every sabbath day, and the old loaves were then eaten by the priests (Lev 24.8-9). David arrived at Nob on the sabbath day when the old loaves were replaced by the new. See v.6: "So the priest gave him hallowed bread; for there was no bread there but the shewbread, that was taken from before the Lord, to put hot bread in the day when it was taken away."

David requested "five loaves" to feed himself and his men. The Lord Jesus fed "five thousand men, beside women and children", from "five loaves and two fishes." See Matthew 14.15-21.

This raises a number of interesting issues. We ought to give some thought to *(i)* The significance of the shewbread; *(ii)* The eating of the shewbread by David and his men; *(iii)* The stipulation of Ahimelech.

i) The significance of the shewbread
"And thou shalt set upon the table showbread before me alway" (Ex 25.30). Young's Concordance explains the word "showbread" as "bread of the presence." It was to be "before me alway." It has also been rendered "the

bread of faces." The showbread comprised twelve loaves (AV. "cakes"): "And thou shalt take fine flour, and bake twelve cakes thereof: two tenth deals shall be in one cake. And thou shalt set them in two rows, six on a row, upon the **pure table** before the Lord. And thou shalt put pure frankincense upon each row, that it may be on the bread for a memorial, even an offering made by fire unto the Lord. Every sabbath shall he set it in order before the Lord continually, being taken from the children of Israel ("on the part of the children of Israel" JND) by an everlasting covenant. And it shall be Aaron's and his sons"; and they shall eat it in the holy place" (Lev 24.5-9).

The twelve loaves are a beautiful picture of our acceptance in Christ. The description of the loaves reminds us of the meal offering, which describes the perfect life of the Lord Jesus. "His offering shall be of **fine flour**, and he shall pour oil upon it, and put **frankincense** thereon" (Lev 2.2). But the fact that the showbread is called "**twelve** cakes" and "**the** bread" (Lev 24.5-7) strongly suggests the union between Christ and His people. "Both **He that sanctifieth** and **they who are sanctified** are **all of one**: for which cause He is not ashamed to call them brethren" (Heb 2.11). "According as He hath chosen us in Him before the foundation of the world, that we should be **holy and without blame before Him**...to the praise of the glory of His grace, wherein He hath made us **accepted in the Beloved**" (Eph 1.4)

The twelve loaves were to be on the table perpetually. "Thou shalt set upon the table showbread before me **alway**" (Ex 25.30). Whilst the loaves were changed, the table was never to be empty. This reminds us that we can never be evicted from the presence of God. That would mean the eviction of Christ Himself. We must also remember that the very bread that the priests were privileged to eat had been on the "pure table **before the Lord**" for the previous week. The priests therefore enjoyed fellowship with God at that "pure table", and received their nourishment from that "most holy" food which had given satisfaction to Him. The Lord Jesus, with whom we are identified and on whom we feed, has brought infinite joy and pleasure to God.

(ii) The eating of the shewbread
Leviticus 24.9 specified that the showbread "shall be eaten by Aaron and his sons; and they shall eat it in the holy place: for it is most holy unto him of the offerings of the Lord made by fire by a perpetual statute." Technically, therefore, David and his men transgressed the law. It is therefore most

significant that the Lord Jesus referred to this incident when combating criticism of His disciples for plucking and eating ears of corn on the sabbath day. See Matthew 12.1-8: "Have ye not read what David did when he was an hungred, and they that were with him; how he entered into the house of God, and did eat the shewbread, which was not lawful for him to eat, neither for them that were with him, but only for the priests?" See also Mark 2.23-28 and Luke 6.1-5. The Lord Jesus therefore makes the point that if in the past, God-given ceremonial laws could be suspended in order to feed hungry people, it was totally wrong to object when man-made laws were violated! The disciples had not infringed any God-given commandments. They had not stolen the farmer's crops. See Deuteronomy 23.25. They had not even violated the fourth commandment. After all, people were still permitted to eat on the Sabbath day!

Notice that in Mark 2.26, the priest's name is given as Abiathar, as opposed to Ahimelech. Various explanations have been given, including the suggestion that Mark suffered "an error of memory." (Keil & Delitzsch). This is definitely not acceptable! The inspiring Holy Spirit does not make mistakes! Very clearly, Ahimelech and his son, Abiathar were **both** present when David came to Nob. Shortly after, Ahimelech was murdered, but Abiathar escaped, fled to David, and became high priest. While it is true that Abiathar was not high priest at the moment the bread was given to David, it is not unusual to refer to people as if they had always carried a title which was not actually bestowed upon them until later. For example, we say that Lord Tennyson studied at Trinity College, Cambridge. But he wasn't Lord Tennyson at the time! It is not surprising that Mark should link David's name with Abiathar as opposed to Ahimelech. After all, Abiathar was high priest during David's reign, and Ahimelech during the reign of Saul.

(iii) The stipulation of Ahimelech.
Ahimelech was prepared to give "the hallowed bread" to David, "if the young men have kept themselves at least from women." David assured Ahimelech that his men met this requirement: "Of a truth, women have been kept from us about these three days, since I came out, and the vessels of the young men are holy." In broad terms, Ahimelech insisted that David's men should be morally pure. The word "vessel" is used of clothing in Deuteronomy 22.15, and it is possible that David is referring to Leviticus 15.16-18. In New Testament terms, the word "vessel" refers to the believer's body. See 1 Thess 4.4: "that every one of you should know how to possess his vessel in sanctification and honour." The overall lesson is clear: "keep

yourselves pure" (1 Tim 5.22). Holy food can only be eaten and enjoyed by holy people.

Notice that David adds, "and the (bread) is in a manner common, and the more so, because today (new) is hallowed in the vessels" (JND). The meaning is not altogether clear. Possibly, David is saying that it was in order for his men to eat the showbread since it was now "common" because it had been replaced by new loaves, although, strictly speaking, this was not true. It remained "hallowed bread."

D) The presence of Doeg (v.7)
We know, with hindsight, that this is an ominous verse. David was aware of the danger at the time: "I knew it that day, when Doeg the Edomite was there, that he would surely tell Saul" (22.22). Notice that he is consistently called "Doeg the **Edomite**." The Edomites were inveterate enemies of God's people. Read Obadiah! It is not without significance that he was "the chiefest of the herdmen ("shepherds" JND) that belonged to Saul". He turned out to be a butcher. It seems rather incongruous that Saul employed an Edomite in the first place, and reminds us that we have to be very careful in our relationships and associations.

The words "detained before the Lord" possibly refer to his presence at Nob for a festival. (A.McShane suggests that he was at Nob as a worshipper). See Gesenius on the word "detained": "To be gathered together (from the idea of restraining, compelling... especially to a festival)." We use the word "detain" in a different way.

E) The sword of Goliath (vv.8-9)
David persisted with his story: "And is there not here under thine hand spear or sword? For I have neither brought my sword nor my weapons with me, because the king's business required haste."

We have already noticed that David's victory over Goliath was displayed in three places. The giant's head was displayed in Jerusalem (reminding us of testimony in public life), his armour was kept in David's tent (reminding us of testimony in private life), and his sword was placed in the tabernacle (reminding us of testimony in heaven). H.L.Rossier writes: "The instrument of David's victory was kept behind the ephod (see Ex 28.4-14), wrapped in a cloth; looked after and set in a place of honour under the very eyes of God. Likewise the testimony of Christ's victory, through death, by which he conquered the prince of death, has been carried as a memorial into the most holy place where Jesus has entered in by His own blood."

We do not know how or when the sword of Goliath found its way to the tabernacle, but "David accepted it as a weapon of greater value to him than any other, because he had not only taken the sword as booty from the Philistine, but had cut off the head of Goliath with it", Keil & Delitzsch. We too have a weapon of which we can say, "There is none like it." Paul wrote: "For the preaching of the cross is to them that perish foolishness; but unto us which are saved it is the power of God…We preach Christ crucified, unto the Jews a stumblingblock, and unto the Greeks foolishness; but unto them which are called, both Jews and Greeks, Christ the power of God, and the wisdom of God" (1 Cor 1.18, 23-24). The weapon with which Satan was defeated is the weapon which we use in delivering men and women from his power. It is rather significant that David's weaponry was located in the sanctuary! Think about it.

While David used a sword to complete his victory over Goliath, the Lord Jesus was victorious because he was subject to the sword of divine judgement. See Zechariah 13.7, "Awake, O sword, against my shepherd, and against the man that is my fellow, saith the Lord of hosts: smite the shepherd, and the sheep shall be scattered."

2. David at Gath (vv.10-15)

The "fear of Saul" (v.10) gave place to "the fear of Achish" (v.12). David's brief stay at Gath achieved nothing. His failure at Nob led to failure at Gath. As A.McShane rightly observes, "The lesson of this brief passage is plain…it often happens that one failure leads to another. Once the path of faith is left, and we begin to depend on self-aid, the road becomes slippery and we can expect to fall." We must notice **(A)** His flight to Gath (v.10); **(B)** His fame at Gath (v.11); **(C)** His fear at Gath (vv.12-13); **(D)** His failure at Gath (vv.14-15).

A) His flight to Gath (v.10)

It seems inconsistent that David should seek refuge in Gath! It was a Philistine city, and, more to the point, the home of Goliath! David arrived at Gath carrying Goliath's sword! He obviously thought that Saul would not attempt to apprehend him in Philistine territory, but it was a very sad situation. It is equally sad if our unkindness and lack of Christian love results in fellow-believers being driven elsewhere, particularly if they go to places where God's word is not honoured and obeyed. On the other hand, we should not allow pressure to drive us into the arms of people with whom we have nothing in common. See 2 Corinthians 6.14-18.

B) His fame at Gath (v.11)
"Is not this David the king of the land? Did they not sing one to another of him in dances, saying, Saul hath slain his thousands, and David his ten thousands?" Compare 29.5. Notice that they called David, "the king of the land!" Whilst this does not mean that they were aware that David had been anointed king by Samuel, it does suggest that David's famous victory gave him precedence over Saul in the eyes of the Philistines.

While it seems that the servants of Achish were pointing out the danger of accommodating David at Gath, and David himself certainly regarded their report in that way, it is quite possible that they were being sarcastic. The very man who was once so famous is now seeking refuge with us! "How are the mighty fallen!" This led to

C) His fear at Gath (vv.12-13)
David's lack of faith in God led him to the wrong place, and to disdain and contempt. "And David laid up these words in his heart, and was sore afraid of Achish the king of Gath. And he changed his behaviour before them, and feigned himself mad in their hands, and scrabbled on the doors of the gate, and let his spittle fall down upon his beard." He feared for his life. The man who "behaved himself wisely" at the court of Saul now acts the fool at the court of Achish.

D) His failure at Gath (vv.14-15)
Whilst the strategy was successful, and David's life was preserved, he left a poor impression behind him when he moved on. "Lo, ye see the man is mad; wherefore then have ye brought him to me? Have I need of mad men, that ye have brought this fellow to play the madman in my presence? Shall this fellow come into my house?"

What kind of impression do **we** make, deliberately or unwittingly, on other people? Do we "adorn the doctrine of God our Saviour in all things?" (Tit 2.10). What about our assembly meetings? It is possible that we could create the wrong impression there as well. "If therefore the whole church be come together into one place, and all speak with tongues, and there come in those that are unlearned, or unbelievers, will they not say that ye are **mad?** But if all prophesy, and there come in one that believeth not, or one unlearned, he is convinced of all, he is judged of all…and so, falling down on his face, will worship God, and report that God is in you of a truth" (1 Cor 14.23-25). We must live, and meet, in a way that enhances the testimony.

We ought now to read Psalms 34 and 56. After his failure at Gath, David evidently returned to faith in God, and attributed his escape to divine overruling. He evidently learned from his mistakes. People who do not learn from their mistakes usually repeat them. It is worth noticing that David wrote Psalms in connection with his mistakes, but he did not write any Psalms in connection with his victory over Goliath. Look at the headings to Psalms 34, 52 and 56. (The superscription to Psalm 34 refers to Abimelech, rather than Achish, but we should remember that Abimelech was the standing **title** of the Philistine princes. Compare Genesis 20.2).

CHAPTER 22

"He became captain over them" (22.1-23)

This chapter records more episodes in the story of David's exile, and there are still more to come. Sadly, he did not exactly distinguish himself either at Nob or at Gath (see Chapter 21), and the consequences of his encounter with Ahimelech at Nob are recorded here. We do have to say, however, that whilst David admitted to Abiathar that he had "occasioned the death of all the persons of thy father's house", he was not **responsible** for the massacre at Nob.

There is a striking contrast between the end of Chapter 21 and the beginning of Chapter 22. We last saw David feigning madness at Gath, where he "scrabbled on the doors of the gate, and let his spittle fall down upon his beard." Back in home territory, he establishes his headquarters in the cave of Adullam, and becomes captain over a rather motley band of four hundred men. Just look at the description: "And every one that was in distress, and every one that was in debt, and every one that was discontented, gathered themselves unto him." It doesn't look very promising! But wait. Read 2 Samuel 23. 13-17. In all his wanderings, the period spent in the cave of Adullam is one of the most interesting and significant. It has been said that God remade the kingdom in the cave. Like David's unlikely men, we can be "more than conquerors through him that loved us" (Rom 8.37).

However, there is more to the chapter than events at Adullam, and we will look at the passage as follows: **(1)** David's escape to Adullam (vv.1-2); **(2)** David's provision for his parents (vv.3-4); **(3)** David's discovery by Saul (vv.5-8); **(4)** David's helpers massacred by Doeg (vv.9-19); **(5)** David's recruitment of Abiathar (vv.20-23).

1. David's Escape to Adullam (vv.1-2)
"David therefore departed thence, and escaped to the cave Adullam: and

when his brethren and all his father's house heard it, they went down thither to him." David must be numbered amongst those described in Hebrews 11.38: "they wandered in deserts, and in mountains, and in dens and **caves** of the earth." The biblical city of Adullam has been identified with Aid-el-Ma, some fifteen miles south-east of Jerusalem. In the vicinity are limestone cliffs which are marked by extensive excavations, one of which may have been David's cave. Since Adullam lay on the lower slopes of the hill country of Judaea, we can understand the statement, "his brethren and all his father's house...went **down** thither to him." Bethlehem is situated in the centre of the highland area. There is a reference to Adullam in Micah 1.15: "The glory of Israel (i.e. its nobles) shall come even to Adullam" (JND). That is, come to Adullam like outcasts.

In our studies, we have noticed the striking parallel between the history of David and "great David's greater Son", the Lord Jesus. Both were anointed, both were overlooked, both won great victories, and both were rejected (the Lord Jesus is still rejected). David ultimately ascended the throne, and the Lord Jesus will soon be recognised as "King of kings and Lord of lords." But now we have a further point in common. In their rejection, both gathered people around them who, in David's case, shared his kingdom, and who, in the case of the Lord Jesus, will reign with Him. "If we suffer, we shall also reign with him" (2 Tim 2.11). We can look at it like this:

A) The attraction of David

Not only "his brethren and all his father's house", but people of all sorts "gathered themselves unto him." While, at first, Eliab was certainly not impressed by his youngest brother (see 17.28), he was there at Adullam! Similarly, the Lord's brethren did not "believe in him", see John 7.5. But they were all there in the "upper room", with His mother Mary! See Acts 1.14.

We must notice that they "gathered themselves **unto him**." Note the expressions "to **him**...unto **him**....with **him**" (vv.1-2). David's personal character, his wisdom and his winsomeness, together with his great victory in the valley of Elah, made him the centre of gathering at Adullam. Need we say more? We sing of the Lord Jesus:

> We love Thee for the glorious worth which in Thyself we see:
> We love Thee for that cruel cross endured so patiently.

He said "For where two or three are gathered together in (unto) my name, there am I in the midst of them" (Mt 18.20). While Genesis 49.10 points to the future, it is always God's will that "unto him (Shiloh) shall the gathering of the people be."

B) The assorted followers of David

"And every one that was in distress, and every one that was in debt, and every one that was discontented, gathered themselves unto him." It is not unlikely that these people were the products of Saul's misrule. Not very promising! But isn't this the way in which God so often works? Compare 1 Corinthians 1.26-29: "For ye see your calling, brethren, how that not many wise men after the flesh, not many mighty, not many noble, are called. But God hath chosen the foolish things of the world to confound the wise; and God hath chosen the weak things to confound the things which are mighty; and base things of the world, and things which are despised, hath God chosen, yea, and things which are not, to bring to nought things that are: that no flesh should glory in his presence."

The categories are most significant. The gospel preacher can certainly have a field day here!

i) "Every one that was in distress." Psalm 107 describes people who were "delivered...out of their ***distresses.***" There were people who had lost their way in life, unsettled and unsatisfied: "They wandered in the wilderness in a solitary way; they found no city to dwell in, hungry and thirsty, their soul fainted in them" (vv.4-5). There were people who were enslaved to sin because they had deliberately rejected God's word: "Such as sit in darkness and in the shadow of death, being bound in affliction and iron, because they rebelled against the words of God, and contemned the counsel of the Most High" (vv.10-11). There were people with ailments, perhaps of both body and mind, as a result of their sinful lives: "Fools because of their transgression, and because of their iniquity, are afflicted. Their soul abhorreth all manner of meat; and they draw near to the gates of death" (vv.17-18). There were people who are buffeted by the storms of life, with no stability or haven of refuge: "They reel to and fro, and stagger like a drunken man, and are at their wits end", (v.27). In each case, they cried "unto the Lord in their trouble, and he delivered them out of their ***distresses.***"

The distressed of Israel found salvation and security with God's anointed king, even in his rejection, and distressed sinners can find salvation and blessing in God's rejected but beloved Son, the Lord Jesus.

ii) "And every one that was in debt. In His pattern prayer, the Lord Jesus taught His disciples to pray, "forgive us our debts, as we forgive our debtors" (Mt 6.12), from which we learn that it is possible to be in debt to God. Compare Luke 11.4, "And forgive us our sins; for we also forgive every one that is indebted to us", from which we learn that sin is a debt. We are liable to recompense God for sin committed against Him in violation of His law. But like the debtors in Luke 7.42, we "had nothing to pay." The Lord Jesus made a payment at Calvary of sufficient value to meet all human indebtedness to God, but the sinner must claim his discharge by "repentance toward God, and faith toward our Lord Jesus Christ" (Acts 20.21).

iii) "And every one that was discontented." Literally, "bitter of soul." Here are some people who were "bitter of soul." The children of Israel, groaning in Egypt, suffered under their taskmasters, who "made their lives bitter with hard bondage." Doesn't this describe so many people today? How many people are bitter because of their circumstances. Naomi, returning from Moab, having lost her husband and her two sons, said, "Call me not Naomi, call me Mara: for the Almighty hath dealt very bitterly with me." How many people are bitter because of sorrow or bereavement? Peter, after denying the Lord Jesus, "went out, and wept bitterly. Failure, falling short of an ideal, can bring bitterness and regret.

In each of the three cases, bitterness was dispelled. Just as David became the succourer of all who were "discontented", or "bitter of soul", so the Lord Jesus can bring relief and hope (1 Tim 1.1) to all who come to Him.

C) The authority of David
"And he became a captain over them." David became captain over this strangely- assorted group of people, but as we have noticed in 2 Samuel 23, his leadership had a transforming effect on them. They may have been ill-assorted initially, but from their ranks emerged a host of "mighty men" (2 Sam 23.8 etc) whose loyalty to the rejected king spurred them on to great exploits. We too can become "mighty men and women" for God if our lives are committed to Christ, and we acknowledge Him as "Lord of all." Notice that "there were **with him** about four hundred men." There's the secret of their prowess! They were so close to him that they knew exactly

what he wanted, even down to a "drink of water out of the well of Bethlehem, which is by the gate!"

It's worth emphasising that there were two contributing factors to the prowess of David's "mighty men." In the first place, they were willing to share his rejection and reproach, and in the second place, they were willing subjects of a man who knew how to lead and inspire others. As A.McShane observes, "His ability to improve men was given scope, and time showed him to be a master in this field." A.McShane continues: "The true ruler ever brings blessing into the lives of those whom he rules, He sees in the low state of the saints an opportunity to prove his worth."

2. David's Provision for His Parents (vv.3-4)
"Let my father and my mother, I pray thee, come forth, and be with you, till I know what God will do for me. And he brought them before the king of Moab: and they dwelt with him all the while that David was in the hold." The "hold" was evidently not the cave of Adullam since David was later instructed to return to Judah. See v.5. Presumably, it was in the land of Moab. It doesn't need too much imagination to conclude why David moved his parents to Moab. Having failed to kill David, Saul might wreak his vengeance on his parents.

Once again, there is an interesting parallel between David and the Lord Jesus. David made provision for his parents, and the Lord Jesus made provision for His mother. See John 19.25-27: "Then saith he to the disciple, Behold thy mother! And from that hour that disciple took her unto his own home."

The scriptures teach very clearly that children should care for their parents. See, for example 1 Timothy 5: "Honour widows that are widows indeed. But if any widow have children or nephews (RV "grand-children"), let them learn first to shew piety at home, and to requite their parents: for that is good and acceptable before God...But if any provide not for his own, and specially for those of his own house, he hath denied the faith, and is worse than an infidel...If any man that believeth hath widows, let them relieve them, and let not the church be charged; that it may relieve them that are widows indeed" (vv.3-4,8,16). The Lord Jesus condemned the way in which the Pharisees used an "escape clause" when it came to responsibility for parents. "Moses said, Honour thy father and thy mother...but ye say, If a man shall say to his father or mother, It is Corban, that is to say, a gift, by whatsoever thou mightest be profited by me; he shall be free, And ye suffer him no more to do ought for his father or his mother; making the word of God none effect through your tradition" (Mk 7.10-13).

The use of the word "Corban" here requires explanation. The teaching of the scribes and Pharisees gave a man freedom to exclude his parents from the support and help required by the fifth commandment, simply by saying, in the form of a vow, "Corban." In using the word, "Corban", the man said in effect to his parents, "The money (or whatever it was) that you expected me to give you has been dedicated as an offering to God." In actual fact, he had no intention of giving it to God, or to anyone else, but so far as the people who hoped to receive it were concerned, it had become dedicated to God, and therefore they couldn't have it. In this way, they were "making the word of God of none effect by their tradition..."

While it is true that there is now financial and physical provision by the State for elderly people, this does not exempt us from responsibility. Caring for them can be time-consuming and taxing in many ways, but we should regard it as an opportunity to show our love for God and His word, as well as our love for our parents. As A.McShane rightly observes, "No man will earn the respect of the saints that has no regard for his private responsibilities."

We must not leave this little section without noticing David's words to the king of Moab: "Let my father and my mother, I pray thee, come forth, and be with you, **till I know what God will do for me."** Ellicott's Commentary has a nice piece here: "This shows that the old trust and love, which in his first moments of care and sorrow had failed him, h ad come back again to the son of Jesse." The Commentary also points out that David does not use the name "Jehovah" when speaking to the king of Moab. He uses "Elohim" (AV "God"). "An idolater had nothing to do with the awful name by which the Eternal was known to His covenant people."

3. David's Discovery by Saul (vv.5-8)
"And the prophet Gad said unto David, Abide not in the hold; depart and get thee into the land of Judah. Then David departed, and came to the forest of Hareth." We are not told why David was to return to Judah (quite obviously, God didn't want him to settle down in Moab!), but when news reached Saul of David's whereabouts, he wallowed in a mixture of anger and self-pity. Saul seemed to have a liking for holding court under trees in

1 Samuel

Gibeah! Compare 14.2. He also seemed very attached to his spear! See (v.6). Gad and Saul make an interesting contrast:

i) Gad was a man who could see. He was a prophet. He is called "David's seer" in 1 Chronicles 21.9. He was present during the last year of David's reign (2 Sam 24.10-14), and was one of three men who wrote about David's life. "Now the acts of David the king, first and last, behold, they are written in the book of Samuel the seer, and in the book of Nathan the prophet, and in the **book of Gad the seer**" (1 Chron 29.29). Now that is most interesting! But we can only speculate!

ii) Saul was a man who could not see. He couldn't even get his facts right. "All of you have conspired against me, and there is none that sheweth me that my son hath made a league with the son of Jesse, and there is none of you that is sorry for me or sheweth unto me that my son hath stirred up my servant against me, to lie in wait, as at this day." His attitude reminds us of Proverbs 28.1, "The wicked fleeth when no man pursueth." We get the impression that Saul was virtually alone. A man out of touch with God is not attractive. Saul was at a low ebb personally, and dragged others down with him. We must remember that we do have an effect on each other, either beneficially or banefully.

4. David's Helpers Massacred by Doeg (vv.9-19)

We must notice the vivid contrast between David and Gad, and Saul and Doeg. David responded to the counsel of a man of God. Saul responded to the information of an evil man. See Psalm 52. Note its heading as well as its contents. Doeg is described as mischievous, deceitful and evil.

This paragraph describes one of the blackest episodes in Saul's history. Doeg's report heaped fuel on the fire of Saul's anger, and he refused to listen to reason. Ahimelech defended himself on two counts;

i) On the basis of David's innocence and integrity, (v.12). "And who is so faithful among all the servants as David, which is the king's son in law, and goeth at thy bidding (JND, "has access to thy secret council), and is honourable in thine house?" We know, of course, that David had falsely told Ahimelech that he was engaged in "the king's business." But the priest appears to be speaking generally about David here. Notice that David told lies to Ahimelech, and lived, whilst Ahimelech told the truth about David, and died. Seems ironical, doesn't it?

ii) On the basis of his ignorance of the true facts, (v.13). "Let not the king impute any thing unto his servant, nor to all the house of my father: for thy servant knew nothing of all this, less or more." The words, "Did I then begin to inquire of God for him? Be it far from me", might mean that this wasn't the first time that Ahimelech had asked God to give guidance for David. There was, therefore, nothing unusual about his enquiry, and certainly no conspiracy against Saul. It has, however, been suggested that the words can be translated, "That was the first day that I enquired of God for him, and I did not know that it was displeasing to thee." (Ellicott's Commentary). On balance, the first suggestion seems correct.

But it was to no avail. "Thou shalt surely die, Ahimelech, thou, and all thy father's house." The cruel massacre follows, not at the hands of Saul's servants who refused to "fall upon the priests of the Lord", but at the hand of Doeg, the Edomite. The man who spared Agag, the Amalekite, and the best of the animals (15.9), utterly destroys the entire priesthood, with their wives, families, babies, oxen, asses and sheep. A.McShane is worth quoting at length here (slightly altered and with paragraphs added): "The lessons to be learned from this action of Saul are weighty:

i) It shows that when a ruler departs in heart from the Lord, he becomes cruel. Communion with God keeps the soul tender and the mind humble.

ii) It shows that when men are helpless to fight the Lord's battles, they wreak their vengeance on the weak and innocent. Not a man at Nob had any means of defence.

iii) It shows just how seared the conscience can become until the most wicked deeds can be practised with impunity. Saul's servants had some respect for the priestly office, but their master had none.

iv) It shows that there is nearly always someone who is prepared to do the foulest deed in order to gain favour with those in high places. The Edomite hatred in Doeg responded to the occasion, and he carried out the dastardly act. The man, who had previously worshipped at the tabernacle (21.7), now defiles it with the blood of those who served therein.

We might add that this awful event takes us back to the prediction, "Behold, the days come that I will cut off thine arm, and the arm of thy father's house, and there shall not be an old man in thine house...and all the increase of thine house shall die in the flower of their age." (2.31-33)

5. David's Recruitment of Abiathar, (vv.20-23)
One man escaped the massacre. "And one of the sons of Ahimelech the son of Ahitub, named Abiathar, escaped, and fled after David." He was assured of security: "Abide thou with me, fear not; for he that seeketh my life seeketh thy life: but with me thou shalt be in safeguard." Compare John 15.18-20. The arrival of Abiathar meant that David now had the help of a prophet **and** a priest. All "the essential elements of his kingdom" were present. We shall see more of Abiathar shortly. He "came down with an ephod in his hand" (23.6).

The chapter ends with a prophet (Gad), a priest (Abiathar) and a king (David). David's men enjoyed great privileges, and so do we! The Lord Jesus is a Prophet (Heb 1.1-2), a Priest (Heb 1.3) and a King (Heb 1.8).

CHAPTER 23

"Jonathan...strengthened his hand in God" (23.1-29)

Saul's animosity against David continues, and in this chapter we follow David as he flees from the forest of Hareth (22.5) to Keilah (23.1-13), from Keilah to the wilderness of Ziph (23.14-23), from the wilderness of Ziph to the wilderness of Maon (23.14-28), and from the wilderness of Maon to En-gedi (23.29). He was hunted "from pillar to post."

1. David at Keilah (vv.1-13)
We can divide this section into two parts: **(A)** Robbing the threshingfloors (vv.1-5), and **(B)** Rewarding David (vv.6-13). David's kindness to Keilah was rewarded with treachery.

A) *Robbing the threshing floors (vv.1-5)*
"Then they told David, saying, Behold the Philistines fight against Keilah, and they rob the threshingfloors." So the Philistines are back. Yet again! As we have seen in past studies, they attacked God's people in all sorts of ways. This calls for a little revision. For example, *(a) They filled wells.* See Genesis 26.15, "For all the wells which his (Isaac's) father's servants had digged...the Philistines had stopped them, and filled them with earth"; *(b) They invaded holy places.* See 1 Samuel 10.5, "After that thou shalt come to the hill of God, where there is a garrison of the Philistines"; *(c) They monopolised weapons.* See 1 Samuel 13.19, "Now there was no smith found throughout all the land of Israel: for the Philistines said, Lest the Hebrews make them swords or spears"; *(d) They despatched spoilers.* See 1 Samuel 13.17, "And the spoilers came out of the camp of the Philistines in three companies"; *(e) They exercised lordship.* See Judges 15.11: "Knowest thou not that the Philistines are rulers over us?" (The men of Judah to Samson). Let's remember that satanically led "principalities and powers" will endeavour to do exactly the same to us. Go over the references again, and think of the way in which they illustrate the tactics of

our spiritual enemies. Remember too that "there was sore war against the Philistines **all the days** of Saul" (1 Sam 14.52). We can expect "sore war" all our days as well!

Now we have another example of enemy strategy. **They robbed God's people of their food!** The Midianites did the same. See Judges 6. We will become impoverished and weakened if we allow the enemy to steal our food. Job certainly didn't allow anything or anybody to rob him in this way. "I have esteemed the words of his mouth more than my necessary food" (Job 23.12). Jeremiah was the same: "Thy words were found, and I did eat them; and thy word was unto me the joy and rejoicing of mine heart" (Jer 15.16). We **all** need to be "nourished up in the words of faith and good doctrine" (1 Tim 4.6).

Don't let anything rob your personal "threshingfloor." Your food supply can be endangered by hobbies and pastimes, sport, business, friends, television. We are all vulnerable in different ways. Notice that David was obliged to take positive action, and fight against the Philistines, which reminds us that we will get nowhere at all if we just "hope" that something will happen: we have to "make" it happen. **See Addendum.**

We must now notice some further lessons of interest and importance in this paragraph:

i) David's concern for others (v.1). They didn't "tell Saul." "They told David!" Saul was far too occupied with his own selfish interests to bother about anybody else. David was a true shepherd. See Psalm 78.70-72, "He chose David also his servant, and took him from the sheepfolds: and from following the ewes great with young he brought him to feed Jacob his people, and Israel his inheritance." Although David was under considerable pressure, he was still concerned about other people. Keilah lay some twenty miles south-west of Bethlehem, and David could have excused himself from involvement on the grounds of his own problems. But there was nothing selfish about him. He exemplified the injunction, "Look not every man on his own things, but every man also on the things of others" (Phil 2.4). David could have excused himself on the grounds that Saul was king, and that it was his responsibility to protect his people! He obviously agreed with Paul when he wrote that "the members should have the same care one for another. And whether one member suffer, all the members suffer with it" (1 Cor 12.25-26).

ii) David's communion with God (v.2). David did not proceed against the Philistines without first seeking divine guidance and help. He asked God for guidance twice (vv.2 & 4). On the first occasion, he was told to proceed against the Philistines: "Shall I go and smite the Philistines? And the Lord said unto David, Go, and smite the Philistines, and save Keilah." On the second occasion, he gained reassurance for his men, which brings us to:

iii) David's consideration for his men, (v.3). "And David's men (now six hundred, v.13) said unto him, Behold we be afraid here in Judah: how much more if we come to Keilah against the armies of the Philistines?" David shines here as a good spiritual leader. Rather than reassuring them personally that all would be well, he "enquired of the Lord yet again." He could then face his men with assurance from **God.** That's first class leadership! Quite obviously, God was as good as His word. The Philistines were defeated, (v.5). We can now understand why God wanted David back in Judah (22.5). In delivering Keilah, David was proving his fitness to lead Israel as king.

We should add that God had every consideration for David! He had already answered David's request, "Shall I go and smite these Philistines?" Wasn't that enough? How glad **we** are that God is not a harsh taskmaster, but gracious and longsuffering. "He knoweth our frame; he remembereth that we are dust" (Ps 103.14). He therefore gives David further reassurance.

B) Rewarding David, (vv.6-13)
This is a sad paragraph. In the first place, Saul showed no gratitude to David for delivering Keilah, a town in his own kingdom, from the Philistines, and in the second, the men of Keilah showed no gratitude to David either. The only bright spot in the dark story is David's recourse to God for guidance. We should therefore notice:

i) Saul's intransigence. It is almost unbelievable. "And Saul said, God hath delivered him into mine hand; for he is shut in, by entering into a town that hath gates and bars. And Saul called all the people together for war, to go down to Keilah, to besiege David and his men. And David knew that Saul practised mischief against him.....thy servant hath certainly heard that Saul seeketh to come to Keilah, to **destroy the city** for my sake." Saul seems to have forgotten the solemn words of Samuel "the Lord...hath also rejected thee from being king" (15.23). He actually believed that God was on his side: "God hath delivered him into mine hand!" But, unlike David, he had neither a prophet nor a priest.

It all began with Saul's jealousy. See 18.8-9. "Jealousy is cruel as the grave; the coals thereof are coals of fire, which hath a most vehement flame" (Song 8.6). We all need to be careful here. It is sadly possible to take a strong dislike to someone, to the extent that we take every opportunity to discredit them.

ii) Keilah's ingratitude. "Will the men of Keilah deliver me and my men into the hand of Saul? And the Lord said, They will deliver thee up." The man who had willingly come to their aid would be disowned and betrayed. The Christians in Galatia received Paul as "an angel of God, even as Christ Jesus", when he first preached the gospel to them. But the advent of false teachers made them change their minds, and Paul was obliged to say, "Am I therefore become your enemy, because I tell you the truth?" (Gal 4.13-16). Later, he wrote, "This thou knowest, that all they which are in Asia be turned away from me" (2 Tim 1.15). "Demas hath forsaken me, having loved this present world, and is departed unto Thessalonica" (2 Tim 4.10).

iii) Abiathar's intervention. David's only resource in the circumstances was the facility of communion with God. It was through the priestly ministry of Abiathar that David was able to obtain divine help and guidance. "And David knew that Saul secretly practised mischief against him; and he said to Abiathar the priest, Bring hither the ephod" As we have noted before, the Urim and Thummin were located in the ephod, and it was by this means that God made known His will. In the perplexities and uncertainties of life, we too have the facility of communion with God:

> Have we trials and temptations?
> Is there trouble anywhere?
> We should never be discouraged;
> Take it to the Lord in prayer.

H.L.Rossier has a nice piece here: "It is lovely to see David take on the character of a servant here. He, to whom the kingdom belonged, claims only the most humble place before God. "Jehovah, God of Israel, **thy servant** hath heard for certain…will Saul come down, as thy **servant** hath heard? Jehovah, God of Israel, I beseech thee, tell **thy servant**" (vv.10-11). In this, is he not a lovely type of Christ Who, knowing that the Father had placed all things into His hands, came not to be served, but to serve God and His own?"

2. David in the Wilderness of Ziph (vv.14-23)

We can divide this section into three parts: *(A)* The flight from Saul (vv.14-15); *(B)* The support of Jonathan (vv.16-18); *(C)* The treachery of the Ziphites (vv.19-23). The structure of these verses is rather like Mark 14.1-10. In both cases, an act of devotion is preceded by animosity, and followed by treachery.

A) The flight from Saul (vv.14-15)

"And David abode in the wilderness in strong holds, and remained in a mountain in the wilderness of Ziph. And Saul sought him, every day, but God delivered him not into his hand. And David saw that Saul was come out to seek his life: And David was in the wilderness of Ziph in a wood." God was on David's side! He is on our side too! "If God be for us, who can be against us?" David wrote: "If it had not been the Lord who was on our side, when men rose up against us: then they had swallowed us up quick, when their wrath was kindled against us:...Blessed be the Lord, who hath not given us as a prey to their teeth" (Ps 124, Read the title).

B) The support of Jonathan (vv.16-18)

"And Jonathan Saul's son arose, and went to David in the wood," We should notice the following:

i) His assistance to David. Jonathan "went to David in the wood": this required some effort on his part. Helping others carries a price-tag. He "strengthened his hand in God." He encouraged David. People like that are worth their weight in gold! When the spies returned from Canaan, the people murmured in their tents and said.....whither shall we go up? Our brethren have discouraged our heart", Deuteronomy 1.27-28. Tychicus was so different: "Whom I have sent unto you for the same purpose, that he might know your estate, and comfort (encourage) your hearts", Colossians 4.8. We need more people like Barnabas. He was a true "son of consolation (encouragement)." See Acts 4.36; 11.22-23.

Jonathan didn't just "strengthen David": he "strengthened his hand **in God.**" This is worth remembering when we are visiting fellow-believers in trouble. It is important to pray and read the Scriptures. Otherwise we are just making a social visit! Notice too the timing of Jonathan's visit. He must have been downcast and disappointed at the behaviour of Keilah. Help and encouragement was available just at the right moment. The timing was perfect!

ii) His assurance about David. "Fear not: for the hand of Saul my father shall not find thee; and thou shalt be king over Israel." He was right there! But notice what follows: "And I shall be next unto thee; and that also Saul my father knoweth." Jonathan was right when he thought of David's future glory, but he was wrong when he anticipated his own prominence. Compare Mark 10.35-40. However, Jonathan did give the place of pre-eminence to David, and he does illustrate Romans 12.10, "In honour preferring one another."

iii) His absence from David. "And they two made a covenant before the Lord.and David abode in the wood, and Jonathan went to his house." (Compare John 7.53 – 8.1). Neither David or Jonathan knew that this was to be their last meeting. Jonathan thought in terms of **future glory** with David, but he wasn't prepared to pay the price of **present rejection** with David. Jonathan ultimately lost his life because he was unwilling to become identified with the rejected king. The Lord Jesus taught that "whosoever will save his life shall lose it; but whosoever shall lose his life for my sake and the gospel's, the same shall save it" (Mk 8.34-38). We should add that David never criticised his friend. See 2 Samuel 1.25-26. Perhaps both David and Jonathan felt that David's best interests could be served by Jonathan remaining at court.

C) The treachery of the Ziphites (vv.19-23)
The men of Keilah would have betrayed David, but the men of Ziph actually went ahead with their betrayal. Once again, Saul used the Lord's name to cover his own iniquity: "Blessed be ye of the Lord; for ye have compassion on me." He describes divine deliverance as David's subtlety: "it is told me that he dealeth very subtilly." David certainly did not attribute his deliverance to his own subtlety. Just read Psalm 54. Notice its title: "A Psalm of David, when the Ziphims came and said to Saul, Doth not David hide himself with us?" "Save me, O God, by thy name, and judge me by thy strength...Behold, God is mine helper...He hath delivered me out of all trouble." Notice that Saul was determined to search for David "throughout all the thousands of Judah." The Lord Jesus was born at Bethlehem which was "little among the thousands of Judah" (Mic 5.2).

3. David in the Wilderness of Maon (vv.24-28)

Saul was on the verge of capturing David, but "man's extremity is God's opportunity", and at the very last moment, a messenger arrives to inform Saul that the Philistines had invaded the land. As usual, God's timing is perfect. David had good cause to write, "My times are in thy hand: deliver me from the hand of mine enemies, and from them that persecute me" (Ps 31.15). Jonathan was right, "the hand of Saul my father shall not find thee" (v.17). (Sela-hammahlekoth means, literally, "the rock of smoothness", i.e. of "slipping away or escaping", Keil & Delitzsch).

4). David at En-Gedi (v.29)

"And David went up from thence, and dwelt in the strong holds at En-gedi. The following chapter describes events in "the wilderness of En-gedi." It wasn't long before Saul continued his hunt for David.

<u>ADDENDUM</u>

A plea for planned reading

On a positive note, here are four ways in which we can get maximum benefit from our Bibles:

i) We should read the Scriptures prayerfully. See Psalm 119.18, "Open thou mine eyes, that I might behold wondrous things out of thy law." We have an excellent example of the attitude we should display in Nehemiah 8.5-6, "And Ezra opened the book…and Ezra blessed the Lord, the great God. And all the people answered, Amen, Amen, with lifting up their hands: and they bowed their heads, and worshipped the Lord with their faces to the ground". The Scriptures were read with reverence, and in a worshipful spirit.

ii) We should read the Scriptures purposefully. While we all have favourite passages, and probably for good reason, we do need to read and study the Scriptures comprehensively. This involves planned reading, and that necessitates planned time. The Scriptures must be read at length, but also in detail It is an excellent practice to read the entire Scriptures once every year. Within this framework of general reading, select particular books for more detailed study.

> Yes I thought I knew my Bible
> Reading piecemeal hit or miss;
> Now a part of John or Matthew,
> Then a bit of Genesis.
>
> Certain chapters of Isaiah,
> Certain Psalms, the 23rd;
> First of Proverbs, 12th of Romans;
> Yes, I thought I knew the word.
>
> But I found that thorough reading
> Was a different thing to do,
> And the way was unfamiliar
> When I read my Bible through.
>
> You who like to play at Bible,
> Dip and dabble here and there,
> Just before you kneel aweary
> Yawning through a hurried prayer
>
> You who treat the crown of writings
> As you treat no other book;
> Just a paragraph disjointed,
> Just a crude impatient look.
>
> Try a worthier procedure,
> Try a broad and steady view
> You will kneel in awesome wonder
> When you read the Bible through.

Bible study involves meditation. We must think about what we read. It is important to be technically accurate, but we must build on that foundation. Hence the instructions given to Joshua, "This book of the law shall not depart out of thy mouth; but thou shalt meditate therein day and night, that thou mayest observe to do according to all that is written therein: for then thou shalt make thy way prosperous, and then thou shalt have good success" (Josh 1.8).

iii) We should read the Scriptures positively. We should read the Scriptures with determination to act on what we read. "To this man will I look, even to him that is poor and of a contrite spirit, and trembleth at my word" (Is 66.2). This is all part of our conduct as "obedient children" (1 Pet 1.14). The word of God should **(i)** inform our minds, **(ii)** warm our hearts, **(iii)** direct our lives.

We must remember that "all scripture is given by inspiration of God, and is profitable for **"doctrine"** (it tells me what is right), **"reproof"** (it tells me when I am not right), **"correction"** (it puts me right), and **"instruction"** (it keeps me right). It is an excellent practice to memorise the Scriptures, but Bible study involves far more than the ability to fire off verses like a machine gun, and become walking Young's Concordances! We are to "adorn the doctrine of God our Saviour in all things" (Tit 2.10).

Notice that the public reading of the Scriptures in Nehemiah 8 was followed by a period of intensive Bible study, and the people concerned "found written in the law which the Lord had commanded by Moses, that the children of Israel should dwell in booths in the feast of the seventh month." This particular command had not been observed for a thousand years ("since the days of Jeshua the son of Nun unto that day had not the children of Israel done so"), but they acted on what they read!

iv) We should read the Scriptures primarily. Don't let the commentaries take over! Refer to them by all means (we do in these studies), but our business is to read and study **the word of God!** We must let the Scriptures speak for themselves. We must make our **own** effort to understand the Bible. Hence 2 Timothy 2.15, "Study (strive diligently) to shew thyself approved unto God, a workman that needeth not to be ashamed, rightly dividing the word of truth." The RV translates "rightly dividing" as "handling aright." Quite obviously, we cannot expect divine approval if we misinterpret, mishandle, or misapply the word of God. It is the "word of truth", as opposed to "words to no profit" (v.14), and as opposed to the "word" of Hymenaeus and Philetus; who "concerning the truth have erred" (vv.17-18). The expression, "the word of truth", emphasises its total accuracy and reliability.

CHAPTER 24

"I know well that thou shalt surely be king"(24.1-22)

The temporary respite for David was soon over. We have no details of Saul's counter-attack on the Philistines (23.27-28), but it wasn't long before he was back in the hunt for David. However, he gained a further respite in his ongoing flight from Saul, but this time it was for a different reason. Once again, it didn't last long. Saul returned to the chase in Chapter 26.

This chapter can be divided as follows: **(1)** David's mercy to Saul (vv.1-7); **(2)** David's appeal to Saul (vv.8-15); **(3)** David's recognition by Saul (vv.16-21); **(4)** David's departure from Saul (v.22).

1. David's Mercy to Saul (vv.1-7)
There are two parts to the opening paragraph: **(A)** David's pursuit by Saul (vv.1-2), and **(B)** David's power over Saul (vv.3-7).

A) David's pursuit by Saul (vv.1-2)
"And it came to pass, when Saul was returned from following the Philistines, that it was told him, saying, Behold, David is in the wilderness of En-gedi. Then Saul took three thousand chosen men out of all Israel, and went to seek David and his men upon the rocks of the wild goats." We do not know for sure who "told him", but the Ziphites look like the culprits. See 23.19 and 26.1. En-gedi lay at the middle of the western coast of the Dead Sea, and we are told (Keil & Delitzsh) that it is now known as Ain-jidy, meaning "goat-fountain." It is sad to see Saul's relentless pursuit of David. It is equally sad when believers take every opportunity to attack each other. "Let all bitterness, and wrath, and anger, and clamour, and evil speaking, be put away from you, with all malice: and be ye kind one to another, tenderhearted, forgiving one another, even as God for Christ's sake hath forgiven you" (Eph 4.31-32). Saul, who "went to **seek** David", resembled his dark master who "walketh about, **seeking** whom he may devour" (1 Pet 5.8).

B) David's power over Saul (vv.3-7)

"And he came to the sheepcotes by the way, where was a cave; and Saul went in to cover his feet (to relieve himself): and David and his men remained in the sides of the cave." It has been suggested that the cave in question lies near the ruined village of Chareitun, but this has been disputed. However, the description of this particular cave is interesting, and will at least help us to imagine the place: "a large cave or chamber in the rock, with a very narrow entrance entirely concealed by stones, and with many side vaults in which the deepest darkness reigns, at least to anyone who has just entered the limestone vaults from the dazzling light of day." Returning to the actual text of our chapter, we should notice:

i) The recommendation to David (v.4).
"And the men of David said unto him, Behold the day of which the Lord said unto thee, Behold, I will deliver thine enemy into thine hand, that thou mayest do to him as it shall seem good unto thee." David's companions mistakenly concluded that God had given David an opportunity to avenge himself. But there is no record that God had ever spoken to David in the way they suggested. In fact, David was quite adamant that the Lord Himself would deal with Saul. See (vv.6,12 and 26.8-11).

Here is yet another way in which the history of David reminds us of the Lord Jesus. David acted most graciously towards the man who sought his life. His men were rather like the Lord's disciples when He was rejected by the Samaritans: "Lord, wilt thou that we command fire to come down from heaven, and consume them, even as Elias did?" To which the Lord replied, "Ye know not what manner of spirit ye are of. For the Son of man is not come to destroy men's lives, but to save them" (Lk 9.51-56).

We must remember that Christians live by different principles. In this case, the principle of Romans 12.16-21 applies: "Recompense to no man evil for evil...Dearly beloved, avenge not yourselves, but rather give place unto wrath: for it is written, vengeance is mine; I will repay, saith the Lord. Therefore if thine enemy hunger feed him; if he thirst, give him to drink: for in so doing thou shalt heap coals of fire on his head. Be not overcome of evil, but overcome evil with good." As A.McShane observes, "It might be expected of Saul that he would slay a man on a sick bed (19.14-15), but for a man after God's own heart (13.14) to slay the Lord's anointed in such circumstances, would have been nothing short of a disaster." David exemplified 1 Peter 4.19, "Let them that suffer according to the will of

God, commit the keeping of their souls to him in well doing, as unto a faithful Creator."

H.L.Rossier makes a telling comment in connection with the "providential" opportunity given to David. "Providential circumstances are not ordained to govern our conduct, or to direct it, but to put our faith to the test." This is very important. We should never judge by circumstances: we must always judge by the word of God. God had not yet executed the sentence pronounced upon Saul, and therefore he remained "the Lord's anointed."

ii) The regret of David (vv.5-6). "Then David arose, and cut off the skirt of Saul's robe privily. And it came to pass afterward, that David's heart smote him, because he had cut off Saul's skirt. And he said unto his men, The Lord forbid that I should do this thing unto my master, the Lord's anointed, to stretch forth mine hand against him, seeing he is the anointed of the Lord." It seems such a minor offence, but David evidently had a very tender conscience. Even the slightest infringement of God's will, and the slightest disservice to Saul, caused him grief. That's not a bad thing. So often we ignore the will of God, and hurt our fellow-believers, without even realising what has happened.

iii) The restraint by David (v.7). "So David stayed his servants with these words, and suffered them not to rise against Saul." It was certainly a victory for restraint, both self-restraint and restraint on others.

At this point we should read Psalm 57. It is headed, "To the chief Musician, **Al-taschith**, Michtam of David, when he fled from Saul in the cave." "Altaschith" means "destroy not", and it has been suggested that this is what David actually said to his men. He was quite confident that God would intervene on his behalf: "Be merciful unto me, O God, be merciful unto me: for my soul trusteth in thee: yea, in the shadow of thy wings will I make my refuge, until these calamities be overpast. I will cry unto God most high; unto God that performeth all things for me. He shall send from heaven, and save me from the reproach of him that would swallow me up. Selah. God shall send forth his mercy and his truth. My soul is among lions: and I lie even among them that are set on fire, even the sons of men, whose teeth are spears and arrows, and their tongue a sharp sword, Be thou exalted, O God above the heavens; let thy glory be above all the earth. They have prepared a net for my steps; my soul is bowed down: they have digged a pit before me, in the midst whereof they are fallen themselves. Selah" (Ps 57.1-6)

2. David's Appeal to Saul (vv.8-15)

Saul was soon made aware of the presence of David and his men in the cave. "Saul rose up out of the cave, and went on his way. David also arose afterward, and went out of the cave, and cried after Saul." We must notice: **(A)** He respected Saul (v.8); **(B)** He reproached Saul (vv.9-11); **(C)** He referred the issue to God (vv.12-15).

A) He respected Saul (v.8)

"David...cried after Saul, saying, My lord the king. And when Saul looked behind him, David stooped with his face to the earth, and bowed himself." Actions speak louder than words! Notice what he **said**: he "cried...My lord the king." Notice what he **did**: he "stooped with his face to the earth, and bowed himself." David exhibited true humility. His attitude to Saul reminds us of 1 Peter 2.18-19, "Servants, be subject to your masters with all fear; not only to the good and gentle, but also to the froward. For this is thankworthy, if a man for conscience toward God endure grief, suffering wrongfully." David showed no animosity towards Saul. Intemperance, however much we think it is justified, achieves nothing, and only serves to bring our testimony into disrepute.

B) He reproached Saul (vv.9-11)

Notice that while David reproached Saul: he did not **revile** him. "Wherefore hearest thou men's word's, saying, Behold, David seeketh thy hurt?" Perhaps David is referring here to men like Doeg (22.8-10), and the Ziphites, who took every opportunity to betray David (23.19-20;26.1). These talebearers evidently deepened Saul's hatred for David, and fuelled his attempts to kill him. This is a warning to us all. One of the obnoxious characters described in the book of Proverbs is the talebearer. See, for example 26.20, "Where no wood is, there the fire goeth out: so where there is no talebearer, the strife ceaseth." Compare 16.28, "A froward man soweth strife: and a whisperer separateth chief friends." Some people simply love stories about others: see 18.8 and 26.22, "The words of a talebearer are as wounds ("dainty morsels", JND), and they go down into the innermost parts of the belly." Beware! Someone who is always running down other people behind their backs to you, will certainly run **you** down behind your back as well! Do remember as well, that even if a story is true, it does not have to be circulated. "Love covers a multitude of sins" (1 Pet 4.8 JND). This does not mean that wrong is "swept under the carpet", but it does mean that we must not go around publicising each other's weaknesses and deficiencies.

Sadly, Saul, like so many people when they listen to a story about somebody else, never checked the facts. Well, the facts now stare him in the face: "Behold, this day thine own eyes have seen how that the Lord hath delivered thee to day into mine hand in the cave: and some bade me kill thee: but mine eye spared thee; and I said, I will not put forth mine hand against my lord; for he is the Lord's anointed. Moreover, my father, see, yea, see the skirt of thy robe in my hand: for in that I cut off the skirt of thy robe, and killed thee not, know thou and see that there is neither evil nor transgression in mine hand, and I have not sinned against thee; yet thou huntest my soul to take it." Notice that he addressed Saul here as "my father." This conveys affection. Saul responded with "my son" in v.16.

Happily, David could appeal to his behaviour without fear of contradiction. When Paul was under attack at Corinth, he could say, "For our rejoicing is this, the testimony of our conscience, that in simplicity and godly sincerity, not with fleshly wisdom, but by the grace of God, we have had our conversation in this world, and more abundantly to you-ward" (2 Cor 1.12).

C) He referred the issue to God (vv.12-15)
Yet again, David's attitude reminds us of the Lord Jesus: "Who when he was reviled, reviled not again; when he suffered he threatened not; but committed himself to him that judgeth righteously" (1 Pet 2.23). This is exactly what David did: "The Lord judge between me and thee, and the Lord avenge me of thee: but mine hand shall not be upon thee. As saith the proverb of the ancients, Wickedness proceedeth from the wicked: but mine hand shall not be upon thee." (The source of David's quotation is not known to us). Compare Proverbs 20.22. A.McShane has a telling comment here: "Those who have put their case into His hands must ever be on their guard, lest they take it out of them."

We should notice David's humility here: "After whom is the king of Israel come out? After whom dost thou pursue? After a dead dog, after a flea." In this way, David describes himself "as a perfectly harmless and innocent man, of whom Saul had no occasion to be afraid, and whom the king of Israel ought to think it beneath his dignity to pursue, A dead dog cannot bite or hurt, and is an object about which the king ought not to trouble himself. See 2 Samuel 9.8 & 16.9, where the idea of something contemptible is included. The point of comparison with a flea is the insignificance of such an animal (see 26.20)", Keil & Delitzsch. The original is even stronger: "a flea" is "a single flea", which is "not easily caught, and easily escapes, and if it is caught, is poor game for the royal hunter." (Quoted in Ellicott's Commentary). In his own eyes, David, is less than nothing, reminding us of 1 Corinthians 3.7, "So then neither is he that planteth any thing, neither he that watereth; but God that giveth the increase."

However, we know that "God resisteth the proud, and giveth grace to the humble (1 Pet 5.5) David was therefore able to say, "The Lord therefore be judge, and judge between me and thee, and see, and plead my cause, and deliver me out of thine hand." Peter continues: "Humble yourselves therefore under the mighty hand of God, that he may exalt you in due time: casting all your care upon him; for he careth for you."

3. David's Recognition by Saul (vv.16-21)
Saul **(A)** Acknowledged David's righteousness (vv.16-19), and **(B)** Anticipated David's reign (vv.20-21).

A) He acknowledged David's righteousness (vv.16-19)
"Is this thy voice, my son David. And Saul lifted up his voice and wept. And he said to David, Thou art more righteous than I: for thou hast rewarded me good, whereas I have rewarded thee evil. And thou hast shewed this day how that thou hast dealt well with me: forasmuch as when the Lord hath delivered me into thine hand, thou killedst me not. For if a man find his enemy will he let him go well away? Wherefore the Lord reward thee good for that thou hast done unto me this day."

In the heat of the moment, Saul acknowledges David's moral superiority, but, sadly, this soon passed. David evidently recognised that Saul had not changed his mind permanently, otherwise he would have not returned to his refuge in the wilderness. See v.22. However, it does give us the opportunity to say that we should act and speak in a way which commends our testimony. "In all things shewing thyself a pattern of good works: in doctrine shewing uncorruptness, gravity, sincerity, sound speech, that cannot be condemned; that he that is of the contrary part may be ashamed, having no evil thing to say of you" (Tit 2.7-8).

B) He anticipated David's reign (vv.20-21)
Saul confirmed what his son Jonathan had already stated: "Thou shalt be king over Israel, and I shall be next unto thee; and that also Saul my father knoweth" (23.17). Notice:

i) He expressed conviction (v.20). "And now, behold, I know well that thou shalt surely be king, and that the kingdom of Israel shall be established in thine hand." Samuel had told Saul that God had given the kingdom to "a man after his own heart" (14.13-14), and it wasn't long before he realised that David was the man in question. See 18.8 & 20.30-31.

We have to note, once again, that these impressive words did not bring an end to Saul's hostility. He still persisted in his murderous hunt for David. See Chapter 26. H.L.Rossier has correctly assessed the situation: "A reprobate heart may be **softened** in the presence of grace without being changed. God does not ask us for **feelings,** however righteous they may be; it is **faith** that counts, for faith alone is able to regenerate and save a sinner."

We can say, in **faith,** of the Lord Jesus, "I know well that thou shalt surely be king, and that the kingdom of Israel shall be established in thine hand." We stand with Nathanael, and say "Rabbi, thou art the Son of God; thou art the King of Israel" (Jn 1.49).

ii) He desired clemency (v.21). "Swear now therefore unto me by the Lord, that thou wilt not cut off my seed after me, and that thou wilt not destroy my name out of my father's house. And David sware unto Saul." It has been pointed out that a change of dynasty was frequently accompanied by the slaughter of the descendants of the original monarch. This happened in 1 Kings 15.29, 16.11 and 2 Kings 10.1-14.

David was as good as his word, witness his kindness to Saul's grandson, Mephibosheth. "And David said, Is there yet any that is left of the house of Saul, that I may shew him kindness for Jonathan's sake?" (2 Sam 9.1) The Lord Jesus, "the root and the offspring of David", showed wonderful clemency to the dying thief. See Luke 23.42-43, "And he said unto Jesus, Lord, remember me when thou comest into thy kingdom. And Jesus said unto him, verily I say unto thee, To day shalt thou be with me in paradise."

4. David's Departure from Saul (v.22)
The chapter ends on a significant note: "And Saul went home; but David and his men gat them up unto the hold."

i) Saul returned home. While Saul may have gone home filled with remorse, he evidently left David to his own devices. There is no mention of David going home, and no mention of his return to court. Saul went home, but David remained an exile. There was no genuine repentance on Saul's part.

ii) David returned to the hold. According to Keil & Delitzsch, "the hold" (a different word is used in 22.5) here denotes "the mountainous part of the desert of Judah." This is confirmed by Gesenius. Keil & Delitzsch explain that David "remained upon the mountain heights, because he did not regard the passing change in Saul's feelings as likely to continue." He was certainly right! It has been nicely said that David was certainly as "wise as a serpent" here, just as he was as "harmless as a dove" in the cave. See Matthew 10.16.

Homeless David reminds us, again, of the Lord Jesus. "Foxes have holes, and the birds of the air have nests; but the Son of man hath not where to lay his head" (Lk 9.58). Compare John 7.53–8.1: "And every man (the Jewish leaders) went unto his own house. But Jesus went unto the mount of Olives."

> No room in the inn for the Saviour was found,
> Who from childhood was treated with scorn;
> No place but the manger where cattle were brought,
> When in Bethlehem Jesus was born.
>
> No home but the mountain of Olives was His,
> Though the bird of the air had its nest;
> No love but the Father's, Whose bosom He left,
> Could give Him refreshment and rest.
>
> No comforters came, when for comfort He looked,
> No pity, when pity He sought;
> For sin He was wounded and smitten of God,
> And sinners did set Him at nought.
>
> And now that He dwells in the mansions of bliss,
> He has room for each trusting one there,
> And His sorrows remembered will heighten the joy
> Which all will eternally share.

CHAPTER 25A

"The man was churlish, and evil in his doings" (25.1-22)

No, **not** David! "The man" in question was Nabal. His own wife, Abigail, had to say, "for as his name is, so is he; Nabal is his name, and folly is with him (v.25). As you can guess from this, Nabal means "fool", or "foolish." It seems unlikely that this was his proper name, but a nickname by which he was known on account of his folly.

This is a long chapter, and deserves two studies. After the death of Samuel (v.1), we will divide the passage as follows: **(1)** Nabal's animosity to David (vv.2-22) and **(2)** Abigail's appeal to David (vv.23-44). As you can see, these are just general titles. We will find a variety of valuable lessons in the chapter.

The chapter begins, as we have noted, with the death of Samuel. "And Samuel died; and all the Israelites were gathered together, and lamented him, and buried him in his house at Ramah." It has been nicely said that "few have left the world with so many virtues, and so few failings." (A.McShane). It is significant that his funeral was attended by all Israel. The entire nation recognised the benefits they had received through his leadership. "Since the days of Moses, no man had arisen to whom the covenant nation owed so much as to Samuel." (Keil & Deliztsch). Through him, God's authority had been re-established in Israel, and the nation had grown in strength and power. His wise counsel had been accompanied by personal godliness.

We cannot avoid the comparison between the death of Samuel and the death of Nabal. See (vv.37-38). Like Jehoram, Nabal "departed without being desired" (2 Chron 21.20). But the nation lamented the passing of Samuel. We are told that "a good name is better than precious ointment; and the day of death than the day of one's birth" (Ecc 7.1). At first glance, this is a curious statement, but on reflection, it is absolutely true! The connection between the "good name" and "the day of death" is clear. The good name is secured by the end of the journey. "The life lived between the two events will determine whether our name leaves behind a lovely fragrance or a foul stench" (W.W.Weirsbe). Samuel certainly left "a lovely fragrance." Nabal certainly left "a foul stench." What will **we** leave behind?

"And David arose, and went down to the wilderness of Paran." Quite obviously, he had no confidence in Saul. He was not deceived by his apparent change of heart, and events proved that he was right. See 26.1-2. Paran, lying south of the Dead Sea, means "cavernous" and was a suitable place for a fugitive. It is interesting to note that Paran was associated with the glory of God. See Deuteronomy 33.2 and Habakkuk 3.3. It is also worth pointing out that the death of Samuel did not spell disaster for David. Some people collapse when human "props" are removed. Look what happened to Joash after the death of Jehoiada! Read 2 Chronicles 24. We should value each other, but our strength and confidence must be in the Lord. This brings us to the first major section of the chapter:

1) Nabal's Animosity to David (v.2-22)
We must notice here *(A)* His household (vv.2-3); *(B)* His ingratitude (vv.4-12); *(C)* His peril (vv.13-22).

A) His household (vv.2-3)
"And there was a man in Maon (see 24.24), whose possessions were in Carmel; and the man was very great, and he had three thousand sheep, and a thousand goats: and he was shearing his sheep in Carmel. Now the name of the man was Nabal; and the name of his wife Abigail: and she was a woman of good understanding and of a beautiful countenance: but the man was churlish and evil in his doings; and he was of the house of Caleb." (Carmel here evidently refers, not to well-known Carmel on the coast, but the present Kurmul on the mountains of Judah, scarcely half an hour's journey to the north-west of Maon. See Keil & Delitzsch). There are at least three things to ponder here:

i) His wealth
The word of God does not condemn wealth *per se*. It **does** censure those that "**will be**" rich" (people who make it their consuming ambition to be rich), and gives good advice to those who "**are**" rich" (1 Tim 6.9 & 17).

Moses reminded Israel of their indebtedness to God for material prosperity: "Thou shalt remember the Lord thy God: for it is he that giveth thee power to get wealth" (Deut 8.18). David recognised this: "But who am I, and what is my people, that we should be able to offer so willingly after this sort? For all things come of thee, and of thine own have we given thee" (1 Chron 29.14).

We look in vain for any suggestion that Nabal was grateful to God for his wealth. He certainly didn't show any gratitude to David for protecting his flocks. See vv.7-8 & 14-16. It reminds us of another rich farmer who said: "What shall I do, because I have no room where to bestow *my* fruits? And he said, This will I do: I will pull down my barns, and build greater; and there will I bestow all *my* fruits and *my* goods." God called him a "fool" too! See Luke 12.16-21.

ii) His wife
Inwardly, Abigail was "a woman of good understanding", and outwardly, she was "of a beautiful countenance." As we shall see, her wisdom was remarkable. Solomon said that "as a jewel of gold in a swine's snout, so is a fair woman which is without discretion", Proverbs 11.22. This did not apply to Abigail! It is worth noticing that Abigail's "good understanding" is mentioned before her "beautiful countenance." It's very important to get our priorities right, especially in choosing a partner in life. Listen to this, "Favour (charm) is deceitful (deceptive), and beauty is vain (passing): but a woman that feareth the Lord, shall be praised. Give her the fruit (reward) of her hands; and let her own works praise her in the gates" (Prov 31.30-31).

iii) His worthlessness
He was wealthy, but worthless. ("Belial" means "worthless"). He was "churlish and evil in his doings." "Churlish" *(quasheh)* means "hard" (see, for example 2 Samuel 3.39) or "obstinate" (see Isaiah 48.4). Then comes a very significant little remark. "And he was of the house of Caleb!" This was the man who, with Joshua, "wholly followed the Lord" (Num 32.12). H.L.Rossier compares the two men with reference to Romans 6.13. Both men were evidently energetic. Caleb was eighty-five when he said, "Give me this mountain." Read Joshua 14. Nabal was energetic in other directions, but he yielded "his members as instruments of unrighteousness unto sin", whereas Caleb yielded his "members as instruments of righteousness unto God." A.McShane has a very telling piece here: "A look at this home in Carmel will show that it was sharply divided. The husband was a fool, and

his wife was prudent. He was exceedingly selfish and speaks of "my bread", "my water", and "my flesh", but she was most generous. He was a drunken sot, and she was a dutiful wife. If she married him for his wealth, or because he belonged to the noble house of Caleb, she must have regretted her choice a thousand times. Alas! She is not the only example of those who have learned when it is too late."

This extraordinary marriage, between two people who evidently had nothing in common at all, is a picture of the old and new natures in every one of us. We are all painfully aware "that in me (that is in my flesh), dwelleth no good thing" (Rom 7.18). That sounds just like Nabal! We are also aware of the new nature and its desires: we "delight in the law of God after the inward man" (Rom 7.22). Paul describes the "works of the flesh" and the "fruit of the Spirit" in Galatians 5.19-23. Nabal exhibited the former, and Abigail the latter.

B) His ingratitude (vv.4-12)
In this section, we should notice *(i)* David's request (vv.4-8), and *(ii)* Nabal's response (vv.9-12).

i) David's request, (vv.4-8)
These verses display David's shepherd heart, and take us back to 16.11, "Behold, he keepeth the sheep." Good leaders must have shepherd hearts. See Acts 20.28. We know that David was a fugitive at this time. He was continually "on the run." But the very man who needed protection himself, was busy protecting others! In his own words, "now thy shepherds which were with us, we hurt them not, neither was there ought missing unto them, all the while they were in Carmel. Ask the young men, and they will shew thee" (vv.7-8). One of the "young men" confirmed the facts: "the men were very good unto us, and we were not hurt, neither missed we any thing, as long as we were conversant with them, when we were in the fields: they were a wall unto us both by night and day, all the while we were with them keeping the sheep." We know from 24.24 that David had been in the area.

David and his men were not so busy looking after their own interests that they ignored the interests of other people. This reminds us of New Testament teaching: "Look not every man on his own things, but every man also on the things of others", Philippians 2.4. The same passage continues by reminding us that the Lord Jesus Himself looked "not on his own things, but...on the things of others." This was true in **His life.** See, for example,

Mark 6.31, "Come ye yourselves apart into a desert place, and rest a while: for there were **many coming and going**, and they had no leisure so much as to eat." When the "band of men and officers" came to arrest Him, the Lord Jesus said, "I have told you that I am he: if therefore ye seek me, let **these** go their way: that the saying might be fulfilled, which he spake, Of them which thou gavest me I have lost none" (Jn 18.8-9). This was true in **His death**. We need say no more. Philippians 2 speaks for itself. But do remember that we are told "Let this mind be in **you,** which was also in Christ Jesus." We should notice as well that like the Lord Jesus, David assisted Nabal's men voluntarily. He was not under any obligation to protect them. Our care for each other should flow from mutual love and devotion, although we **do** have a duty to each other!

But there is another important lesson here. Even in exile and adversity, David's ability to control men was developing. He was welding the most unlikely people (see 22.2) into a disciplined fighting force. They were certainly not brigands! David was deeply concerned for the welfare of God's people, and protected them from harm and danger. God was preparing the future king for rule. See Psalm 78.70-72. How are **we** getting on in God's "prep school?" Difficulty and opposition didn't halt David in his tracks. So often, we resemble the seed which fell on "stony places." The Lord Jesus said, "the same is he that heareth the word, and anon with joy receiveth it; yet hath he no root in himself, but dureth for a while: for when tribulation or persecution ariseth because of the word, by and by he is offended" (Mt 3.21-21). But not David! He did not "throw in the towel!" Do **we?**

It was certainly "a good day" for Nabal (v.8), and David was not unreasonable in requesting some recognition for services rendered. Notice his courtesy: "Greet him in my name: and...say to him...Peace be to thee, and peace be to thine house, and peace unto all that thou hast" (vv.5-6). Notice his tone of voice. He did not demand his rights: "Wherefore let the young men find favour in thine eyes" (v.8). Notice his humility: "Give, I pray thee, whatsoever cometh to thine hand unto thy **servants,** and to thy **son** David" (v.8). We should notice similar courtesy in Paul's letter to Philemon. Paul prefaced his request with "Grace to you, and **peace,** from God our Father and the Lord Jesus Christ" (v.3). Paul did not command Philemon to receive Onesimus: "Wherefore, though I might be much bold in Christ to enjoin thee that which is convenient, yet for love's sake I rather **beseech** thee" (vv.8-9). Paul did not trumpet his apostolic authority. He described himself as "Paul the aged, and now also a prisoner of Jesus Christ" (v.9). Paul gently reminded Philemon of his indebtedness to him: "Albeit I do not say to thee how thou owest unto me even **thine own self** besides" (v.19). All this reminds us that our "moderation (gentleness)" should "be known unto all men" (Phil 4.5).

Let's look at it another way. The Lord Jesus has every right to our love and devotion in view of all that He has done for us. Although at present rejected, He continues to shower us with divine blessing. He is "a wall unto us both by night and day." He "hath said, I will never leave thee nor forsake thee. So that we may boldly say, The Lord is my helper, and I will not fear what man shall do unto me" (Heb 13.5-6).

> What can I bring Thee my Saviour
> In return for Thy great love to me,
> For redemption so full and so precious,
> By the blood shed on Calvary"s tree?
> What can I offer Thee, Saviour
> When the whole of creation is Thine?
> Take my heart, my life, and my all, dear Lord
> To be fashioned by Thy love divine.

ii) Nabal's response (vv.9-12)

It does not make happy reading. "And Nabal answered David's servants, and said, Who is David? And who is the son of Jesse? There be many servants nowadays that break away every man from his master". (Perhaps Nabal was alluding to the breach between Saul and David here). Shall I then take my bread, and my water, and my flesh that I have killed for my shearers, and give it unto men, whom I know not whence they be?"

The centuries pass, and we hear a similar voice: "We know that God spake unto Moses: as for this *fellow,* we know not **from whence he is"** (Jn 9.29). Their contempt for the Lord Jesus is clear when we omit the italicised word *"fellow."* Nabal rejected the "man after God's own heart", and men and women generally have no time for the Lord Jesus. They say in effect, with Pharaoh, "Who is the Lord, that I should obey his voice...I know not the Lord" (Ex 5.2). Nabal referred to "**my** bread, and **my** water, and **my** flesh", and placed himself, therefore under the same condemnation as Belshazzar: "the God in whose hand thy breath is, and whose are all thy ways, hast thou not glorified" (Dan 5.23). Or, to put it in hymnology:

> Room for pleasure, room for business;
> But for Christ, the crucified,
> Not a place that He can enter,
> In the heart for which He died!

Humanly speaking, the "writing was on the wall" for Nabal as well as Belshazzar, and this brings us to:

C) His peril, (vv.13-22)
In these verses, we must notice *(i)* David's intention (v.13) and *(ii)* Abigail's intervention (vv.14-22).

i) David's intention (v.13)
"And David said unto his men, Gird ye on every man his sword. And they girded on every man his sword: and there went up after David about four hundred men; and two hundred abode by the stuff." A very angry man rode towards Carmel. "Now David had said, Surely in vain have I kept all that this fellow hath in the wilderness, so that nothing was missed of all that pertained unto him: and he hath requited me evil for good. So and more also do God unto the enemies of David, if I leave of all that pertain to him by the morning light any that pisseth against the wall" (vv.21-22). David intended to kill all the men. (The last sentence is not easy to follow: it could mean, "as truly as God will punish the enemies of David, so certainly will I not leave till the morning...", Keil & Delitzsch. Or, bearing in mind that Nabal was not actually present, in which case David would have said, "So and more also do God **unto thee**", it could mean that even if David left some alive, God would judge them). Angry David cried, "Gird ye on every man his sword." The Lord Jesus said to Peter, "Put up again thy sword into his place" (Mt 26.52). David complained that his work in protecting Nabal's interests had been "in vain." We are assured that our "labour is not in vain in the Lord" (1 Cor 15.58).

As A.McShane rightly observes, "Slander is not easily borne, and lies told by those we have befriended eat deeply into our souls, but it is not our right, anymore than David's, to avenge ourselves." James reminds us that "the wrath of man worketh not the righteousness of God" (1.20). See also Romans 12.19, "Dearly beloved, avenge not yourselves, but rather give place unto wrath: for it is written, (vengeance is mine; I will repay, saith the Lord." David certainly learnt this lesson in the previous chapter, but he appears to have forgotten it here! Just like us! How quickly **we** forget the lessons God teaches us! Abigail, a "woman of good understanding" rightly assessed the situation. Notice what she said to David in (v.26).

It is unwise, sometimes disastrous, to take decisions "in the heat of the moment." Our judgment is often severely impaired when we are angry. Listen to this (from *"Springs in the valley"*):

"Keep still! When trouble is brewing, keep still! When slander is getting on its legs, keep still! When your feelings are hurt, keep still till you recover from your excitement at any rate! Things look different through an unagitated eye. Nothing is lost by learning to keep still."

Solomon puts it like this: "He that hath no rule over his own spirit is like a city that is broken down, and without walls" (Prov 25.28); "Be not hasty in thy spirit to be angry: for anger resteth in the bosom of fools" (Ecc 7.9).

ii) Abigail's intervention (vv.14-22)
We will listen to Abigail's advice to David in our next study. This paragraph describes her preparation to intercept him en route to Carmel. A wise woman sets out to meet a very angry man! Abigail's cool hand is about to be laid on David's hot head! Notice the following;

a) Abigail was approachable. Unlike Nabal, who was "such a son of Belial, that a man cannot speak to him" (v.17), Abigail was prepared to listen. The young man was able to share his concerns with her without fear, even though it involved unpleasant facts about her husband. Nabal had a terrible reputation, but the young man knew that Abigail would not "fly off the handle", and could be relied upon to act wisely. "Now therefore know and consider what thou wilt do; for evil is determined against our master, and against all his household" (v.17). Sadly, even some Christians are very "off-putting." We can all be "prickly" at times, but we ought to be people who are willing to listen sympathetically to others. Elders, of course, should be people whom we can approach with confidence, and since we are talking about Abigail, how much we need wise women as well as wise men! Read 1 Timothy 3.11 and Titus 2.3-5.

b) Abigail was urgent. "Then Abigail made haste" (v.18). This is the first of four references to her "haste." See also (v.23, v.34, and v.42). Perhaps there's a sermon here somewhere! While David was wrong to act hastily,

Abigail was quite justified in "making haste." Lives were at stake, including, apparently, her own! See (v.34). The "Preacher" tells us, amongst many other things, that there is "a time to keep silence, and a time to speak" (Ecc 3.7). For Abigail, it was "a time to speak!"

This reminds us that we should lose no time in putting matters right if we have caused someone offence. Apologising is not a sign of weakness! Some of us know what Solomon meant when he said, "A brother offended is harder to be won than a strong city" (Prov 18.19). But we should do all that we can to ease the situation. Bearing in mind that David was on his way to avenge Nabal's insult, it also reminds us that judgment is coming, and therefore we should preach the gospel with urgency. Once again, lives are at stake. "Preach the word; be instant (urgent) in season, out of season" (2 Tim 4.2).

c) Abigail was unselfish. Unlike her selfish husband ("*my* bread...*my* water...*my* flesh"), she "took two hundred loaves, and two bottles of wine, and five sheep ready dressed, and five measures of parched corn, and an hundred clusters of raisins, and two hundred cakes of figs" (v.18). Nabal wouldn't give the "man after God's own heart" anything. Abigail gave liberally! Like Abigail, we should hold our possessions lightly for the Lord. See 1 Timothy 6.17-18.

> Naught that I have my own I call,
> I hold it for the Giver:
> My heart, my strength, my life, my all,
> Are His, and His for ever.

d) Abigail met David alone. Colin Lacey (*"Abigail, The Father's Joy"*, Precious Seed, May 2002) puts it like this: "She knew **where** to find David. Not in the bright lights of the city, but in the wilderness, "by the covert (secret place) of the hill." She knew **how** to find him. Without her husband: "But she told not her husband Nabal", (v.19). He would have been a hindrance to her. Without her servants: "And she said unto her servants, Go on before me; behold I come after you" (v.19). They would not understand. This was a personal matter between her and the king." We all recognise the importance of public prayer. The assembly prayer meetings are vital. But we all have personal concerns which are rightly brought to the Lord privately. After all, Abigail had some very personal things to say about her husband (see vv.25-26) and it would not have been wise to let everybody hear! Some things must remain confidential. Remember that the risen Lord appeared to Peter privately (Lk 24.35, 1 Cor 15.5), and that's all we know!

In our next study, we will listen to Abigail's advice to David, and see the outcome of their meeting.

CHAPTER 25B

"Blessed be thy advice" (25.23-44)

We come now to our second study in this long chapter. As we have seen, after recording the death of Samuel (v.1), the passage can be divided as follows: **(1)** Nabal's animosity to David (vv.2-22), and **(2)** Abigail's appeal to David (vv.23-44).

1. Nabal's Animosity to David (vv.2-22)
Nabal was unaware that his life was in jeopardy. David, accompanied by four hundred armed men, was on his way to Carmel with the sole object of avenging Nabal's insult. David appears to be muttering angrily to himself in (vv.21-22), "Surely in vain have I kept all that this fellow hath in the wilderness, so that nothing was missed of all that pertaineth unto him: and he hath requited me evil for good. So and more also do God unto the enemies of David, if I leave of all that pertain to him by the morning light any that pisseth against the wall." We have noticed that David was quite wrong to "take the law into his own hands." He acted in "the heat of the moment", with no reference to God at all. Highly dangerous! But as we shall see, God did not stand on the touchline, and let David ruin his good name.

Nabal was also unaware that his wife had left Carmel to avert the coming disaster, having been warned by one of the young men: "evil is determined against our master, and against all his household" (v.17). This brings us to:

2. Abigail's Appeal to David (vv.23-44)
Spiritual wisdom does not belong exclusively to men! We read about the "wise woman" of Tekoah (2 Sam 14.2), and the "wise woman" of Abel (2 Sam 20.16). Proverbs 31.10-31 describes "a virtuous woman" who, amongst other things, "openeth her mouth with wisdom" (v.26). Whilst Abigail certainly provisioned David and his men (vv.18,27,35), it was her **wisdom**

that led David to say, "Blessed be the Lord God of Israel, which sent thee this day to meet me: and blessed be thy advice, and blessed be thou, which hast kept me this day from coming to shed blood, and from avenging myself with mine own hand" (vv.32-33). We must never think that the only work that sisters can do in the church is to make sandwiches and cakes for conferences, provide cups of tea, and wash up afterwards! For a start, read Philippians 4.3 and Titus 2.3-4.

We can divide this section of the chapter as follows: **(A)** Abigail's advice (vv.23-31); **(B)** David's appreciation (vv.32-35); **(C)** Nabal's death (vv.36-38); **(D)** Abigail's marriage (vv.39-44).

A) Abigail's advice (vv.23-31)
Abigail did not harangue David. Good advice can be spoilt by the way in which it is given. Paul didn't fall into that trap. Just look at the way he prefaces his remarks to Euodias and Syntyche in Philippians 4.1-2. Abigail acted in the spirit of Galatians 6.1. David had certainly been "overtaken in a fault!" We must therefore notice:

i) Her attitude towards David. "And when Abigail saw David, she hasted, and lighted off the ass, and fell before David on her face, and bowed herself to the ground" (v.23). In vv.24-31 she calls David "my lord" fourteen times, and describes herself as "thine handmaid" six times. Abigail displayed true humility in the presence of David. She recognised his authority, and placed herself at his disposal.

The Lord Jesus is the Son of David, yet David's Lord: Matthew 22.41-46. He is the "root and offspring of David" (Rev 22.16). He is, without any reserve whatsoever "the man after God's own heart." Can we really say with Thomas, **"My Lord** and my God?" Are we really vessels "unto honour, sanctified, and meet for the master's use, and prepared unto every good work?"

ii) Her intercession before David. "Upon me, my lord, upon me let this iniquity be: and let thine handmaid, I pray thee, speak in thine audience, and hear the words of thine handmaid. Let not my lord, I pray thee, regard this man of Belial, even Nabal: for as his name is, so is he; Nabal is his name, and folly is with him: but I thine handmaid saw not the young men of my lord, whom thou didst send" (vv.24-25). Notice that in her intercession, she did not minimise Nabal's guilt. She appealed to the grace and mercy of David, and pleaded with him to withhold judgement.

iii) Her confession of blame to David. "Upon me, my lord, upon me let this iniquity be" (v.24). She did not disassociate herself from Nabal. It is noteworthy that godly people never take a "holier than thou" attitude. Nehemiah was not responsible for the ruin of Jerusalem, but he prayed, "Let thine ear now be attentive and...hear the prayer of thy servant...both *I* and my father's house have sinned" (Neh 1.6). Daniel did the same: "And whiles I was speaking, and praying, and confessing **my** sin and the sin of my people Israel" (Dan 9.20).

iv) Her confidence in David. "Now therefore, my lord, as the Lord liveth, and as thy soul liveth, seeing the Lord hath withholden thee from coming to shed blood, and from avenging thyself with thine own hands, now let thine enemies, and they that seek evil to my lord, be as Nabal" (v.26). Abigail knew that the Lord had already intervened, and answered her appeal to David, before he even uttered a word! She was confident that her intercession had been effective, even without supporting evidence. Now there's faith for you!

v) Her assurance about David's future. "The Lord will certainly make my lord a sure house ("a lasting house', JND); because my lord fighteth the battles of the Lord, and evil hath not been found in thee all thy days. Yet a man is risen up to pursue thee, and to seek thy soul: but the soul of my lord shall be bound in the bundle of life ("the bundle of the living", JND) with the Lord thy God; and the souls of thine enemies, them shall he sling out, as out of the middle of a sling" (vv.28-29). Abigail seems to be alluding to 17.49 here. Colin Lacey ("*Abigail, The Father's Joy"*, Precious Seed, May 2002) sums it up nicely: "She had a clear vision of David's coming glory. No one looked less like a king than he did. He was rejected, and the dust of the wilderness was upon him. But she saw beyond his rejection to the time of his coming glory."

Her assurance about David's future mirrors the certainty surrounding the future of "Great David's greater Son." **He** has a "sure (enduring) house." See Luke 1.32-33, "He shall be great, and shall be called the Son of the Highest: and the Lord God shall give unto him the throne of his father David: and he shall reign over the house of Jacob for ever; and of his kingdom there shall be no end." **He** has fought "the battles of the Lord." See, for example, Luke 11.21-22, Acts 10.38, and particularly, Hebrews 2.14-15. It is true of **Him,** above all others, that "evil hath not been found in thee all thy days." Events proved, sadly, that this was not always true of

David. But the Lord Jesus "knew no sin" (2 Cor 5.21), "did no sin" (1 Pet 2.22), and "in him is no sin", 1 Jn 3.5. (Please do quote this correctly: it is often quoted as, "in him **was** no sin"). The work of the Lord Jesus ("fighteth the battles of the Lord") and the perfect life of the Lord Jesus ("evil hath not been found in thee") gives Him the moral right to reign. One day, another man will rise against God's anointed. His appearance is described in Revelation 13.1-2. In fact, the whole world will unite "against the Lord, and against his anointed." Read Psalm 2. The language describing the defeat of this man, called "the beast", does not allude to a sling, but the result is the same: the Lord will consume him "with the spirit of his mouth", and shall destroy him "with the brightness of his coming." See also Isaiah 11.4.

vi) Her desire for the well-being of David. She did not want him to have any regrets when he became king. "And it shall come to pass, when the Lord shall have done to my lord according to all the good that he hath spoken concerning thee (Abigail obviously knew that David was God's appointed king), and shall have appointed thee ruler over Israel; that this shall be no grief unto my lord, either that thou hast shed blood causeless, or that my lord hath avenged himself" (vv.30-31) This is beautiful. Abigail was not only concerned for the lives of other people; she was concerned for David himself. She wanted him to live and act in a way that would not cause him shame later. That was good advice! We all look back with regrets. Not many of us can say with Paul, "And herein do I exercise myself, to have always a conscience void of offence toward God, and toward men" (Acts 24.16). We should live so that, "when he shall appear, we may have confidence, and not be ashamed before him at his coming", (1 Jn 2.28). We do need to think and pray carefully about our decisions, and their possible consequences. Take time to "think things through."

vii) Her desire to share in David's glory. "When the Lord shall have dealt well with my lord, then remember thine handmaid" (v.31). Colin Lacey puts it like this: "She was prepared to be associated with him in his rejection, but she also wanted to share with him in his coming glory...She did not need to worry about that: David could never forget her!" The Lord Jesus has promised to honour all who serve and follow Him: "If any man serve me, let him follow me; and where I am, there shall also my servant be: if any man serve me, him will my Father honour" (Jn 12.26). For a time, Pharaoh's butler forgot Joseph's plea, "Think on me when it shall be well with thee", (Gen 40.14). But the Lord Jesus will never forget! "If we suffer, we shall also reign with him" (2 Tim 2.12).

1 Samuel

B) David's appreciation (vv.32-35)
"**Blessed** be the Lord God of Israel, which sent thee this day to meet me: and **blessed** be thy advice, and **blessed** be thou, which hast kept me this day from coming to shed blood, and from avenging myself with mine own hand." This is a lovely "threefold cord" (Ecc 4.12).

i) "Blessed be **the Lord God of Israel**, which sent thee this day to meet me." Both Abigail and David recognised the hand of God in the circumstances. Abigail: "Now therefore, my lord, as the Lord liveth, and as thy soul liveth, seeing **the Lord** hath withholden thee from coming to shed blood..." (v.26). Now David recognised the hand of God as well. He continues: "For in very deed, as the Lord God of Israel liveth, which hath kept me back from hurting thee..." (v.33). There was far more to the success of Abigail's mission than her initiative and intervention, although we must not minimise her role in the least. God put it in her heart to intercept David, just as He put it in the heart of Titus to care for the Corinthians. See 2 Corinthians 8.16, "But thanks be to **God,** which put the same earnest care into the heart of Titus for you." In both cases, God was glorified.

ii) "Blessed be **thy advice**." David appreciated her advice, which meant that he recognised his own shortcomings. Abigail wasn't a "big name", but what she **said** was valuable. It's not who people are, but what they say that's important! We don't always say, "Blessed be thy advice", do we?! Rehoboam was given some good advice by his senior counsellors, but followed the recommendation of "the young men that were grown up with him." Disaster followed! Read 1 Kings 12.1-19. We should welcome good scriptural advice. You can't improve on the word of God. Read Psalm 19.7-11.

iii) "Blessed be **thou**." David valued the advice, but he also valued the person who gave it. Paul urged the Christians at Thessalonica to "know them which labour among you, and are over you in the Lord ('take the lead among you in the Lord', JND), and admonish you; and to esteem them very highly in love for their work's sake" (1 Thess 5.12-13).

"So David received of her hand that which she had brought him, and said unto her, Go up in peace to thine house; see, I have hearkened to thy voice, and have accepted thy person." Notice that David withdrew from his mission against Nabal, not for his sake, but for Abigail's sake. "I have...accepted thy person." Years later, David acted on the same principle: "Is there yet any that is left of the house of Saul, that I may shew him kindness **for Jonathan's sake?**" (2 Sam 9.1). Centuries later, God acted on the same principle: "Be ye kind one to another, tenderhearted, forgiving one another, even as God **for Christ's sake** hath forgiven you" (Eph 4.32).

C) Nabal's death (vv.36-38)
The section speaks for itself. Abigail evidently foresaw the death of her husband. "Now let thine enemies, and they that seek evil to my lord, be as Nabal" (v.26). We should notice:

i) His drunkenness. "And Abigail came to Nabal; and, behold, he held a feast in his house, like the feast of a king; and Nabal's heart was merry within him, for he was very drunken: wherefore she told him nothing less or more, until the morning light", (v.36). David certainly wouldn't have found much resistance if he had arrived with his four hundred armed men! Nabal was quite insensible, and Abigail could not have "got through" to him, even if she had tried. All right-minded Christians condemn drunkenness, and thoroughly agree with Ephesians 5.18, "And be not drunk with wine, wherein is excess; but be filled with the Spirit." We should also remember Romans 14.21, "It is good neither to eat flesh (that is, flesh offered to idols), nor to drink wine, nor anything whereby thy brother stumbleth, or is made weak." It has been nicely said that "the best way to keep out of harm, is to keep out of harm's way." An alcoholic was once asked, "Which drink did the damage?" He replied, "The first one!" There are other forms of drunkenness. Some people are drunk with power. Others are drunk with success. Beware of the heady wine of popularity! Notice too that Nabal threw himself into the celebrations, but Abigail threw herself into intercession (v.23). It is important to be enthusiastic in the right thing, isn't it!

ii) His dread. "But it came to pass in the morning, when the wine was gone out of Nabal, and his wife had told him these things, that his heart died within him, and he became as a stone" (v.37). " Keil & Delitzsch say, " he was smitten with a stroke." Gordon L. Bissett *("The Unwanted Husband"*, Precious Seed, May 2002) puts it like this: "It was not precisely that night that "his soul was required of him", but the end was very near. The next day, when his "hang-over" began to wear off, his wife Abigail broke the news...Nabal's blood ran cold. But for her intervention, his party would have ended, like Belshazzar's feast in Babylon, in a horror of blood and death and destruction."

iii) His death. "And it came to pass about ten days after, that the Lord smote Nabal, and he died." Notice David's comments: "Blessed be the Lord, that hath pleaded the cause of my reproach from the hand of Nabal, and hath kept his servant from evil: for the Lord hath returned the wickedness of Nabal upon his own head" (v.39). Now read (again) Romans 12.19, "Dearly beloved, avenge not yourselves, but rather give place unto wrath: for it is written, vengeance is mine; I will repay, saith the Lord." But that wasn't the end of the story.

D) Abigail's marriage (vv.39-44)
Abigail was now free to marry again. She was "loosed from the law of her husband." Here is the full quotation: "Know ye not, brethren…how that the law hath dominion over a man as long as he liveth? For the woman which hath an husband is bound by the law to her husband so long as he liveth; but if the husband be dead, she is loosed from the law of her husband. So then if, while her husband liveth, she be married to another man, she shall be called an adulteress: but if her husband be dead, she is free from that law; so that she is no adulteress, though she be married to another man", Romans 7.1-3. Very clear, isn't it?

So, after the death of Nabal, "David sent and communed with Abigail, to take her to him to wife. And when the servants of David were come to Abigail to Carmel, they spake unto her, saying, David sent us unto thee, to take thee to him to wife" (vv.39-40).

i) Abigail's response. She "arose, and bowed herself on her face to the earth, and said, Behold, let thine handmaid be a servant to wash the feet of the servants of my lord" (v.41). She was prepared to take the lowest place. Just like John the Baptist: see Mark 1.7

ii) Abigail's reward. She "arose, and rode upon an ass, with five damsels of her's that went after her; and she went after the messengers of David, and became his wife" (v.42). She was given an honoured place. "Before honour is humility" (Prov 15.33, 18.12). However, let's remember that Abigail left a prosperous farm to share the hardships of life with David (see 27.3 & 30.5), and that she was prepared to undertake the most menial tasks. It would be some years before the fugitive became king. She was glad that David had remembered his "handmaid" **before** the Lord "dealt well" with him (v.31), and she was there when he was crowned "king over the house of Judah" at Hebron. See 2 Samuel 2.1-4. (She must have been "glad" because she "hasted" to return with David's messengers!). For the record, Abigail became the mother of Chileab (2 Sam 3.3), who seems to be the same as Daniel (1 Chron 3.1). Incidentally, we mustn't mix up David's wife with another lady of the same name. See 1 Chronicles 2.16-17.

The chapter ends on a rather sad note. "David also took Ahinoam of Jezreel; and they were also both of them his wives. But Saul had given Michal his daughter, David's wife, to Phalti the son of Laish, which was of Gallim." As A.McShane *(Lessons for Leaders)* observes, "here we have another case of polygamy, an evil which God allowed, but as we have already pointed out, He never commended. Wherever it appears, it is ever followed by a crop of sorrow." Ahinoam became the mother of Amnon, who was guilty of a despicable crime against his half-sister, and was murdered by his half-brother, Absalom. David was not content with two wives. Read 2 Samuel 3.2-5 and 1 Chronicles 3.1-4.

Addendum

The case of David's first wife, Michal, makes sad reading. The story begins with her love for David (1 Sam 18.20). But in the end, she "despised him in her heart", and then publicly scorned him for his zeal and devotion to the Lord. She certainly "left her first love."

While, initially, Michal protected and helped David, she weakened under pressure, and insinuated to her father that she would have hindered David's flight, but he threatened to kill her. See 1 Sam.19.8-17. Does **our** "first love" begin to wane under pressure? Do **we** begin to think of our own welfare rather than the honour of Christ?

That was sad enough, but worse was to follow. We have just read that "Saul had given Michal his daughter, David's wife, to Phalti the son of Laish, which was of Gallim." The precise details are not given, but Ellicott's Commentary is probably right in saying "that this high-handed act showed on the part of Saul a fixed determination to break utterly and forever with David." This evidently took place without any protest on Michal's part. She was evidently content with her estrangement from David. Does distance from Christ trouble **us?**

When David became king, he demanded the return of his wife, and "her husband went with her along weeping behind her to Bahurim" (2 Sam 3.14-16). Saul, Michal, and Phalti ignored God's marriage laws, with harrowing consequences. We cannot expect to tamper with God's word, and escape unscathed. Do remember that our disobedience can involve pain for other people as well.

So Michal was returned to her rightful position, but there is no evidence that she ever regained her "first love" for David. She made this clear by her criticism of David's enthusiasm when the ark was carried into Jerusalem. See 2 Samuel 6.14-16, 20-23. We know that the ark is a beautiful picture of the Lord Jesus, and Michal's attitude reminds us that even some Christians try to dampen the love and enthusiasm of other believers for Him. As a result, Michal was barren "unto the day of her death", and ended up caring for her sister's children. Compare 2 Samuel 21.8 with 1 Samuel 18.19. In New Testament terms, there was no "fruit for God", which is exactly what we can expect if we "leave our first love" for Christ.

CHAPTER 26

"Thou shalt...do great things" (26.1-25)

Although there was "a great space between them" (v.13), we now come to the final meeting between Saul and David. Before they parted, Saul spoke about himself. He said, "I have played the fool, and have erred exceedingly" (v.21). He never spoke a truer word! But he also spoke about David: "Blessed be thou, my son David: thou shalt both do great things, and also shalt still prevail" (v.25). He was right about this as well! In this chapter we discover that while David learnt from his experiences in chapter 25, Saul did not learn from his experiences in chapter 24.

The chapter can be divided as follows: **(1)** David's betrayal by the Ziphites (vv.1-3); **(2)** David's restraint on Abishai (vv.4-12); **(3)** David's rebuke to Abner (vv.13-16); **(4)** David's appeal to Saul (vv.17-20); **(5)** David's recognition by Saul (vv.21-25). Do remember that paragraph headings are not always exact! Their main purpose is to provide a framework for orderly study.

1. David's Betrayal by the Ziphites (vv.1-3)

We have met the Ziphites before. They certainly didn't have any love for David. Compare 23.19-29. David escaped on that occasion, but now they had another opportunity to betray him. "And the Ziphites came unto Saul to Gibeah, saying, Doth not David hide himself in the hill of Hachilah, which is before Jeshimon?" (v.1). The Ziphites hadn't changed, and neither had Saul. "Then Saul arose, and went down to the wilderness of Ziph, having three thousand chosen men of Israel with him (again: see 24.2), to seek David in the wilderness of Ziph" (v.2). Saul's tears and fine words at En-gedi (24.16-22) didn't impress David then, and events here proved him right! The leopard had not changed his spots. Saul was "after him" again (v.3).

This just reminds us that, like Saul, **our** spiritual enemies **never give up.**

Don't expect them to "throw in the towel", and go away. Satan didn't even give up with the Lord Jesus. "And when the devil had ended all the temptation, he departed from him *for a season"* (Lk 4.13). In due course, he returned. See, for example, John 14.30: "The prince of this world cometh, and hath nothing in me." It also reminds us that, like Saul, our spiritual enemies *never change.* Right at the "end-time", our great spiritual adversary is described as "the great dragon…that old serpent, called the Devil, and Satan" (Rev 12.9). He will never change. The "old nature" within us doesn't change either. We will remain subject to temptation from without and within, until we enter heaven. Notice too that David was aware of Saul's intentions (v.4), and we must not be "ignorant of his (Satan's) devices" (2 Cor 2.11).

2. David's Restraint on Abishai (vv.4-12)
For the second time, David has Saul in his power. But the two incidents are not identical. On the first occasion, Saul fell inadvertently into David's hands (24.3), but now David deliberately penetrates Saul's headquarters. The words, "Saul lay in the trench, and the people pitched round about him", can be rendered, "Saul lay within the wagon-defence, and the people pitched round about him" (JND). See also 17.20. As before, there are important lessons for us here:

i) David took the initiative
"Who will go down with me *to Saul* in the camp?" He took the battle to Saul, but not with the intention of killing him. Bearing in mind that it was night, and we are not told that he was aware that "a deep sleep from the Lord was fallen upon them" (v.12), David evidently wanted to prove, yet again, that he had no evil intentions towards Saul. It is often said that "the best means of defence is attack" and this is certainly true in the spiritual battle. Saul was accompanied by a hand-picked army, but that did not deter David. We too are faced by overwhelming odds, but that should not deter us either. We must not forget 1 John 4.4. If we just "sit tight", and let the enemy hurl everything at us, it will not be too surprising if we eventually "go out of business." David took the offensive, and we must "preach the word" and be "instant (urgent) in season and out of season." Paul and Silas were not called, "these that have turned the world upside down" (Acts 17.6), for nothing! They took the gospel to the people. They didn't even have halls in which to hide!

ii) David was accompanied by Abishai
This is the first time we meet David's nephew, Abishai. His mother was

Zeruiah, David's sister (1 Chron 2.16), but we don't have a note of his father's name. His two brothers were Joab and Asahel. See 2 Samuel 2.18. He eventually commanded a third of David's army against Absalom, rescued David from Ishbi-benob the giant, and was captain of the second three of David's mighty men. See 2 Samuel 18.2; 21.16-17; 23.18. We don't know anything about "Ahimelech the Hittite".

Here is another example of an older man and a younger man working together. Remember Jonathan and his armour-bearer? Refresh your memory by reading 14.1-16 again. Don't forget Moses and Joshua, and Paul and Timothy. Notice that Abishai was willing to go with David ("I will go down with thee" v.6). Like Priscilla and Aquila (Rom 16.4), he was ready to risk his life. The habits of a lifetime are formed in early years, and Abishai certainly exposed himself to plenty of risk later on!

iii) David instructed Abishai
Abishai learnt "a thing or two" from his expedition with David. To his credit, he was wise enough not to "hit first, and ask questions afterwards." Notice that the two men communicated with each other. "Then said Abishai to David (v.8)…And David said to Abishai (v.9)." A lot of difficulties can be avoided in this way, especially when you are young! Whilst older believers should give every encouragement to younger brothers and sisters, they also have a duty to steer them away from wrong suggestions and ideas.

One thing that Abishai learnt here was the danger of circumstantial evidence. After all, everybody was fast asleep, and Saul's spear was most convenient! Abishai therefore leapt to the conclusion that "God hath delivered thine enemy into thine hand this day." But David knew otherwise. He read the circumstances quite differently. Be careful about "circumstances." Don't let "favourable circumstances" override the word of God. After all, Jonah must have thought the circumstances were right when he "went down to Joppa; and…found a ship going to Tarshish" (Jonah 1.3). But he was running away from God!

Do notice that David **explained** his prohibition to Abishai. That's important too! It was not a case of "do as I say": he set out the reasons for sparing Saul (vv.9-11). Let's sum it up by saying that David was willing to give Abishai good advice, and Abishai was willing to take it. That places responsibility on us **all** in one way or another!

1 Samuel

iv) David had learnt from experience
As A.McShane observes, "Repeating lessons can be irksome enough at school. When God is teaching, He will not allow us to pass on to new subjects until we have fully learned those He is seeking to teach us. Like David, our actions often indicate that what we thought we knew is still outside our grasp. His attempt to slay Nabal all but nullified his previous sparing of Saul, so he was given another chance to prove his development."

David's faith was under subtle attack. Abishai unwittingly set a trap for David, probably for the best of reasons. Knowing that David would not avenge himself, he offered to do the job for him. But David was equal to the situation: "Destroy him not: for who can stretch forth his hand against the Lord's anointed, and be guiltless?…As the Lord liveth, the Lord shall smite him; or his day shall come to die; or he shall descend into battle, and perish. The Lord forbid that I should stretch forth mine hand against the Lord's anointed."

Let's be warned by this. It's all too easy to sidestep our responsibilities by shifting responsibility to other people. If Abishai had killed Saul, David could have argued that his companion was actually responsible! But that would not have absolved him from responsibility. "The Lord forbid that *I* should stretch forth **mine hand** against the Lord's anointed." We must admire David's long-suffering. His patience with Saul could have snapped. As it was, he was consistent to the end. See 2 Samuel 1.14.

As we have noted, unlike Abishai, David used the circumstances, not as an opportunity to kill Saul, but to prove that he had no evil intentions towards him. "Take now the spear that is at his bolster, and the cruse of water, and let us go." As A.McShane observes, "Now that Saul had lost his spear, his most prized possession of war, he is symbolically shown that his power to fight had been removed from him, yea more, that David had taken his place as captain of the armies of Israel."

Abishai must have wondered what was happening. He did not have long to wait for the answer.

3. David's Rebuke to Abner (vv.13-16)
"Art not thou a valiant man? And who is like to thee in all Israel? Wherefore then hast thou not kept thy lord the king? For there came one of the people in to destroy the king thy lord. This thing is not good that thou hast done. As

the Lord liveth, ye are worthy to die, because ye have not kept your master, the Lord's anointed. And now see where the king's spear is, and the cruse of water that was at his bolster."

Keil & Delitzsch explain this nicely: "These reproaches that were cast at Abner were intended to show to Saul, who might at any rate possibly hear, and in fact did hear, that David was the most faithful defender of his life, more faithful than his closest and most zealous servants." His rebuke to Abner certainly supported his plea: "Wherefore doth my lord thus pursue after his servant? For what have I done? Or what evil is in mine hand?" (v.18).

H.L.Rossier makes the thought-provoking observation that David showed Abner "that there is more interest and care for the world in a child of God, than in those who pretend to support, help, or defend it." The Lord Jesus said, "Ye have heard that it hath been said, Thou shalt love thy neighbour, and hate thine enemy. But I say unto you, Love your enemies, bless them that curse you, do good to them that hate you, and pray for them which despitefully use you, and persecute you" (Mt 5.43-44). You won't find too much of that in the world! Can people detect that *we* live by higher standards?

4. David's Appeal to Saul (vv.17-20)
David is answered, not by Abner, but by Saul. "Is this thy voice, my son David?" Unfortunately, Saul had said it all before! See 24.16. We can therefore assume, with some justification, that David was probably unimpressed by Saul's tenderness! It didn't mean very much at En-gedi, and it obviously didn't mean too much on this occasion either, for in spite of Saul's fine words, he remained intent on David's death, and didn't give up the chase until David had fled to Achish, king of Gath. See 27.4. It's very easy, in the heat of the moment, to say things we don't mean! However, David did not accuse Saul of insincerity. We should notice the following:

i) His courtesy
"And David said, It is my voice, my lord, O king...Wherefore doth my lord thus pursue after his servant?...Now therefore, I pray thee, let my lord the king hear the words of his servant." He certainly illustrates 1 Peter 3.9, "Not rendering evil for evil, or railing for railing." In fact, Peter continues by emphasising that Christians are to display courtesy and respect even under pressure. "But and if ye suffer for righteousness' sake, happy are ye: and be not afraid of their terror, neither be troubled; but sanctify the Lord God in

your hearts: and be ready always to give an answer to every man that asketh you a reason of the hope that is in you with meekness and fear" (vv.14-15). The word "fear" means "reverential fear." When Peter refers to "every man that asketh you a reason of the hope that is in you", he is not thinking about a casual enquirer, but about Christians answering for their faith before a tribunal. However, in all circumstances, we are to show courtesy to our fellow-men. The gospel is not commended by rudeness, disrespect, ill-temper, or an offensive attitude. When the Lord Jesus was "reviled", He "reviled not again."

ii) His conscience

"Wherefore doth my lord thus pursue after his servant? For what have I done? Or what evil is in mine hand?" No legitimate charge could be brought against him, and this reminds us that we must give "none occasion to the adversary to speak reproachfully" (1 Tim 5.14). In later years, David gave "great occasion to the enemies of the Lord to blaspheme" (2 Sam 12.14). Paul was able to write to the church at Corinth and say, "for our rejoicing is this, the testimony of our conscience, that in simplicity and godly sincerity, not with fleshly wisdom, but by the grace of God, we have had our conversation in the world, and more abundantly to you-ward" (2 Cor 1.12).

iii) His conclusion

In view of his own innocence, David concludes that there were only two possible causes for Saul's hostility: either **(a)** that "the Lord have stirred thee up against me", or **(b)** that "the children of men" had done so.

a) That the Lord had stirred up Saul against David. "If the Lord have stirred thee up against me, let him accept an offering." This has been explained as follows: "If the Lord hath stirred thee up against me for any fault of mine, let me know mine offence, and I am ready to make an offering for it to the Lord, that I may be forgiven." (According to Ellicott's Commentary, this is the reading given by the Arabic version of the Chaldee Targum!). While this seems to dispose of any difficulties, it is not what the Bible actually says! It is always tempting, when confronted by a difficult passage, to rewrite it to suit our interpretation!

But what **does** this statement mean? Is it right to suggest that the Lord could actually have provoked Saul to persecute David? There can be little doubt that David believed that this was possible: "If the **Lord** have stirred thee up against me. This could mean that God had stirred up Saul against David **directly**. See 16.14, "But the Spirit of the Lord departed from Saul, and an evil spirit **from the Lord** troubled him." See also 18.10. Compare 2 Thessalonians 2.11. We have a similar situation with Pharaoh: "the Lord hardened Pharaoh's heart" (Ex 9.1). He first hardened his own heart (Ex 7.13 JND), with the result that he became more and more entrenched in his opposition to Moses. In Saul's case, the Lord evidently "stirred him up" against David to bring about his own destruction. In persecuting David, Saul was hastening his own death. David was not at hand to deliver him on mount Gilboa. Saul disobeyed God, and reaped the solemn consequences. Alternatively, it could mean that God had stirred up Saul against David **indirectly**. See, for example, Psalm 81.11-12, "But my people would not hearken to my voice; and Israel would have none of me. So I gave them up to their own hearts lust: and they walked in their own counsels." Compare Romans 1.24,26,28.

Either way, the "offering" was required from Saul, not David, and it is significant that the Hebrew word *minchah* is used for the meal offering, which was a bloodless offering, and denoted sanctity and purity of life. The offering that God required from **Saul** was "a broken spirit...a broken and a contrite heart" (Ps 51.17).

b) That other people had stirred up Saul against David. "But if they be the children of men, cursed be they before the Lord; for they have driven me out this day from abiding in the inheritance of the Lord, saying, Go, serve other gods." (Compare Deuteronomy 4.27-28). Doeg, the Edomite (7.10 etc), and the Ziphites, were certainly guilty in this way. Ellicott's Commentary says all that is necessary: "He means that, far away from the only country where Jehovah is loved and honoured, away from the influence of Jehovah's prophets and beloved priests, he and his would be tempted to serve other gods, and to share in the foul and impious practice of the nations." Calvin is probably correct in suggesting that David's enemies did not actually **say,** "Go, serve other gods", but that this would be the result of their opposition to him.

It is worth adding that we must be very careful how we treat other people. Misguided words or actions, perhaps a bad example, could have a detrimental effect on them. After all, we would not want to become responsible for either discouraging nor stumbling a fellow-Christian, would we?

iv) His concern
"Now therefore, let not my blood fall to the earth before the face of the Lord ("far from the face of Jehovah", JND): for the king of Israel is come out to seek a flea, as when one doth hunt a partridge in the mountains."

In the first place, David did not want to die in a foreign land. He loved the place where God dwelt. See Romans 9.4. How much do we value "the place where thine honour dwelleth?" (Ps 26.8). In the second place, he was an insignificant quarry. This is the second occasion on which David describes himself as a flea (a single flea)! See 24.15. It is a most insignificant insect, which is "not easily caught, and easily escapes, and if it is caught, it is poor game for the hunter!" (Quoted in Ellicott's Commentary). Changing the metaphor, "no one would think it worth his while to hunt a single partridge that had flown to the mountains, when they may be found in coveys in the fields." (Quoted by Keil & Delitzsch). Once again, notice David's deep humility. He felt that he just wasn't worth Saul's trouble!

5. David's Recognition by Saul (vv.21-25)
We come now to the last exchange between Saul and David, and even here it is difficult to accept Saul's sincerity. It sounds good, "I have sinned: return my son David (no need to flee to a foreign country): for I will no more do thee harm." But David didn't believe it, and he was right. As we have already noted, Saul only gave up the chase when he was told that David had "fled to Gath" (27.4). With this in mind, we must notice the following:

i) Saul's admission
"Then said Saul, I have sinned: return, my son David: for I will no more do thee harm, because my soul was precious in thine eyes this day: behold, I have played the fool, and have erred exceedingly." Although he was unaware of it, Saul was approaching the end of his life, and he was forced to confess that he had "played the fool...and erred exceedingly." Preachers have often contrasted the declaration by Saul the son of Kish, with the declaration, also at the end of his life, by Saul of Tarsus. The first man said, "I have played the fool, and have erred exceedingly." The second man said, "I have fought a good fight, I have finished my course, I have kept the faith" (2 Tim 4.7). What will **we** say at the end of life's journey?

There will be countless people in eternity who will sadly confess, "I have played the fool." Like Saul, so many people have every opportunity, and receive every encouragement. Like Saul, they disobey God's word, and reject the very Man whose victory over the enemy has made deliverance from bondage possible. Like Saul they reject His longsuffering and tender mercy. Like Saul, they die without hope.

ii) David's answer
David was obviously unimpressed. He asked for "one of the young men" to retrieve the spear. He didn't trust Saul. This is not surprising. He knew only too well that Saul was likely to throw the spear at him! Notice that David does not commit himself to Saul, but to the Lord. He makes no appeal to Saul at all. "The Lord render to every man his righteousness and his faithfulness: for the Lord delivered thee into my hand today, but I would not stretch forth mine hand against the Lord's anointed. And, behold, as thy life was much set by this day in mine eyes, so let my life be much set by in the eyes of the Lord, and let him deliver me out of all tribulation." Saul had vindicated David ("my soul was precious in thine eyes this day"), and pledged his safety ("I will no more do thee harm"). But David turned to the Lord for vindication ("the **Lord** render to every man his righteousness and his faithfulness"), and for safety ("so let my life be much set by in the eyes of the Lord, and let **him** deliver me out of all tribulation"). He had no confidence whatsoever in Saul. But he knew that his life, even if akin to "a flea" and "a partridge on the mountains", was of "great price in the eyes of Him who had chosen him, called him, and kept him as the apple of his eye." (H.L.Rossier). He knew that "it is better to trust in the Lord than to put confidence in man. It is better to trust in the Lord than to put confidence in princes" (Ps 118.8-9).

iii) Saul's acknowledgement
"Then said Saul to David, Blessed be thou, my son David: thou shalt both do great things, and also shalt still prevail." Once again, impressive words! But how much did they really mean? After all, the man who said **"Blessed** be thou, my son David", had recently said to the Ziphites, **"Blessed** be ye of the Lord; for ye have compassion on me" (23.21). The man who said to David, "thou shalt do great things, and also shalt still prevail", had said to Jonathan, "thou hast chosen the son of Jesse to thine own shame" (20.30). Saul's prediction was certainly right, but it didn't carry any moral weight, for "out of the same mouth proceedeth blessing and cursing" (Jas 3.10). "There is no sinner so hardened, but that God gives him now and then some rays of light, which show him all his error. But, alas! When they are awakened by such divine movings, it is only for a few moments; and such impulses are no sooner past, than they fall back again immediately unto

their former life, and forget all that they have promised." (Quoted by Keil & Delitzsch).

We can say, however, with utmost confidence and with great sincerity, that the "Son of David" will "do great things…and prevail!"

"So David went on his way, and Saul returned to his place." A.McShane makes the solemn comment: "Thus the two men parted, never to meet on earth again, and as far as we know, never to be together again for all eternity."

CHAPTER 27

The Recovery of Ziklag (27.1-12)

While the recovery of Ziklag makes exciting reading, it is worth pointing out that, strictly speaking, David should not have been there in the first place. 1 Samuel 27 should therefore be read in preparation for 1 Samuel 30.

Saul had said to David, "Blessed be thou, my son David: thou shalt both do great things, and also shalt still prevail" (26.25). But David was not impressed by Saul's fine words! He had heard it all before, and he didn't trust Saul for one moment. Now, for the second time (compare 21.10-15), the relentless pressure became too great for him, and this chapter chronicles a further lapse of faith. God has faithfully recorded the weaknesses of His servants, as well as their strengths, to teach us valuable lessons. It's always worth remembering that the great men and women of Scripture were "subject to like passions as we are" (Jas 5.17), but this did not disqualify them from serving God. Jonah, "rose up to flee unto Tarshish from the presence of the Lord", but God did not "strike him off": "The word of the Lord came unto Jonah the second time." What an encouragement to us! He can use us too, with all our limitations and deficiencies. We all have good reason to thank God for his grace, mercy and longsuffering towards us.

1 Samuel 27 can be divided as follows: **(1)** David's reversal of faith (v.1); **(2)** David's refuge with Achish (vv.2-3); **(3)** David's relief from persecution (v.4); **(4)** David's residence at Ziklag (vv.5-7); **(5)** David's raids on the south (vv.8-12).

1. David's Reversal of Faith (v.1)

"And David said in his heart, I shall now perish one day by the hand of Saul: there is nothing better for me than that I should speedily escape into the land of the Philistines; and Saul shall despair of me, to seek me any more in any coast of Israel: so shall I escape out of his hand." In a nutshell, David looked at his circumstances instead of God, and his faith failed.

It all happened so quickly! The man who cried, "So let my life be much set by in the eyes of the Lord, and let **him** deliver me out of all tribulation" (26.24), now says, "I shall now perish one day by the hand of Saul." When we look at David's victory at the camp on the hill of Hachilah, we can scarcely believe that he would so soon be heard to cry, "I shall now perish one day by the hand of Saul." "Perhaps we forget that almost as sure as night follows day, so do failures follow successes. These words of despondency did not spring from his communion with God, but were doubtless the expression of his own unbelieving heart, nor were they supported by a single statement from the lips of any of the Lord's servants." (A.McShane, *Lessons for Leaders*).

Without being over-critical of David (if we criticise him, it is a case of "the pot calling the kettle black!") we should notice the following:

i) He forgot the promise of God. He had been anointed king, and God's purposes cannot fail. Abraham was "fully persuaded that, what he (God) had promised, he was able also to perform" (Rom 4.21). Humanly speaking, it didn't look like that at the time, but "Abraham believed God." Abraham's faith was sorely tested in Genesis 22, but he was absolutely certain that even if Isaac's ashes were scattered to the four winds, he would return with him. "I and the lad will go yonder and worship, and **come again** to you." David lacked the faith of Abraham here. But don't we all? We must never forget that despite appearances, "all things work together for good to them that love God, to them who are the called according to his purpose" (Rom 8.28). Remember,

> He cannot fail, for He is God:
> He cannot fail, He's pledged His word;
> He cannot fail, He'll see you through;
> He cannot fail, He'll answer you.

ii) He forgot the preserving care of God. C.H.Spurgeon *(Morning & Evening: Morning, October 17th)* has a delightful piece on this verse. Here is part of his meditation: "On no one occasion had the Lord deserted His servant; he had been placed in perilous positions very often, but not one instance had occurred in which divine interposition had not delivered him. The trials to which he had been exposed had been varied: they had not assumed one form only. Yet in every case, He who had sent the trial had also graciously ordained a way of escape. David could not put his finger upon any entry in his diary, and say of it, 'Here is evidence that the Lord will forsake me', for the entire tenor of his past life proved the very reverse. He should have argued from what God *had* done for him, that God would be his defender still." In the words of the hymn:

> His love in times past forbids me to think
> He'll leave me at last in ruin to sink:
> Each sweet Ebenezer I hold in review
> Confirms His good pleasure to see me right through.

David made no attempt to consult God about his movements. That was bad enough, but did you notice that God is **not even mentioned in the chapter?!** That really clinches the lesson, doesn't it!

2. David's Refuge with Achish (vv.2-3)
"And David arose, and he passed over with the six hundred men that were with him unto Achish, the son of Maoch, king of Gath. And David dwelt with Achish at Gath, he and his men, every man with his household, even David with his two wives, Ahinoam the Jezreelitess, and Abigail the Carmelitess, Nabal's wife."

So David became an asylum-seeker! Quite up to date, isn't it? As we have already noted, he had been to Gath before, and for the same reason. See 21.10-15. On that occasion, Achish called David a "mad man." But now he certainly appears to have extended a kindly welcome to David. It has been suggested that whilst, on the first occasion, "he was a fugitive, almost unattended, now he was at the head of an army of trained and devoted soldiers. Such a guest might be of the greatest service to the Philistines in their perpetual wars with Saul, with whom David had apparently broken off all relations."

It seems incredible that the man who defeated the Philistine champion should now seek refuge in one of the five royal Philistine cities. Gath, above all places. That's where Goliath came from! The Philistines were Israel's inveterate enemies. David's decision illustrates Proverbs 29.25, "The fear of man bringeth a snare: but whoso putteth his trust in the Lord shall be safe." As we shall see, this led to deceit (vv.8-12), and ultimately he faced the prospect of fighting against his own people. See Chapter 29. One false step can annul past triumphs, and lead to unforeseen consequences. It all resulted from a breakdown in David's communion with God. The man who "inquired of the Lord", and "inquired of the Lord again" (23.1-4), failed to seek divine help and guidance here. He had already made up his mind. As A.McShane points out, "David was more culpable in going astray at this time than ever before, for he had with him the priest and the ephod whereby he could have enquired of God."

David's decision to seek asylum with Achish, reminds us that "the friendship of (JND 'with') the world is enmity with God. Whosoever therefore will be a friend of the world is the enemy of God" (Jas 4.4). Unlike Abraham, who is called "the friend of God!" Where do **we** go when life gets difficult? Whose company do **we** keep when the future looks uncertain? But we mustn't confine this to the difficult times. Whose help and companionship do we seek as a **matter of course?** Remember that "evil communications (the word means 'company') corrupt good manners" (1 Cor 15.33).

It is not without significance that we are told that "David dwelt with Achish at Gath, he and his men, every man with his household, even David with his two wives, Ahinoam the Jezreelitess, and Abigail the Carmelitess, Nabal's wife." David led his family and followers to the wrong place! Although he didn't know it at the time, he exposed them to grave danger. Read Chapter 30.1-5. This is a lesson for all leaders, and potential leaders. Do be careful where you take people. Don't lead them into worldly pleasures and pursuits, and expose them to unnecessary risks. Set them the best possible example. It's not a case of, "Can *I* take the Lord there?", but "Would **He** take me there?"

3. David's Relief from Persecution (v.4)
"And it was told Saul that David was fled to Gath: and he sought no more again for him." Perhaps Saul thought that he had won at last! After all, David was out of the country, and therefore no longer a threat to him. It does remind us, however, that Satan never gives up. He will hinder and harry us to the very end!

Success! It worked! David achieved his object. The end justified the means. Or did it? While David's flight to Gath brought him short-term benefits, it also brought him long-term problems.

We cannot stress the lesson too much. For a few months, David led a more settled life, but without the consciousness of God's presence. As we have noticed, He is not even mentioned in this chapter. That was a high price to pay for a start! David gained some respite, but he lost so much. What a good thing that it was only for "a full year and four months" (v.7)! But they were lost months all the same.

This also reminds us that, unlike David here, we do need to make decisions in the light of the long-term future. What do we want to achieve? What are our objectives in life, and in the Lord's work? We need to ask these questions about our gospel work. Short-term measures (musical evenings, drama, etc) can attract large crowds, but produce little, if anything, in the long-term. Remember, "he that goeth forth and weepeth, bearing **precious seed**, shall doubtless come again rejoicing, bringing his sheaves with him" (Ps 126.6). Enduring results, in terms of salvation and spiritual growth, can only be achieved by faithfully sowing the word of God.

4. David's Residence at Ziklag (vv.5-7)

"And David said unto Achish, If I have now found grace in thine eyes, let them give me a place in some town in the country, that I may dwell there: for why should thy servant dwell in the royal city with thee? Then Achish gave him Ziklag that day: wherefore Ziklag pertaineth to the kings of Judah unto this day." Goliath would have been delighted to hear David say "thy servant!" It would have implied Israel's defeat. See 17.9. But now David describes himself in this way to another Philistine!

But why did David make this request? It seems quite obvious that David had a "hidden agenda." Ellicott's Commentary puts it like this: "The real reason why David wished a separate residence was that he might conduct his forays and other affairs apart from the supervision of his Philistine friends. **They** had one purpose in welcoming him and his band, **he** had quite another." The following paragraph (vv.8-12) certainly confirms these observations.

Things are getting worse. Loss of fellowship with God is a slippery slope, and David's honesty and integrity are now in question. This reminds us that Christians should not resort to duplicity. The Lord Jesus had no "hidden agendas." "I spake openly to the world; I ever taught in the synagogue, and in the temple, whither the Jews always resort; and in secret have I said nothing." False teaching is characterised, at least initially, by secretiveness.

1 Samuel

See Galatians 2.4, 2 Peter 2.1, Jude 4. Notice the words "privily" and "crept in unawares." There is no need to hide the truth. We have no reason to be "ashamed of the gospel of Christ."

It has been rightly said that "this year and four months were among the darkest days of David's life." The reason follows:

5. David's Raids on the South (vv.8-12)
The Geshurites, Gezrites, and Amalekites (v.8) were evidently located close to the southern boundary of Judah (this is clear from the reference to Shur: see also 15.7), which enabled David to make Achish believe that he had attacked southern Judah itself. We must consider:

A) The destruction of the tribes (v.9)
"And David smote the land, and left neither man nor woman alive, and took away the sheep, and the oxen, and the asses, and the camels, and the apparel, and returned, and came to Achish." Whilst it is true that God commanded Israel to completely destroy the original inhabitants of Canaan on account of their wickedness, David's ferocity is explained in v.11: "And David saved neither man nor woman alive, to bring tidings to Gath, saying, Lest they should tell on us, saying, So did David." Usually, prisoners would have been taken as part of the spoils of war, but not here. David's "atrocious acts of murder" (Ellicott) cannot be justified, and it is possible that it was these "acts of ruthless cruelty" that disqualified David from building the temple. See 1 Chronicles 28.3.

We can only add that Paul warned the Galatians against "spiritual cannibalism." "But if ye bite and devour one another, take heed that ye be consumed one of another" (5.15). Even Christians, alas and alas, have been known to wage war against fellow-believers.

B) The deception of Achish (vv.10-12)
It has been rightly said that "a half truth is as bad as a downright lie." David was deliberately ambiguous in replying to Achish: "Whither have ye made road today? And David said, against the south of Judah, and against the south of the Jerahmeelites, and against the south of the Kenites." He had certainly gone in that direction! But the booty had come from elsewhere. Achish was given the impression that the sheep, oxen, asses, camels and apparel, had come from Judah!

In this way, David intended to convince Achish that he had severed his loyalty to Israel, and now fully espoused the Philistine cause. He was eminently successful! "And Achish believed David, saying, He hath made his people Israel utterly to abhor him (literally, 'made his name stink'); therefore he shall be my servant for ever." See also 29.3,6,9. The rest of the Philistine princes were not so sure! See, again, Chapter 29. Events proved that they were right!

Are we creating false impressions about ourselves? Ananias and Sapphira did that, only to hear Peter say, "Why hath Satan filled thine heart to lie unto the Holy Ghost…thou hast not lied unto men, but unto God" (Acts 5.1-11). Do remember that whilst we can deceive each other, at least for part of the time, we cannot deceive God. Like David, we can create the desired impression of ourselves, especially when we use the right words, and do the right things, but God knows our unseen motives and assesses our inward reality. See, for example, Matthew 15.8, "This people draweth nigh unto me with their mouth, and honoureth me with their lips; but their heart is far from me" (Mt 15.8).

1 Samuel 27 therefore commences with David's loss of fellowship with God, and traces the sad **results** in his life.

CHAPTER 28

"Bring me up Samuel" (28.1-25)

This chapter deals with a unique event. A man returns from the dead without a body! So it cannot be classified as resurrection: but more of this later.

Before we examine the passage in detail, it might be helpful to notice its structure. The main "story-line" begins with (vv.1-2) and continues in chapter 29.1-11. These verses describe preparation for battle by the Philistines. The intervening verses (vv.3-25) are a parenthesis. You could put them in brackets. They describe Saul's reaction to the Philistine invasion.

For ease of study, we can divide the chapter as follows: **(1)** David's invidious position (vv.1-2); **(2)** Relevant information about Samuel and Saul (v.3); **(3)** Saul's intense fear (vv.4-6); **(4)** Saul's interview with Samuel (vv.7-25).

1. David's Invidious Position (vv.1-2)
David never anticipated that his flight to Gath would result in a summons to fight his own people! "And it came to pass in those days (see 27.7), that the Philistines gathered their armies together for warfare, to fight with Israel. And Achish said unto David, Know thou assuredly, that thou shalt go out with me to battle, thou and thy men" (v.1). This put David in a dilemma. On one hand stood **Achish,** who believed that David, who had been wronged and insulted by Saul, would now fight against him. On the other hand stood **Israel,** over whom he expected to reign. A.McShane is certainly right in saying, "One wrong step usually leads to others which often prove more serious. In Ziklag, he was clear of Saul's sword, but this did not shield him from greater dangers, which indeed involved his whole future."

David's position reminds us that it is much easier to enter a wrong pathway than it is to leave it. Failure to declare "whose we are, and whom we serve" (Acts 27.23), can put **us** in a difficult position as well. How would you feel if someone spoke disparagingly, or blasphemously, in your presence about the Lord Jesus, and you had never made it clear that you were a Christian? Or, even worse, if you had not been living a Christian life? It would be very difficult to protest, wouldn't it? How would you feel if you got mixed up with people who profess Christianity, but began to pour scorn on Christians who love and practise Bible teaching? Far better to "nail your colours to the mast" from "day one!" Remember Nicodemus: John 7.50-52.

But that wasn't all. Do notice the significant words, "Thou shalt go out with me to battle, thou **and thy men**." This just emphasises one of the lessons we noticed in the previous chapter: "And David dwelt with Achish at Gath, he and his men, every man with his household, even David with his two wives" (v.3). As we said then, David led his family and his followers to the wrong place, and now his men are being lined up to fight their own flesh and blood! Do remember, again, that it's not a case of, "Can *I* take the Lord there?", but "Would *He* take me there?"

David's answer is deliberately ambiguous: "Surely thou shalt know what thy servant can do?" Achish interpreted this as a pledge of loyalty to him: "And Achish said to David, Therefore will I make thee keeper of mine head (body guard) for ever." Thankfully, God overruled, and David was relieved of his dilemma. See Chapter 29. But the lessons remain.

2. Relevant Information about Samuel and Saul (v.3)
This is certainly not a "throw-away" line! There are no "throw-away lines" in the Bible! It does seem that these two pieces of information are more than statements of fact. After all, we **do** know that Samuel was dead! See 25.1. It therefore seems likely that the death of Samuel, and the execution of mediums and wizards by Saul, are mentioned to emphasise Saul's desperation. He was driven to seek help and guidance from a dead man through one of the very people he had previously opposed! However, the facts are worth amplifying:

A) The death of Samuel
"Now Samuel was dead, and all Israel lamented him, and buried him in Ramah, even in his own city." He was mourned by "all Israel", and this emphasises his greatness. On two occasions, he is linked with Moses. See Psalm 99.6 and Jeremiah 15.1. It has been rightly said that after Moses, Samuel was the greatest leader in Israel's history. He must have kept records. See 1 Chronicles 29.29, "Now the acts of David the king,

first and last, behold, they are written in **the book of Samuel** the seer, and in the book of Nathan the prophet, and in the book of Gad the seer." It seems likely that the man who wrote 1 & 2 Samuel used these sources of information.

B) The decree of Saul
"And Saul had put away those that had familiar spirits (mediums), and the wizards, out of the land." The close connection with Samuel here may well infer that Saul did not do this out of personal conviction, but under Samuel's influence. The Scriptures are very clear about the occult. See Exodus 22.18, "Thou shalt not suffer a witch to live": "Regard not them that have familiar spirits, neither seek after wizards, to be defiled by them: I am the Lord your God" (Lev 19.31): "A man also or woman that hath a familiar spirit, or that is a wizard, shall surely be put to death" (Lev 20.27) "There shall not be found among you any one that...useth divination, or an observer of times, or an enchanter, or a witch, or a charmer, or a consulter with familiar spirits, or a wizard, or a necromancer. For all that do these things are an abomination unto the Lord: and because of these abominations the Lord thy God doth drive them out from before thee." (Deut 18.10-12). This is sufficient warning for us. We must never become involved in "the black arts."

Ellicott's Commentary suggests that the word "*oboth*" (familiar spirits) could be connected with "*ob*", meaning "a hollow thing" or "bag", and came to signify "one who speaks with a hollow voice." The Septuagint (version (the Greek translation of the Hebrew Old Testament) uses the word "ventriloquist." A "familiar spirit" was the spirit possessed by the medium through which contact was allegedly made with dead people. The word "wizards" means, literally, "the wise people", and "seems to have been given in irony to those dealers in occult and forbidden arts."

Talking about "irony", the most "ironical" thing here is that after vigorously implementing the word of God, Saul consulted a woman with "a familiar spirit." However, we must not let this pass without saying that Saul wasn't the last man to practice something that he once condemned. Sadly, many Christians now teach and practice the very opposite of things they once held dear, and therefore imply that they were wrong in the first place. Referring to false teaching, Paul puts it like this: "If I build again the things which I destroyed, I make myself a transgressor" (Gal 2.18). We must not allow pressure, from people or circumstances, to push us in the wrong direction. This brings us to:

3. Saul's Intense Fear (vv.4-6)

"And the Philistines gathered themselves together, and came and pitched in Shunem: and Saul gathered all Israel together, and they pitched in Gilboa." This is frightening. The Philistines were now strong enough to strike a blow at the centre of the kingdom. They probably marched north along the coastal plain, turned eastward through the valley of Jezreel, or Esdraelon, and advanced further east to Shunem, on the slopes of one of the mountains to the north-east of the valley. Saul and his army camped on Mount Gilboa, also to north-east of Jezreel, a few miles to the south of the Philistines. A map will be helpful! But the spiritual lesson is more important than the geography. The Philistines had got to the heart of the land. Let's say it again! Failure to deal with the Philistines years before (see Joshua 13.1-3), had far-reaching results. The Philistines, despite various defeats, had no intention of withdrawing from the field. Israel, without David, was weak and vulnerable at this time. The enemy (Eph 6.11-12) still knows how and when to exploit our weakness.

We must notice that Saul had **(A)** No assurance in himself (v.5), and **(B)** No answer from God (v.6).

A) No assurance in himself (v.5)

"And when Saul saw the host of the Philistines, he was afraid, and his heart greatly trembled." Disobedience had robbed him of divine assurance. He did not enjoy the promise made to Joshua: "Be not afraid, neither be thou dismayed: for the Lord thy God is with thee whithersoever thou goest" (Josh 1.9). He did not have the confidence of Jehoshaphat: "We have no might against this great company that cometh against us; neither know we what to do: but our eyes are upon thee" (2 Chron 20.12). The Lord Jesus was "heard in that he feared" (JND-because of his piety (Heb 5.7). He could say, "For the Lord God will help me; therefore shall I not be confounded", (Is 50.7). We must remember the words of Azariah to Asa, "The Lord is with you, while ye be with him: and if ye seek him, he will be found of you: but if ye forsake him, he will forsake you" (2 Chron 15.2).

B) No answer from God (v.6)

"And when Saul enquired of the Lord, the Lord answered him not, neither by dreams, not by Urim, nor by prophets." This is not surprising. "If I regard iniquity in my heart, the Lord will not hear me" (Ps 66.18). Notice: not "the Lord will not **answer** me", but "The Lord will not **hear** me." It has been said that there is no such thing as unanswered prayer (the answer might be "no"), but there is such a thing as unheard prayer. How dreadful! Disobedience robbed Saul of divine assurance, and divine help. In v.6, the word "enquired" is *shaal*, to ask in a formal way: in v.7, the word "enquire" is *darash*, to seek. He formally asked the Lord for help, but earnestly sought help from the medium!

On a technical point, considerable discussion has arisen over reference to "Urim" here. The Urim and Thummim were located in the breastplate worn by the high priest (Exodus 28.30). While we are not given any further details about the Urim and Thummim, we do know that God revealed his will through them. We have discussed this in past studies. See, for example, our comments on 1 Samuel 14.18-19. Note Numbers 27.21, "And he (Joshua) shall stand before Eleazar the priest, who shall ask counsel for him after the judgement of Urim before the Lord." Two questions arise:

a) Did Saul have a priest with him? After all, following the murder of Ahimelech, the high priest, Abiathar, Ahimelech's son, "fled to David...with an ephod in his hand" (1 Sam 22.18-21, & 23.6-9). This left Saul without a priest, or did it? It is usually suggested (but not specifically stated) that Zadok succeeded Ahimelech as Saul's high priest, and that the tabernacle was moved from Nob to Gibeon. Hence, early in David's reign, we read, "And Zadok the priest, and his brethren the priests, before the tabernacle of the Lord in the high place that was at Gibeon", 1 Chronicles16.39. This would also account for the repeated allusions to two high priests in David's time. See, for example, 2 Samuel 8.17, "And Zadok the son of Ahitub, and Ahimelech the son of Abiathar, were the priests." See also 2 Samuel 15.24, 29, 35.

b) Did Saul have the Urim with him? After all, we know that David sought God's help by using the ephod, and that the original ephod was permanently united to the breastplate (Ex 28.28, 1 Sam 23.6-9). But, at the same time, Saul evidently possessed the Urim, which was located in the breastplate. Quite obviously, it could not have been in two places at once! Perhaps the answer lies in the fact that Abiathar "fled to David...with **an** ephod in his hand." The Bible does **not** say "**the** ephod", and it certainly does **not** mention the breastplate, containing the Urim and Thummin. Bearing in mind the extraordinary circumstances, it seems that God communicated with David through Abiathar, **without** the Urim, which remained with Saul. But, not surprisingly, God did not reply to Saul's enquiry.

As "the Lord answered him not", Saul turned for guidance to "a woman that hath a familiar spirit." Hebrew *Baalath-ob*: "the mistress (or possessor) of a conjuring spirit" (Keil & Delitzsch). It would have been better if God's refusal to answer Saul led him to repentance.

4) Saul's Interview with Samuel (vv.7-25)
We come to the lowest point in the life of Saul. The man of whom Samuel said, "there is none like him among all the people", consults a witch at En-dor. What a shipwreck! But "let him that thinketh he standeth take heed lest he fall" (1 Cor 10.1). Notice **(A)** His consultation with the witch (vv.7-14); **(B)** His conversation with Samuel (vv.15-19); **(C)** His constraint to eat (vv.20-25).

A) His consultation with the witch (vv.7-14)
We'll call her a witch, although the Bible does not actually use the term here. In fact, M.C.Unger (writing in "The Word") thoroughly deplores the expression, and states that the word "sorceress" is a better translation of the Hebrew word where it does occur. According to Ellicott's Commentary (quoting Conder: *"Tent Life in Palestine"*), the journey from Mount Gilboa to En-dor, a journey of some ten miles, meant passing the Philistine camp. Rather hazardous! Watch him as he sets out: "without a star in his black sky, he decided to resort to Satan's agent for whatever glimmer of light she could give", A.McShane. Notice the following:

i) Saul's disguise (v.8)
"And Saul disguised himself...and they came to the woman by night." Quite obviously, Saul wished to escape detection by the woman. As we shall see, she certainly wouldn't have practised her "art" in the presence of Saul! Evil intentions are usually cloaked with secrecy. "Every one that doeth evil hateth the light, neither cometh to the light, lest his deeds should be reproved" (Jn 3.19-20). We are to "walk as children of light...and have no fellowship with the unfruitful works of darkness, but rather reprove them. For it is a shame even to speak of those things which are done of them in secret" (Eph 5.8-12).

ii) Saul's assurance (vv.9-10)
We already know that Saul had "cut off those that have familiar spirits, and the wizards, out of the land" (v.3), but listen to Saul's reply. It is quite unbelievable: "As **the Lord liveth**, there shall no punishment happen to thee for this thing." As A.McShane observes, "The Lord's Name is introduced

into some rare quarters, but never was more out of place than on this occasion!" God had said, "Thou shalt not suffer a witch to live" (Ex 22.18), and now Saul assures the woman in the name of the Lord, that she would not be punished! Saul was utterly hardened! Let's remember that no one has the right to alter God's word, and let's be careful how we use the Lord's name. Do remember that the Lord will not lead you to do anything which contravenes His word.

iii) Saul's request (v.11)
"Bring me up Samuel." We'll confine ourselves here to the word "up." So "Bring me **up** Samuel." This raises the interesting question, "Where was Samuel?" We can be certain that his body was in the grave, unlike Enoch and Elijah, who went - body, soul, and spirit - to heaven. But where was his spirit? Was it beneath the ground? Or was he in heaven, with "the spirits of just men made perfect" (Heb 12.23), and "ascended out of the earth" (v.13) as an indication that he had returned from the dead? The woman's words, "I saw gods (JND has "a god", but "or gods" in the margin) ascending out of the earth" (v.14), may help us here. Keil & Delitzsch render this, "I saw a celestial being come up from the earth', and continue, "Elohim does not signify gods here, nor yet God; still less an angel or a ghost, or even a person of superior rank, but a celestial (super-terrestrial), heavenly, or spiritual being." All this suggests that Samuel came from heaven! This leads to a wider question, "Where did the Old Testament saints go at death?" We know where Elijah went, but what about Moses? Both were present at the Lord's transfiguration. Did Elijah come down, and Moses come up, and then return to their different locations? It seems unlikely, doesn't it?

iv) The woman's alarm (v.12)
"And when the woman saw Samuel, she cried with a loud voice: and the woman spake to Saul, saying, why hast thou deceived me? For thou art Saul." Another interesting question! "How did the woman now realise that it was Saul?" There are plenty of answers in the commentaries, but we don't really know! Perhaps she "put two and two together." We'll leave it there, because we now have an even greater problem.

v) Samuel's appearance (vv.12-14)
"And when the woman saw **Samuel,** she cried with a loud voice." We now come to the biggest question of all: "Was it really Samuel? There are three schools of thought: **(a)** that it was Samuel; **(b)** that the woman pretended

it was Samuel, describing him appropriately and using appropriate words; **(c)** that it was a spirit impersonating Samuel.

As you can imagine, all three suggestions have attracted plenty of support. We must notice, however, that there is nothing in the narrative to suggest that it was anybody else, or anything else, but **Samuel himself.** The woman's cry implies that Samuel appeared contrary to her expectation, and this may suggest that she was "not really able to conjure up departed spirits or persons who had died, but that she either merely pretended to do so, or if her witchcraft was not mere trickery and delusion...the appearance of Samuel differed essentially from everything she had experienced and effected before." (Keil & Delitzsch). Throughout the passage, the writer refers, not to a ghost, but to Samuel himself. See (vv.12, 14, 15, 16 & 20). The words of Samuel to Saul (vv.16-19) certainly create the impression that it is Samuel himself who is speaking, and his announcement of Saul's death is so distinct that it is "impossible to imagine that it can have proceeded out of the mouth of an impostor, or have been an inspiration of Satan" (Keil & Delitzsch). As M.C.Unger has said, "Most purported communications from the dead are vague and cryptic, couched in abstruse language calculated to deceive and at the same time leave a favourable impression. This was far from the case with Samuel. In the severest terms he announced that the Lord had wrested the kingdom from Saul, and that on the morrow Saul and his sons would suffer death." This raises a number of further questions:

a) How was Samuel "brought up." Certainly not by any satanically-imparted power of the woman! The appearance of Samuel must be attributed solely to divine power. M.C.Unger puts it very clearly: "Evil spirits may impersonate the dead, but they cannot recall them from the spirit-world. Only God can do that, as He did in this case. Moreover, the incident is the only example in all Scripture where God permitted a deceased person to come back as a spirit to hold communication with the living. Others have come back from the dead, but not as spirits, but as raised persons." He adds, "Moses and Elijah...were present, not as "spirits", but in glorified bodies." Note that Luke 16.27 "does not affirm that the appearance of a dead man is a thing impossible of itself, but only describes it as useless and ineffective, so far as the conversion of the ungodly is concerned." (Keil & Delitzsch). "Satan himself cannot call up the dead. Those who have not believed and who have died, are and remain "the spirits in prison." God alone by making an exception can permit Samuel to come forth from the realm of the invisible and appear." (H.L.Rossier).

b) Why was Samuel "brought up." After all, this was exceptional. M.C.Unger again: "It was for the unique intent of divine rebuke and warning to all who resort to occultism, and particularly, to pronounce immediate sentence on Saul for this, his final plunge into ruin." See 1 Chronicles. 10.13, "So Saul died for his transgression which he committed against the Lord, even against the word of the Lord…and also for asking counsel of one that had a familiar spirit, to enquire of it; and enquired not of the Lord: therefore he slew him, and turned the kingdom unto David the son of Jesse."

c) Why was Samuel "brought up" in the form described.? "An old man cometh up; and he is covered with a mantle." Compare 15.27. Ellicott's Commentary quotes Bishop Wordsworth here: "God designed that the spirit of Samuel should be recognised by human eyes; and how could this have been done but by means of such objects as are visible to human sense." That will do nicely!

B) His conversation with Samuel (vv.15-19)
This section is quite self-explanatory. Little comment is needed here. Saul received no answer from living prophets, so he seeks help from a dead one! We should, however, notice the following:

i) Samuel's interruption
"Why hast thou disquieted me, to bring me up?" (Very clearly, Samuel was at rest, and had no desire to return to earth). This agrees very nicely with New Testament teaching. For example, "I am in a strait betwixt two, having a desire to depart, and to be with Christ; which is **far better**" (Phil 1.23).

ii) Samuel's intelligence
He was able to recall the past with accuracy (vv.16-18), and to predict the future with accuracy (v.19). Remember, he was dead! He "rested from his labours" (Rev 14.13). Now read Luke 16.19-31. Here is another dead man. But he can see, feel, speak and remember. Solemn, isn't it? We should thank God every day that we're saved. We who are alive can recall the past: but we can't predict the future. But Samuel could! Does this mean that believers who are dead can do more than they could when they were alive?! Notice too, that Samuel names David, for the first time, as Saul's "neighbour" (v.17). That's more than he did when he was alive! Fascinating, isn't it? When Samuel says, "tomorrow shalt thou and thy sons be with me", he means "with me" in death, not in the same place in death. Now, finally

C) His constraint to eat, (vv.20-25)

No comment is necessary here. Everything speaks for itself. There is no response from Saul to the announcement of pending disaster. "In this sole example of one from another world speaking to the living, there was no call to repentance, neither was there any sign of it in the hearer's heart. Remorse there certainly was, but this falls far short of repentance" (A.McShane). Saul leaves En-dor to face the Philistines on Mount Gilboa. His doom is sealed. David evidently learned from this. He prayed "Take not thy Holy Spirit from me" (Ps 51.11). As A.McShane observes, "Surely these words imply that he dreaded being left as this man was." Saul had to say, "God is departed from me, and answereth me no more" (v.15). How terrible! "Then he arose, and went away that **night**." It was night in every sense. It was night in every sense too in John 13.30.

CHAPTER 29

"What do these Hebrews here? (29.1-11)

As we noticed in our last study, the main "story-line" was interrupted by Saul's visit to the witch at En-dor. In this chapter, we resume the sequence of events which commenced at the beginning of chapter 28. To get the overall picture, read 29.1 immediately after 28.2, as if there were no intervening verses.

David was in deep trouble. It looked as though he would be engaged in a battle against his own countrymen but, as we shall see, God mercifully overruled his circumstances, and delivered him from that awful prospect. We know that David fled to Achish to save himself, but it brought him untold trouble, reminding us of the Lord's teaching in Mark 8.35. This short chapter can be divided as follows, **(1)** The preparation for battle (vv.1-2); **(2)** The protest of the princes (vv.3-5); **(3)** The preservation of David (vv.6-11). We should notice that God's name is only mentioned twice in this chapter, and on both occasions it is by Achish! Need we say more? Remember Chapter 27.

1. The Preparation for Battle (vv.1-2)
These opening verses describe a paradoxical situation. In the first place, we have Israel **against** the Philistines (v.1), and in the second, David **with** the Philistines (v.2).

A) Israel against the Philistines (v.1)
"Now the Philistines gathered together all their armies to Aphek.and the Israelites pitched by a fountain which is in Jezreel." According to Keil & Delitzsch (they quote another authority), "this fountain is the present Ain Jalud, or Ain Jalut (meaning 'Goliath's fountain'), a very large fountain that issues from a cleft in the rock at the foot of the mountain on the north-eastern border of Gilboa, forming a beautiful limpid pool of about forty or fifty feet in diameter, and then flowing in a brook through the valley." Note

that the Old Testament mentions several places called Aphek, and it is tempting to think that the Philistines had returned to the very place where they had defeated Israel before. See Chapter 4.1. We are told however, (Keil & Delitzsch, Morrish's Bible Dictionary) that the two places are not identical. Pity!

Leaving aside the geography, there is nothing unusual here. Conflict with the enemy is normal. We know, of course, that in this particular case, Israel's weakness in the past had resulted in ongoing trouble from the Philistines. Failure to deal with the "old life" in Canaan was disastrous for God's people, and failure on our part to deal with our "old life" will be equally disastrous. The old nature within us (the Bible calls it "the flesh") will constantly rear its ugly head unless we "mortify (put to death) our members which are upon the earth" (Col 3.5). The ability to do this lies in the power of the Holy Spirit: "Walk in the Spirit, and ye shall not fulfil the lusts of the flesh", (Eph 5.16). Having said this, warfare is normal. We are constantly under attack from one direction or another. But what follows should never be normal:

B) David with the Philistines (v.2)
"And the lords of the Philistines passed on by hundreds, and by thousands.but **David and his men** passed on in the rereward with Achish." Although David was not in the front line (he was part of the rearguard: "the rereward"), he lined up with the enemies of God's people. We must make sure that we don't do the same. For example, don't "line up with the Philistines" by criticising or slandering fellow-Christians in the presence of non-Christians. (Even better, don't criticise or slander fellow-Christians in the presence of **anybody!).** Don't "line up with the Philistines" by bringing the word of God into disrepute by bad behaviour. It is very difficult to witness for Christ in a place where a fellow-Christian has dishonoured Him. It isn't easy trying to "pick up the pieces." We must "give none occasion to the adversary (whoever he is) to speak reproachfully" (1 Tim 5.14). We must ensure that "the word of God be not blasphemed" (Tit 2.5). Don't "line up with the Philistines" by joining, or associating yourself, with any organisation which involves compromising or denying the word of God. Notice what God says about the Philistines in Ezekiel 25.15-16: "Because the Philistines have dealt by revenge, and have taken vengeance with a despiteful heart, to destroy it for **the old hatred**...I will stretch out mine hand upon the Philistines." That was written almost five hundred years after events in 1 Samuel! The enemy never changes!

We must mark, learn and inwardly digest the solemn lesson here. Compromise with the world will almost certainly bring pressure on us to support things that we know are wrong. We will be asked, and expected, to do and say things, and go to places, which would never have been expected of us had we made our allegiance to Christ clear in the first place.

A.McShane makes an interesting, albeit sad, comparison between David and Saul. "Is it not strange that in these two chapters both David and Saul acted contrary to their convictions of previous days? The former turned for help to witchcraft, that which he had earlier destroyed, and the latter joined with the Philistines, whose armies he had once routed."

2. The Protest of the Princes (vv.3-5)
Achish was more than happy for David to accompany the Philistine army, but his colleagues were not impressed! "Then said the princes of the Philistines, What do these Hebrews here?" Notice the conversation between Achish and his fellow-princes:

A) Achish defended David (v.3)
"And Achish said unto the princes of the Philistines, Is not this David, the servant of Saul the king of Israel, which hath been with me these days, or these years, and I have found no fault in him since he fell unto me unto this day?" A very nice testimony indeed! We could almost say that David had "a good report of them which are without" (1 Tim 3.7). But Achish didn't know that David had deceived him. See 27.8-12. Let's just say that some people are very good at creating the right impression! It has been well said that "you can fool some of the people all of the time, and all the people some of the time, but you can't fool all of the people all of the time!" We ought to live with reference to the fact that "Thou God seest me" (Gen 16.13). He cannot be fooled!

B) The princes doubted David (vv.4-5)
It is most interesting to notice what they said about David and his men. We can summarise their comments as follows:

i) Their description of David's men (v.3). "What do these Hebrews here?" The Philistine lords did not expect to find David and his men there, which reminds us that people don't expect to find **us** in certain places! In the Old Testament, the name "Hebrews" was usually employed by non-Israelites. (Saul was the exception: see 13.3). Morrish's Bible Dictionary puts it like this: "The name is first met with when Lot had been carried away prisoner, and one came and told Abram 'the Hebrew', Genesis 14.13. Hence it is applied to Abraham's descendants through Isaac and Jacob, in distinction to the name 'Israelites' (from the name of Israel given to Jacob), which is their covenant name, the name of promise" The word "Hebrew" comes from a root meaning "to pass over", which is precisely what Abraham did en route to Canaan.

So the Philistine princes failed to recognise the unique calling of God's people, and **we** must not be surprised that non-Christians have little, if any, appreciation whatsoever of **our** spiritual identity. There can be no doubt that they regard us as "peculiar people", but not in the Biblical sense! See 1 Peter 2.9.

ii) Their reservations about David's loyalty (v.4). "Make this fellow (the word '*ish*', simply means 'man') return, that he may go again to his place which thou hast appointed him, and let him not go down with us to battle, lest in the battle he be an adversary to us: for wherewith should he reconcile himself unto his master? Should it not be with the heads of these men?" That is, the heads of the Philistine soldiers. The presence of David created uncertainty in the minds of the Philistine lords.

We can understand this. After all, David had "changed horses" once. He might do it again! Especially, they argued, if he could see an opportunity for reconciliation with Saul. Uncertainty breeds suspicion. Most people would rather listen to someone with whom they disagreed, than to someone who constantly changes their mind, particularly when they trim their views to suit their company! Perhaps the Philistine lords remembered that the "Hebrews" had changed sides before. See 14.1. We should make it perfectly clear "whose we are and whom we serve" (Acts 27.23). We should not be "ashamed of the testimony of our Lord" (2 Tim 1.8).

iii) Their awareness of David's reputation (v.5). "Is not this David, of whom they sang one to another in dances, saying, Saul slew his thousands, and David his ten thousands?" It was this that first aroused Saul's anger against David. See 18.7-9. According to the dates given in the Scofield Bible, about seven years had passed since David slew Goliath, so his victory was still quite fresh in the Philistines' memory. As H.L.Rossier observes, "Why should he be for Achish today, rather than for Saul? The lack of a clear-cut position in regard to the world can only produce conclusions like these. Our very faithfulness in the past is turned against us."

1 Samuel

Behind all this lay the providence of God. He solved David's dilemma by silently and unobtrusively intervening in the situation. Our word "providence" comes from the Latin *provideo,* "to see beforehand", *"pro",* meaning "before", and *"video",* meaning "I see." Behind God's providence was God's love for David. The hymn says:

> Though I forget Him, and wander away,
> Still He doth love me wherever I stray.

3. The Preservation of David (vv.6-11)
There are at least four things to notice in this section. *(A)* The commendation of David (vv.6-7); *(B)* The remonstrance of David (v.8); *(C)* The pressure on David (vv.9-10); *(D)* The departure of David (v.11).

A) The commendation of David (vv.6-7)
For the second time in this chapter, Achish reveals how much he valued David. On the first occasion (v.3) he told his colleagues: now he tells David himself. It was a glowing testimonial: "Surely, as the Lord liveth (what about that!), thou hast been upright, and thy going out and thy coming in with me in the host is good in my sight: for I have not found evil in thee since the day of thy coming unto me unto this day." Taken in isolation, this would make a splendid reference for any Christian! Achish regarded David as an exemplary employee! If he had known about some of David's activities he would not have been so effusive in his praise.

This is the second time in which the Lord's name has been used in most unusual circumstances. See 28.10. Now Achish, a Philistine, uses the expression, "As the Lord (Jehovah) liveth." A little later, he says, "I know that thou art good in my sight, as an angel of God" (v.9). Keil & Delitzsch suggest that Achish swore by Jehovah to convince David of his sincerity. Ellicott's Commentary says something similar about the expression "angel of God", and suggests that Achish used it as a "graceful courtesy...likely to be acceptable to David."

While Achish, sadly, drew wrong conclusions about David, we must remember that "all things are naked and opened unto the eyes of him with whom we have to do", Hebrews 4.13. The Lord is thoroughly aware of unseen motives and objectives, as well as visible actions and audible words. Read 1 Corinthians 4.1-5.

B) The remonstrance of David (v.8)

David could not understand the refusal of the Philistine lords to include him in the coming battle with Israel. At least, it looks like that! "But what have I done? And what hast thou found in thy servant so long as I have been with thee unto this day, that I may not go fight against the enemies of my lord the king. David could say with a clear conscience, "What have I done?", to Jonathan (20.1), and to Saul (26.18), but not to Achish. Bearing in mind that David had no intention of harming "the Lord's anointed", we can only conclude that David's protest was insincere, akin to Shakespeare's, "Methinks the lady doth protest too much!"*(Hamlet: Act 3 Scene 2)*. Achish assumed that the "enemies of my lord the king" were Saul and Israel, but was David being deliberately ambiguous? Compare 28.2.

C) The pressure on David (vv.9-10)

"And Achish answered and said to David, I know that thou art good in my sight, as an angel of God: notwithstanding the princes of the Philistines have said, He shall not go up with us to the battle. Wherefore now rise up early in the morning with thy master's servants that are come with thee: and as soon as ye be up early in the morning, and have light, depart." The precise identity of "thy master's servants" is not altogether clear. Keil & Delitzsch say that it refers to "Saul, whose subjects David's men all were", but this seems most unlikely! Perhaps it refers to servants of Achish who attended David.

Quite obviously, to satisfy the Philistine princes, Achish wanted David out of the way as soon as possible. The battle was imminent. But it is equally true to say that God wanted David out of the area as soon as possible! His providential care for David is clear. David got himself into the mess, and God got him out of it!

D) The departure of David (v.11)

"So David and his men rose up early to depart in the morning, to return into the land of the Philistines. And the Philistines went up to Jezreel." A simple statement of fact, but, as usual, full of lessons! We should notice *(i)* The leadership, *(ii)* The land, and *(iii)* The leave-taking.

i) The leadership

"So David and **his men** rose up early to depart in the morning." The chapter begins and ends with "David and his men." He led them **into** danger at the beginning of the chapter (v.2) and **out** of danger at the end. It would be a little while before David returned to Judah (see 2 Samuel 2.1), but this was a start! At least, his men would not be involved in a battle against their own countrymen.

ii) The land
It was a great pity that he had to lead them back to "the land of the Philistines", but that's where he left the wives and children, and they were in terrible trouble! See Chapter 30. As we shall see, his involvement with the enemies of God's people, left his dependants exposed to danger. David should not have been in "the land of the Philistines" in the first place." David not only put his fighting men in the wrong position, he put the vulnerable members of their families in the wrong place as well. We must be very careful where we lead people: we must not expose weaker and defenceless believers to danger.

iii) The leave-taking
The chapter ends with David and the Philistines going in opposite directions. Keil & Delitzsch are surely right in saying that "David returned...no doubt very light of heart, and praising God for having so graciously rescued him out of the disastrous situation in to which he had been brought, and not altogether without some fault of his own, rejoicing (and here they quote another commentator) that he had not committed either sin, i.e. he had neither violated the fidelity which he owed to Achish, nor had to fight against the Israelites." But "the Philistines went up to Jezreel." In the remaining chapters, we follow David back to Ziklag, and trouble (Chapter 30), and the Philistines to Mount Gilboa, and victory over Israel (Chapter 31).

CHAPTER 30

"David encouraged himself in the Lord his God" (30.1-31)

The previous three chapters have not painted an impressive picture of David at all. Whilst we can sympathise with him when he said, "I shall now perish one day by the hand of Saul: there is nothing better for me than that I should speedily escape into the land of the Philistines", it remains that he did abandon his faith in God, who had protected and preserved him. David went to the wrong place, and ended up in deep trouble. God providentially saved him from fighting with the Philistines against Israel, but now he is in even deeper trouble. David hits rock-bottom in this chapter, but we also come to the turning-point in the story. There is no record of David seeking divine help in Chapters 27-29, and there is no record of God communicating with David. Thankfully, this now changes. The lesson is very clear, isn't it? When we stray from the will of God, our fellowship with Him is impaired. We don't speak to Him, and He doesn't speak to us, except to warn us. Abraham had no fellowship with God in Egypt. See Genesis 12.10-20. He had to go back to the "place where his tent had been at the beginning" before his communion with God was resumed.

David and his men return to Ziklag, only to find that the Amalekites had "burnt it with fire, and had taken the women captives." David and his men reach their lowest ebb: they "wept, until they had no more power to weep." We can divide the chapter in the following way: *(1)* David faces a disaster (vv.1-5); *(2)* David seeks the Lord (vv.6-8); *(3)* David pursues the Amalekites (vv.9-17); *(4)* David rescues the captives (vv.18-20); *(5)* David rewards his men (vv.21-25); *(6)* David distributes the spoils (vv.26-31).

1. David Faces Disaster (vv.1-5)
If David and his men returned with relief from Aphek, their light hearts soon became heavy. We must notice *(A)* The discovery (vv.1-3), followed by *(B)* The despair (vv.4-5).

1 Samuel

A) *The discovery, (vv.1-3)*
"So David and his men came to the city, and, behold, it was burned with fire; and their wives, and their sons, and their daughters, were taken captives." The Amalekites had sacked Ziklag. Perhaps they were on a revenge mission. David had invaded them, amongst others, and had "left neither man nor woman alive" (27.8-9). It seems rather significant that the young Egyptian (vv.11-15) specifically mentions Ziklag, as if it had been singled out for attack. We do know that the Amalekites made a point of concentrating on weak and vulnerable people. See Deuteronomy 25.17-19. Amalek was the grandson of Esau, Genesis 36.12. The Scofield Bible says that Esau was "born after the flesh", but his supporting verse, Galatians 4.29, actually refers to Ishmael! Make sure that you have good Berean blood in your veins! (Acts 17.11). Well, the Amalekites were running true to form. David and his men were out of the way, so the women and children were easy pickings.

By supporting the Philistine offensive against Israel, David and his men left their dependants exposed to danger. Now we have another clear lesson. When we stray from the will of God, other people are put at risk. This is especially true when the leadership is involved. It is very important for elders to spend time with the flock, and not, to use Paul's language, to become "entangled in the affairs of this life." See 2 Timothy 2.4. The elders at Ephesus were urged to "take heed" and to "watch", in view of the intrusion of "grievous wolves", and the influence of "men...speaking perverse things" (Acts 20.28-31). Amongst other things, elders are to "support the weak" (1 Thess 5.14). It is tragic when believers, of whatever age, are "carried...away" (v.2). Even Barnabas was "carried away" by the "dissimulation" (hypocrisy) of other people (Gal 2.13).

While David and his men recovered everything looted by the Amalekites, the destruction of Ziklag, where David should have never been in the first place, reminds us that the "fire shall try every man's work of what sort it is." If we have been building in the wrong place, or with the wrong materials, or from wrong motives, we will "suffer loss" (1 Cor 3.11-15).

B) *The despair (vv.4-5)*
"Then David and the people that were with him lifted up their voice and wept, until they had no more power to weep." How do **we** react when fellow-believers are "carried away" by temptation or false teaching? Paul wept over the assembly at Corinth. His first letter to them was stained with his tears. See 2 Corinthians 2.4.

Chapter 30

It is rather significant that David's wives are specifically mentioned: "And David's two wives were taken captives, Ahinoam the Jezreelitess, and Abigail the wife of Nabal the Carmelite." (Abigail is possibly called "the wife of Nabal the Carmelite" to distinguish her from a lady of the same name in 2 Samuel 17.25. See also 2 Samuel 2.2 and 3.3). The leadership was not exempted from trial and sorrow. David could sympathise with his men, because he was in the same position, which reminds us that "we have not an high priest which cannot be touched with the feeling of our infirmities; but was in all points tempted like as we are, yet without sin" (Heb 4.15).

2. David Seeks The Lord (vv.6-8)

Things look grim for David. "And David was greatly distressed; for the people spake of stoning him, because the soul of all the people was grieved, every man for his sons and for his daughters." This does remind us that when things go wrong, it is all too easy to "lash out" at other people. We look for someone to blame because of our circumstances. It happened to Moses time and time again! In this case, David's men were evidently blaming him for the calamity. You can almost hear them shouting at David: "If we had stayed in Judah, this would never have happened!" Things couldn't get much worse for him. But remember the providence of God! Nobody, "either great or small", had been harmed (although David and his men probably didn't know this at the time), which is amazing in view of what David had done to the Amalekites (27.9), and we can only conclude that God used the captivity of the wives and children to accomplish David's spiritual restoration. He does work like that, doesn't He? The desperate straits of the prodigal son made him say, "I will arise and go to my father" (Lk 15.18). Sometimes, it takes a hard knock to bring us to our spiritual senses! As H.L.Rossier pertinently observes: "God, no longer able to lead him by His eye, used the 'bit and bridle' (Ps 32.9), that is to say, a set of circumstances contrary to the will of His servant, in order to preserve him from an irremediable fall." Ellicott's Commentary suggests that the women and children had "a marketable value, and were carried off to be sold into slavery, probably in Egypt", but God was in control of the situation.

Now look at the effect this had on David: **(A)** He "encouraged himself in the Lord his God" (v.6); **(B)** He "enquired at the Lord" (v.8). When David had lost everything, He found his resource in God. We must remember that God didn't automatically bless David in his distress. He did have to turn to God, reminding us of James 4.8, "Draw nigh to God, and he will draw nigh to you."

A. He "encouraged himself in the Lord his God" (v.6)

It was David who wrote, "Hear my cry, O God; attend unto my prayer. From the end of the earth will I cry unto thee, when my heart is overwhelmed; lead me to the rock that is higher than I" (Ps 61.1-2). We are not told who wrote Psalms 42 & 43, but we can almost hear David speaking, "Why art thou cast down, O my soul? And why art thou disquieted within me? Hope thou in God" (42.6,11; 43.5). David had no one else to whom he could turn. God used the Amalekites to chasten him, and "no chastening for the present seemeth to be joyous, but grievous: nevertheless afterward it yieldeth the peaceable fruit of righteousness unto them which are exercised thereby" (Heb 12.11).

No doubt, David "encouraged himself in the Lord his God" by recalling the promises of God (he had been anointed king by Samuel) and the preserving care of God. This is clear from the words, "the Lord **his** God." David's encouragement did not rest on pious sentiment, but on solid fact. This led to a further move in the right direction:

B) He "enquired at the Lord" (v.8)

"And David said to Abiathar the priest, Ahimelech's son, I pray thee, bring me hither the ephod...And David enquired at the Lord , saying, Shall I pursue after this troop? Shall I overtake them? And he answered him, Pursue: for thou shalt surely overtake them, and without fail recover all." Abiathar had been with David throughout the stay in Philistia, but this is the first time that David had asked for his help in securing divine guidance.

The contrast between Saul and David cannot be greater. "When Saul enquired of the Lord, the Lord answered him not, neither by dreams, nor by Urim, nor by prophets" (28.6). But here, God answered immediately. We do not have to look far for the reason.

i) Saul had deliberately and persistently disobeyed God. He was marked by "envy, jealousy and a murderous spirit to all who opposed him. He had the whole house of Aaron mercilessly and unrighteously butchered in one day, though one of them did escape. He attempted David's innocent life again and again", Wm.Hoste *(Bible Problems and Answers).* There was no sign of repentance on Saul's part.

ii) David had spent sixteen months out of contact with God, but fellowship with Him had now resumed, and look at the welcome he received! The Lord did not say in effect, "You didn't seek me, so why should I help you?" We all have cause to thank Him for His grace to us. How glad we are that "The Lord is merciful and gracious, slow to anger, and plenteous in mercy… hath not dealt with us after our sins: nor rewarded us according to our iniquities. For as the heaven is high above the earth, so great is his mercy toward them that fear him…Like as a father pitieth his children, so the Lord pitieth them that fear him. For he knoweth our frame; he remembereth that we are dust" (Ps 103.8-14). The Lord "healed David's backsliding" (Hos 11.4), and He will be "merciful and gracious" to us as well when we turn to Him. Remember

> Though I forget Him, and wander away,
> Still He doth love me wherever I stray;
> Back to His dear, loving arms would I flee,
> When I remember that Jesus loves me.

With fellowship restored, God now assures David that the tragedy would become a triumph: "Pursue: for thou shalt surely overtake them, and without fail recover all."

3. David Pursues the Amalekites (vv.9-17)
There are at least four things to notice in this piece of narrative: **(A)** The assurance (v.9); **(B)** The exhaustion (v.10); **(C)** The assistance (vv.11-15); **(D)** The attack (vv.16-17).

A) The assurance (v.9)
"**So** (in view of God's promise) David went, he and the six hundred men that were with him, and came to the brook Besor, where those that were left behind stayed." David set out in hot pursuit of the Amalekites with divine assurance that it would be a totally successful mission. God had pledged His word, and David knew that He would not fail. We too must stand on the promises of God. Abraham was "fully persuaded that, what he (God) had promised, he was able also to perform" (Rom 4.21).

B) The exhaustion (v.10)
"But David pursued, he and four hundred men: for two hundred abode behind, which were so faint that they could not go over the brook Besor." Gideon and his three hundred men were "faint, yet pursuing" (Jud 8.4), but two hundred of David's men were totally exhausted. Notice, **not** unwilling to go further! Had they attempted to take part in the pursuit, they would have

hindered the expedition against the Amalekites. Men in the wrong place are always a hindrance! Keil & Detizsch explain their weariness as follows: "As Ziklag was burnt down, of course they found no provisions there, and were consequently obliged to set out in pursuit of the foe without being able to provide themselves with the necessary supplies." (Notice, however, that the four hundred men who continued the chase certainly had food: see vv.11-12). As we shall see, their fatigue did not mean that they were useless. Although they were not in the "front line", David valued their contribution to the "war effort", and later rewarded them accordingly. We shall say more about this later, but it is worth remembering that God's work does involve laborious toil. The Lord Jesus, "being wearied with his journey, sat thus on the well" (Jn 4.6). Epaphroditus, Paul's "companion in labour", was "sick nigh unto death", and not because he succumbed to a virus! "For the work of Christ he was nigh unto death, not regarding his life, to supply your lack of service toward me" (Phil 2.25-30).

How far are **we** prepared to go in our service for Christ? Soul-winning and evangelism are hard and exhausting work. Door to door visitation is tiring. Seeking lost men and women is costly in time and energy. Bible study is always rewarding beyond measure, but it can be tiring! When Paul spoke about building with "gold, silver, precious (costly) stones", he referred to materials which have to be mined (gold and silver) or quarried (costly stones). That's hard work! Spiritual materials are not easily acquired either! It involves hard work. It means "labouring in the word and doctrine" (1 Tim 5.17).

Whilst, like David's men, we may tire physically, we should not faint spiritually. The Lord Jesus taught that "men ought always to pray, and not to faint" (Lk 18.1). The apostle Paul was so thrilled with the gospel that he wrote, "Therefore seeing we have this ministry, as we have received mercy, we faint not" (2 Cor 4.1). The secret lies in Isaiah 40.31, "They that wait upon the Lord shall renew their strength; they shall mount up with wings as eagles; they shall run and not be weary; and they shall walk, and not faint"

C) The assistance (vv.11-15)
Enter a young Egyptian. His Amalekite master would have been accused of wrongful dismissal today! Just listen to this: "my master left me, because three days agone I fell sick" (v.13). That was bad enough. But that wasn't all, "he had eaten no bread, nor drunk any water, three days and three nights" (v.12). So it looks as though he was left to die! We know, of course, that all this happened in the providence of God. A little tender loving care

(TLC) from David and his men (they acted as good shepherds and in the spirit of Romans 12.20) revived him, and subject to assurances about his life, he was only too pleased to guide them to the Amalekite camp. That's not surprising, is it?! His treatment by the Amalekites is very far removed from New Testament teaching that "the members should have the same care one for another" (1 Cor 12.25). People are quickly thrown on the scrap-heap in business and elsewhere. It should never happen amongst God's people: "Nay, much more those members of the body, which seem to be feeble, are necessary" (v.22).

The Egyptian's description of the Amalekite invasion is interesting: "We made an invasion upon the south of the Cherethites, and upon the coast that belongeth to Judah, and upon the south of Caleb, and we burned Ziklag with fire" (v.14). The Cherethites (or "Crethites", possibly indicating that they came originally from Crete) were either Philistines, or connected with the Philistines: See Zephaniah 2.5. (1 Chron 18.17 makes interesting reading!) Notice, particularly, the expression, "the south of Caleb." The man who "wholly followed the Lord" certainly left his mark. (Sadly, he didn't leave his mark on Nabal! See 25.3). It is also rather interesting to notice that the young Egyptian was discarded by his Amalekite master at about the same time that David and his men left Aphek. Compare v.1 and v.13. Is this another example of the providence of God?

D) The attack (vv.16-17)
It is interesting to contrast the rejoicing Amalekites with the rejoicing Israelites in Exodus 15. The former were celebrating their success with godless drinking and dancing: the latter celebrated their deliverance from Egypt with songs of praise. We must be careful that we rejoice in the right way, and for the right reasons!

The arrival of David and his men reminds us of the unexpected judgement of the "day of the Lord." See 1 Thessalonians 5.3: "When they shall say, Peace and safety; then sudden destruction cometh upon them." See also Matthew 24.38-39, "For as in the days that were before the flood they were eating and drinking, marrying and giving in marriage, until the day that Noe entered into the ark, and knew not until the flood came, and took them all away; so also shall the coming of the Son of man be." The "carousing and dancing enemy" (A.McShane) were easy prey for David and his men. A.McShane continues, "Neither the long march nor the deep mourning at Ziklag seemed to hinder his army. They appear to have been reinvigorated by the help of the Lord and by the hopes of success." We must not forget the "four hundred young men, which rode upon camels, and fled." It reminds us that whilst we may win spiritual victories, the enemy is "down but not out." Our spiritual enemies have remarkable staying power! They survive to fight another day. However, there was no doubt about the outcome here:

4. David Rescues the Captives (vv.18-20)
God had said, "Thou shalt surely…**recover all**" (v.8). That is precisely what happened: "And David recovered all that the Amalekites had carried away: and David rescued his two wives. And there was nothing lacking to them, neither sons nor daughters, neither spoil, nor anything that they had taken to them: David **recovered all.**" Whilst, here, innocent wives and children were rescued from unjust captivity, the New Testament refers to the recovery of believers from captivity. See 2 Timothy 2.25-26. One function of "the servant of the Lord" is to instruct "those that oppose themselves; if God peradventure will give them repentance to the acknowledging of the truth; and that they may recover themselves out of the snare of the devil, who are taken captive by him at his will." This could be rendered: "And that they may recover themselves (awake up) out of the snare of the devil, having been taken captive by him, to the will of God", see RV margin. Suffice to say here that, amongst other things, Bible teaching has delivering power for believers, just as it has delivering power for unbelievers.

5. David Rewards His Men (vv.21-25)
On returning to "the brook Besor", David saluted the two hundred men who were too exhausted to pursue the Amalekites, but some of his victorious army slandered them. "Then answered all the wicked men and men of Belial, and said, Because they went not with us, we will not give them ought of the spoil that we have recovered, save to every man his wife and children, that they may lead them away, and depart." This exhibited greed and heartless covetousness. Notice how David deals with these "men of Belial." He points out:

A) *That they owed everything to the Lord*
The "men of Belial" spoke about **their** victory; "the spoil that **we** have recovered", (v.22). David spoke about the **Lord's** victory; "Ye shall not do so, my brethren, with that which **the Lord** hath given us, who hath preserved us, and delivered the company that came against us into our hand" (v.23).

B) That they owed a great deal to their brethren

"As his part is that goeth down to the battle, so shall his part be that tarrieth by the stuff: they shall part alike." Notice how the apostle John refers to this principle when writing to Gaius in connection with hospitality for itinerant preachers: "Because that for his name sake they went forth, taking nothing of the Gentiles. We ought therefore to receive such, that we might be fellow-helpers to the truth" (3 Jn 7-8). When writing to the Philippians, Paul was so thankful to God for their "fellowship in the gospel from the first day until now" (Phil 1.4). He gives us more details later in the epistle: see 4.4-18. We may not be missionaries or evangelists, but we have a vital role to fulfil by "tarrying by the stuff." This includes our ongoing prayer and financial support. Remember that Moses, praying on the hill, contributed to the victory over Amalek even more than Joshua fighting in the plain! See Exodus 17.11.

The oft-quoted words of Milton *(Heavenly Church of God: Sonnet xix)* are perhaps not exactly appropriate, but here they are for what they are worth:

> His state is kingly;
> Thousands at his bidding speed,
> And post o'er land and ocean without rest;
> They also serve who only stand and wait.

6) David's Distribution of the Spoils (vv.26-31)

"And when David came to Ziklag, he sent of the spoil unto the elders of Judah, even to his friends, saying, Behold a present for you of the spoil of the enemies of the Lord." As A.McShane observes, "Instead of holding on to his newly-acquired wealth (see v.20), he begins to scatter it abroad." Notice, nothing for the Philistines! Nothing for the Ziphites either! The people who had supported David in his adversity now benefit from his generosity. Gifts went to "all the places where David himself and his men were wont to haunt." It is both interesting and instructive to notice "that we find amongst those employed by David in offices of trust at the height of his power, so many inhabitants of these obscure places, where he found friends in the days of his early difficulties." (Quoted in Ellicott's Commentary). Notice, for example, Shimei from Ramah, and Zabdi from Siphmoth (1 Chron 27.27).

This reminds us that willingness to be identified with the Lord Jesus in His rejection does not pass unnoticed. Our devotion to Him will be recognised and rewarded.

It also reminds us that although we do not share the spoils of war with each other in quite the same way as David, we should certainly share our acquisitions from the scriptures. The Psalmist said, "I rejoice at thy word, as one that findeth great spoil", (Ps 119.162). The "great spoil" must be shared with fellow-believers. The Bible teacher must share "the spoils" too: "The things that thou hast heard of me among many witnesses, the same commit thou to faithful men, who shall be able to teach others also" (2 Tim 2.2).

CHAPTER 31

"So Saul died" (31.1-13)

In chapter 30, David is victorious in battle, and "sent of the spoil unto the elders of Judah, even to his friends, saying, Behold a present for you of the spoil of the enemies of the Lord" (v.26). In Chapter 31, Saul is defeated in battle, and Israel was spoiled by the Philistines.they "stripped the slain" (v.8). Bearing in mind that it took two or three days to get from Gilboa to Ziklag, we get the strong impression that the two battles took place at the same time. See 2 Samuel 1.1-2.

David anticipated that Saul would die in one of three ways: "the Lord shall smite him; or his day shall come to die; or he shall descend into battle and perish" (26.10). We now know that he "descended into battle and perished." The man who began his reign with victory over the Ammonites at Jabesh-gilead (ch 11), ended his forty-year reign (Acts 13.21) with defeat by the Philistines on mount Gilboa. He could not say, with Paul, "I have fought a good fight, I have finished my course, I have kept the faith." Paul "finished his course with joy" (Acts 20.24).Saul ended his life in misery. On the basis of your current track record, how do *you* expect to end life's journey? Searching, isn't it?

For the purpose of orderly study ("let all things be done decently and in order") we will divide the chapter into five paragraphs : **(1)** The defeat of Israel (v.1); **(2)** The death of Saul (vv.2-6); **(3)** The dispossession of Israel (v.7); **(4)** The decapitation of Saul (vv.8-10); **(5)** The devotion of Jabesh-gilead (vv.11-13). The details given in the chapter are repeated, almost word for word, in 1 Chronicles 10.1-12. A commentary is added in (vv.13-14). There is one major difference: only 1 Samuel tells us what the Philistines did to Saul's body, and only 1 Chronicles tells us what the Philistines did with Saul's head.

1. The Defeat of Israel (v.1)

"Now the Philistines fought against Israel: and the men of Israel fled from before the Philistines, and fell down slain in mount Gilboa." The narrator does not give the precise location of the battle, but it must have been somewhere in the valley of Jezreel, at the foot of the hills occupied by the hostile camps. Israel was defeated, and fled upwards towards their original position on the slopes of Gilboa. See 28.4. Notice the significant sequence: "fought...fled...fell."

Throughout our studies in 1 Samuel, we have stressed the lesson that the Philistines never "waved the white flag", and surrendered. They were defeated time and time again, but they kept coming back, and now they inflict a devastating defeat on Israel. While this is not the end of the story, for David "smote and subdued" them (2 Sam 8.1), we must not miss the lesson. The Philistines were far more than a mere nuisance. They could be devastatingly successful, and so can our spiritual enemies. Think of Demas. "Demas hath forsaken me, having loved this present world (fallen in love with this present world)" (2 Tim 4.10). Think of Hymenaeus and Alexander, who "made shipwreck" and who Paul "delivered unto Satan, that they may learn not to blaspheme" (1 Tim 1.19-20). Think about the assembly at Corinth: "It is reported commonly that there is fornication among you" (1 Cor 5.1). Think of the assemblies in Galatia: "I marvel that ye are so soon removed from him that called you into the grace of Christ unto another gospel" (Gal 1.6). We must not underestimate the power of our enemies. They have one ambition – to defeat us.

The defeat of Israel was a solemn indictment of Saul's misrule. At his death, he left Israel "in ruins, in weakness, in subjugation to the enemy, and without a single prospect for the future." He left a divided nation, and we know that "if a kingdom be divided against itself, that kingdom cannot stand" (Mk 3.24). No wonder the Psalmist (David) said, "Behold, how good and how pleasant it is for brethren to dwell together in unity...for there the Lord commanded the blessing, even life for evermore" (Ps 133.1-3). David, on the other hand, left Israel "in its healthiest state, in supremacy over all around it, in full confidence of the future, and with plans and preparation for the building of God's house. The nation never rose higher than its king, nor will assemblies rise higher than their leaders." A.McShane *(Lessons for Leaders)*. If you aspire to leadership, remember that "unto whomsoever much is given, of him shall be much required" (Lk 12.48).

2. The Death of Saul (vv.2-6)

This sad passage describes the death **(A)** of Saul's sons (v.2); **(B)** of Saul himself, (vv.3-4); **(C)** of Saul's armour-bearer (v.5). It is summarised in v.6: "So Saul died, and his three sons, and his armourbearer, and all his men ("all his house" 1 Chronicles 10.6), that same day together." Samuel's prophecy was fulfilled, "Moreover the Lord will also deliver Israel with thee into the hand of the Philistines: and tomorrow shalt thou and thy sons be with me: the Lord also shall deliver the host of Israel into the hand of the Philistines" (28.19).

A) The death of Saul's sons (v.2)

"And the Philistines followed hard upon Saul and upon his sons; and the Philistines slew Jonathan, and Abinadab, and Mechi-shua, Saul's sons." Ish-bosheth (called Ishui 14.49) survived: presumably, he was not involved in the battle. He became king over Israel, as opposed to Judah in the south, and reigned for two years. See 2 Samuel 2.8-10.

The death of Jonathan caused David particular grief. His touching lament over Saul and Jonathan is recorded in 2 Samuel 1.17-27. See particularly; "I am distressed for thee, my brother Jonathan: very pleasant hast thou been unto me: thy love to me was wonderful, passing the love of women." (v.26). David never forgot Jonathan. Some fifteen years later, when he became king of all Israel, he provided for Jonathan's son, Mephibosheth. See 2 Samuel 9, which begins with the question, "Is there yet any that is left of the house of Saul, that I may shew him kindness for **Jonathan's** sake?"

Sadly, Jonathan was only partly right when he said to David, "thou shalt be king over Israel, and I shall be next unto thee" (23.17). The men who shared David's glory were the men who shared his rejection, reminding us that "If we suffer we shall also reign with him" (2 Tim 2.12).

B) The death of Saul (vv.3-4)

"And the battle went sore against Saul, and the archers hit him; and he was sore wounded of the archers. Then said Saul unto his armourbearer, Draw thy sword, and thrust me through therewith; lest these uncircumcised come and thrust me through, and abuse me. But his armourbearer would not; for he was sore afraid. Therefore Saul took a sword, and fell upon it." Some render the words, "he was sore wounded of the archers", as, "he was much terrified by the archers." It must have been like the battle of

Agincourt! (How's your history?) Since Saul was a very tall man, and was evidently wearing his crown (2 Sam 1.10), he must have been a prime target! Sadly, Saul knew that the battle would end in defeat for Israel and death for him. See 28.19. He did not have the refuge described by Solomon: "The name of the Lord is a strong tower: the righteous runneth into it, and is safe" (Prov 18.10)

Saul's reference to the Philistines as "these uncircumcised", is rather ironic. He was clearly "uncircumcised in heart and ears" (Acts 7.51). The apostle Paul defined a true Jew as follows: "For he is not a Jew, which is one outwardly; neither is that circumcision, which is outward in the flesh: but he is a Jew, which is one inwardly; and circumcision is that of the heart, in the spirit, and not in the letter" (Rom 2.28-29). Circumcision was the outward sign of faith in God. It was the sign of "no confidence in the flesh" (Phil 3.3). Saul had left the pathway of faith. His own circumcision meant nothing. What about **us**? We can hardly condemn the conduct and behaviour of unsaved people, if we live like them!

We have another record of Saul's death, and it is quite different to the passage here and the parallel passage in 1 Chronicles 10. Read 2 Samuel 1.1-16. See, particularly, vv.9-10 where the Amalekite recounts the death of Saul as follows: "And he said unto me again, Stand, I pray thee upon me, and slay me: for anguish is come upon me, because my life is yet whole in me. So I stood upon him, and slew him, because I was sure that he could not live after that he was fallen." C.I.Scofield *(The Scofield Reference Bible)* makes a valiant attempt to reconcile the two accounts, but it isn't very convincing!

It does seem more than likely that the Amalekite was somewhat "economical with the truth" in order to extract a fat reward from David. Keil & Delizsch put it like this: The Amalekite's account of Saul's death "has an air of improbability, or rather of untruth in it, particularly in the assertion that Saul was leaning upon his spear when the chariots and horsemen of the enemy came upon him, without having either an armourbearer or any other Israelitish soldier by his side, so that he had to turn to an Amalekite who accidentally came by, and ask him to inflict the fatal wound. The Amalekite invented this, in the hope of thereby obtaining the better recompense from David. The only part of his statement which is certainly true, is that he found the king lying dead upon the field of battle, and took off the crown and armlet, since he brought these to David. But it is by no means certain whether he was present when Saul expired, or merely found him after he was dead." A.McShane adds that the Amalekite "must have been near the scene of Saul's death to obtain the crown from his head and the bracelet from his arm, otherwise the Philistines would have claimed these treasures. He could well have been searching the dead for any spoil available, and when he found the king and took his crown, he assumed that he had obtained the greatest of all spoils, something that would establish him as one of the most honourable of David's men." So, on one hand, we have facts given by two historians (in 1 Samuel and 1 Chronicles), and on the other, the story of the Amalekite. 2 Samuel 4.10 will settle the problem.

We should now read the commentary that follows the record of Saul's death in 1 Chronicles 10: "So Saul died for his transgressions, which he committed against the Lord, even against the word of the Lord, which he kept not, and also for asking counsel of one that had a familiar spirit, to enquire of it; and enquired not of the Lord, therefore he slew him, and turned the kingdom unto David the son of Jesse" (vv.13-14). This is a fitting introduction to 2 Samuel, which is devoted to the reign of David.

C) The death of Saul's armour-bearer (v.5)
"Then said Saul unto his armourbearer, Draw thy sword, and thrust me through therewith...But his armourbearer would not; for he was sore afraid...And when his armourbearer saw that Saul was dead, he fell likewise upon his sword, and died with him." Perhaps it was his love and devotion for Saul that stopped the armour-bearer "from carrying out his fallen master's last terrible command" (Ellicott's Commentary), or possibly he dreaded the personal consequences. Look what happened to the Amalekite! See 2 Samuel 1.14-16.

Both Jonathan and Saul had devoted armour-bearers. Jonathan's armour-bearer shared his master's victory. See 14.1-15. Saul's armour-bearer shared his defeat. How glad we are that our Master is triumphant. "Now thanks be unto God, which always causeth us to triumph in Christ (leadeth us in triumph in Christ), and maketh manifest the savour of his knowledge by us in every place" (2 Cor 2.14). Let's make sure that our loyalty is not misplaced. Saul's armour-bearer supported the wrong man, and **we** can so easily support the wrong cause, with devastating results.

3. The Dispossession of Israel (v.7)
"And when the men of Israel that were on the other side of the valley, and

1 Samuel

they that were on the other side of Jordan, saw that the men of Israel fled, and that Saul and his sons were dead, they forsook the cities, and fled; and the Philistines came and dwelt in them." When Israel entered Canaan, God gave them "great and goodly cities, which thou buildest not, and houses full of all good things, which thou fillest not, and wells digged, which thou diggest not, vineyards and olive trees, which thou plantedst not" (Deut 6.10-11). But now the Philistines have taken possession! Notice that the "Philistines came and **dwelt** in them." This wasn't a "hit and run" raid: they took up residence. There's a solemn lesson here, isn't there! God's people lost their inheritance. It had happened before. See, for example Judges 5.6, "In the days of Shamgar the son of Anath, in the days of Jael, the highways were unoccupied, and the travellers walked through byways." They couldn't enjoy their own main roads. It's a graphic picture of what the enemy can do in our lives. Have we lost the joy of **our** inheritance?

Who would have thought that the Philistines, living along the Mediterranean seaboard, would have reached and crossed the Jordan? Never think that you are out of the enemy's reach!

4. The Decapitation of Saul (vv.8-10)

"And it came to pass on the morrow, when the Philistines came to strip the slain, that they found Saul and his three sons fallen in mount Gilboa. And they cut off his head, and stripped off his armour, and sent it into the land of the Philistines round about, to publish it in the house of their idols, and among the people. And they put his armour in the house of Ashtaroth: and they fastened his body to the wall of Beth-shan." Beth-shan means, "the house of rest." If you can make something out of that, go ahead! It lay about four miles west of the Jordan and about twelve miles south of the Sea of Galilee. A good map will show you that this was quite near Mount Gilboa.

Ellicott's Commentary sums it up like this: "The historian with extreme brevity records the savage treatment of the royal remains, which, after all, was but a reprisal. The same generation had witnessed similar barbarous procedure in the case of Goliath, the great Philistine champion! We must notice what the Philistines did with **(A)** Saul's head; **(B)** Saul's armour; **(C)** Saul's body.

A) *Saul's head*

See 1 Chronicles 10.10: "And they...fastened his head in the temple of

Dagon." David took Goliath's head to Jerusalem. See 17.54. This was the second occasion on which the spoils of war were deposited in Dagon's temple. On the first occasion, it was the ark of the covenant, and the Philistines discovered that the God of Israel was very much alive! Now it is the head (or skull) of the king of Israel, and that was a lifeless trophy!

Like the ark of the covenant, the head of Saul was deposited in Dagon's temple as a thank-offering for victory over the enemy, and to demonstrate the superiority of their god over the God of Israel. Nebuchadnezzar did the same. See Daniel 1.2. It just reminds us that we should do nothing to bring the Lord's name into disrepute.

B) Saul's armour
Saul's armour became the occasion of thanksgiving in idol temples, and was deposited in the "house of Ashtaroth." The historians tell us that there was a famous temple dedicated to Astarte at Askelon. Herodotus describes it as the most ancient of the temples dedicated to the worship of the Syrian (Venus). The goddess was also known as the "Heavenly Aphrodite, and is called the "queen of heaven" in Jeremiah 7.18. (Isn't it interesting that the Encyclical announcing the Marian Year in 1954 proclaimed that Mary had been crowned "Queen of Heaven!"). Under the name Ishtar, she was a chief goddess of the Assyrians, and had famous temples at Nineveh and Arbela.

Bearing in mind that the "house of Ashtaroth" was at Askelon, plus the fact that Goliath came from Gath, we can understand why David said, "Tell it not in Gath, publish it not in the streets of Askelon; lest the daughters of the Philistines rejoice, lest the daughters of the uncircumcised triumph" (2 Sam 1.18).

C) Saul's body
"They fastened his body to the wall of Beth-shan." The bodies of his three sons were exhibited in the same way. It was a gruesome reminder that the Philistine war machine had triumphed over Israel. It also presupposes that the Philistines had captured the city. See v.7. The bodies of Saul and his sons were saved from further indignities by the men of Jabesh-gilead:

5. The Devotion of Jabesh-Gilead (vv.11-13)
"And when the inhabitants of Jabesh-gilead heard of that which the Philistines had done to Saul; all the valiant men arose, and went all night, and took

the body of Saul and the bodies of his sons from the wall of Beth-shan, and came to Jabesh, and burnt them there. And they took their bones, and buried them under a tree at Jabesh, and fasted seven days."

The men of Jabesh-gilead never forgot that it was Saul who delivered them from Nahash the Ammonite. See Chapter 11. They crossed the Jordan under cover of darkness to retrieve the four bodies. It was certainly not the custom in Israel to burn the dead. This was reserved for people guilty of gross immorality. See Leviticus 20.14, 21.9. In this case, it seems that the mutilated bodies, which would have been in an advanced state of decay, were burnt to avoid further desecration by the Philistines. The bones were buried under, we are told, a tamarisk *(eshel)*.

David recognised the kindness of the men of Jabesh-gilead. "Blessed be ye of the Lord, that ye have shewed this kindness unto your lord, even unto Saul, and have buried him. And now the Lord shew kindness and truth unto you: and I also will requite you this kindness, because ye have done this thing" (2 Sam 2.4-6). This wasn't Saul's last resting place. David eventually transferred the bones of Saul and Jonathan from their grave at Jabesh-gilead to the sepulchre of Kish at Zelah, in Benjamin. See 2 Samuel 21.12-14

1 Samuel ends with the **ruin** of Saul. 2 Samuel describes the **reign** of David. As H.L.Rossier observes, "This defeat, this judgment, this ruin of man are, for God, the dawn of the reign of the beloved!" It reminds us that God will soon terminate the "old order" of this world by judgment, and introduce the "new order" when, under Christ, the "earth shall be filled with the knowledge of the glory of the Lord, as the waters cover the sea" (Hab 2.14).

1 Samuel

form
1 Samuel